TARIFF DETERMINATION IN THE GENERAL EQUILIBRIUM OF A POLITICAL ECONOMY

To my parents

Tariff Determination in the General Equilibrium of a Political Economy

A bargain-theoretic approach to policy modelling

HOM MOORTI PANT
Centre for Regional Economic Analysis,
University of Tasmania, Hobart, Australia

Routledge
Taylor & Francis Group

LONDON AND NEW YORK

Contents

Figures and tables

ix

Preface and acknowledgements

As a student I was exposed to a wide variety of economic models, ranging from simple macro-economic models to highly complex micro-based models of the general equilibrium class. They had one feature in common; they all treated government policies as exogenous. They were used to compare policy alternatives and then to make recommendations about the policies that should be followed to achieve some stated policy objective. I was intrigued by the fact that these policy recommendations seemed to make little impact on policy making. For example, the models showed that tariffs were distortionary and hence that 'welfare' would be enhanced by their removal. But, the process of dismantling tariff barriers had never been very effective, they were still very much with us.

On the other hand, these models seemed to be highly useful in one important respect. They showed very neatly how government policies determined the environment within which all agents make their choices and the way in which the market allocates resources. They did so by showing to any decision maker the consequences of his actions and making it clear that the global efficiency of the market depends critically on the policies apparently chosen by the government. By treating policies exogenously in this way, however, these models ignored a very important question. To summarize in a catch phrase the question 'why do governments do what they do?' was one which worried me and probably worried many other economists, then and since.

I have always believed that policies are not made in a vacuum; they have their basis in the politico-economic system which economists have been modelling and analyzing for a very long time. There must, I felt, be some way of taming this beast. It was this belief which motivated me to attempt to build an economic model in which a model of the policy-formation process was grafted on to an economic model of the traditional kind. This book is the outcome of this exercise.

xi

In the book I have followed a bargain-theoretic approach to policy modelling, which postulates that government policies (even a country's constitution) reflect a state of social unity. This unity arises from a process of hard-nosed bargaining, leading to an equilibrium between the interested individuals or groups. I hope that readers will find this approach novel and thought provoking.

The book originated in a doctoral thesis, which I submitted to the Australian National University in 1992. Professor Peter Warr supervised the thesis with Dr Rod Falvey and Dr George Fane. I am greatly indebted to all three for their constant constructive criticism, helpful suggestions and encouragement. I am also indebted to Dr Neil Vousden and Professor Ngo Van Long, who read the first draft of the thesis and made various invaluable comments. I am also grateful to Professors David Vines, Ross Garnaut, Thomas Hertel, and Lisa Rutstrom, who played a key role in making me persevere with an often frustrating topic. A team of Professors, James Cassing, Professors Long and Rutstrom also anonymously provided encouraging comments as did Professor James Cassing. It was these comments which first made me think of turning the thesis into a book. To them I also extend my thanks. I am also grateful to Dr S. Mahendrarajah, Dr Soonthorn Cahiyindeepum and Mr Ramchandra Acharya, who painstakingly went through successive drafts, identified mistakes and made valuable suggestions.

I am deeply indebted to my colleague Dr Alf Hagger at the Centre for Regional Economic Analysis, University of Tasmania, who read the final draft of the book and made many suggestions, which in total caused it to be a much better book.

I am also grateful to Dr John Madden, Director of the Centre for Regional Economic Analysis, for his encouragement and for providing the excellent research environment in which the final version of the book was completed.

Though I have benefited very much from the above-mentioned persons, I alone am responsible for any errors and faults that may remain.

Finally, I would like to thank Tribhuvan University of Nepal, particularly the Economics Department at Patan Multiple Campus, for granting me leave, the Ford Foundation and the Australian National University for generous financial support, and my wife Ambika and children Sushil and Jyoti for their long-suffering and loving support throughout the entire journey.

Hom Moorti Pant
January 1, 1997

1 An overview

1.1 An introduction to the main issues

Government policies have redistributive implications. Therefore, policy changes often invite many social and political conflicts. A striking example is the European farm subsidy program in which the level of conflict has crossed national frontiers. Carbon taxes and opposition to it; a proposal to reduce tariffs and non-tariff barriers to trade by a certain date and often violent demonstration against it; and recent protests against various changes proposed in the Australian Federal Budget 1996 are other examples. These real world examples suggest that changing policies is not an easy task. People are affected by policy changes and they take them seriously. How government policies in general, and redistributive policies in particular, are formed and why and how do they change, are vexing questions.

All the sophistication, positivity and clarity of economics starts to crumble once it is asked to explain how and why policy changes are made, particularly when redistributive issues are involved. This is so because alternative purely redistributive policies cannot be ranked by the Pareto rule, since each one of them is Pareto efficient. The result is that in any serious economic modelling exercise either some rule of social choice, such as maximization of a social welfare function, has to be specified to rank policy alternatives and explain policy choices or the policies have to be taken as exogenous. Since there are serious logical problems in specifying a social choice rule, positive economic models generally regard government policies as exogenous.[1] The question of policy determination therefore has largely remained outside the scope of these models.[2] The class of policy-exogenous models has already evolved into a class of very complex and sophisticated models, such as computable general equilibrium (CGE) models. These models are being used to trace and explain how the Pareto efficient allocation of resources and the distribution of income will change because of a given change in government policies and other exogenous variables.[3]

1

However, if policies are endogenously determined as the recent literature suggests then, as far as the effects of changes in non-policy exogenous variables on endogenous variables are concerned, the predictions of a policy-exogenous CGE model may be incorrect. Policy-exogenous models do not allow for the second round effect that would take place after the policies respond to the exogenous shocks. Hence, the full effects of, say, a world price change on sectoral employment, output and income distribution would be different from that predicted by a policy-exogenous CGE model. The performance of these CGE models would greatly be enhanced and our questions answered, if the policy formation process could be included and policy variables endogenized in these models.

So in addition to the vexing questions posed above, we have got another live question to answer: how the policy formation process can be modelled in the framework of a CGE model? This book, by focusing on a particular redistributive policy, attempts to answer all of the above questions thoroughly. More precisely, assuming that trade taxes/subsidies are the only redistributive policies available to a government, this book describes a very simplified model that is capable of answering the following two specific questions. How are tariff rates in a small open economy determined? How would tariff rates change if the exogenous environment changes?

The choice of the tariff policy as the subject matter of this study is motivated by the following reasons. First, tariff policy is in itself one of the important forms of government policy. Second, it has distributive implications. Third, its existence is difficult to explain on social welfare grounds under complete and perfect market conditions because, as is well known it is not the first-best policy. Finally, tariff policy has been a favourite subject matter of previous studies on political economy, and there consequently exists a basis of previous work upon which further extensions can be made.

Clearly, this study is not the first that has raised questions concerned with the formation of redistributive policies in general, and tariff policy in particular. There exists a large body of literature on rent seeking, public choice and political economy that has addressed these questions in one way or another.[4] This class of literature argues that policy changes can alter the welfare levels of private agents, who, therefore, have incentives to behave strategically in order to influence the policy choices of the government. The government, on the other hand, survives on political support and therefore supplies policies strategically in order to maximize its political support. This class of literature culminates in the contention that government policies are determined in the political market, where the policy variables play the role of balancing the opposing political forces that are guided by the economic interests of the self-interested agents.

These studies have recognized that the political and the economic spheres are interconnected (for example, Gardner, 1983). Political activities of economic agents or some institutional mechanism that translates economic interests into political preferences provide the link between the two spheres. The agents in such a political economy face a simultaneous choice problem in both spheres such that

2

the choice made in one sphere affects the opportunities available on the other sphere. It is therefore natural to expect that rational actors would behave strategically in the political sphere to enhance their position in the economic sphere and vice versa. This means, however, that the choice of a specific policy in the political sphere and, consequently, the allocation of resources in the economic sphere depend on the joint action of all players. Therefore, an individual's welfare no longer depends only on his or her actions but also on the actions of other individuals as well. For this reason previous studies almost invariably have adopted a game-theoretic framework to study the policy formation process and the individual choice problem in the context of a political economy.

Moreover, once the political sphere is modelled in conjunction with the economic sphere and individuals are allowed to behave strategically the price taking assumption of the Arrow-Debreu model is violated. Agents can choose their lobbying levels (strategies) in the political sphere to affect the prices they face in the economic sphere. Hence, the question of existence of an equilibrium in such a political economy becomes a nontrivial issue.

Previous authors who have studied the policy formation process in the framework of a political economy either have not addressed the question of the existence of equilibrium at all (Yeldan and Roe, 1991; Magee, Brock and Young, 1989) or have had no success (Findlay and Wellisz, 1982, 1983, 1984; Wellisz and Willson, 1986; Hall and Nelson, 1992) or have been able to show it only for an exchange economy (Coggins, 1989; Coggins, et al., 1991). Therefore, an attempt to answer the questions posed above in the framework of a political economy begs another more basic question - the question of the existence of an equilibrium. This question is important for models of a political economy for two reasons. First, an analysis based on the equilibrium behaviour of a political economy makes sense only if an equilibrium exists. Second, a prior knowledge of the conditions under which an equilibrium exists is useful in constructing a computable general equilibrium model of a political economy.

Hence, this book also addresses the following additional questions. Does an equilibrium exist in a productive political economy? Under what conditions can one be assured of an equilibrium? Is it necessary that a political economy in equilibrium should deviate from free trade? How would the tariff rates in such a political economy respond to exogenous shocks?

The existing literature on political economy has modelled the political process of conflict resolution concerning the government's (tariff) policies as a noncooperative game. Such a model does not allow the players to communicate and negotiate with each other and agree on a strategy combination even if that is mutually beneficial. Therefore an outcome of the noncooperative tariff game may not necessarily be Pareto efficient, since a cooperative outcome may Pareto dominate it. The assumption that the players are rational goal maximizers and the assumption that their political behaviour can be characterized by a noncooperative game thus appear to be potentially inconsistent.

In contrast to the existing literature, this book maintains that the political process provides enough opportunities to negotiate a cooperative strategy through bargaining if the players find it rational to do so. Implementation of a cooperative solution does not appear to be a problem in our model of a political economy. It is because a cooperative strategy would be the one agreed to by all conflicting parties, and the government would maximize its political support by enforcing it. Therefore, even in situations when a cooperative solution is not self-enforcing, the presence of a politically motivated government guarantees its enforcement. Hence, this study finds enough reason to view that tariff determination is essentially a bargaining problem. The choice of bargain-theoretic framework constitutes a major departure of the present study from the existing literature on endogenous tariff formation. To justify this choice, this study, nevertheless, analyses the noncooperative behaviour in the political sphere and shows that there is an incentive to each player to look for a cooperative solution of the game.

As a by-product, this study also attempts to answer the following additional questions. How is a bargaining problem defined in the tariff game? What would induce the players to agree during a bargaining process? How can a bargaining equilibrium be characterized? What would be the bargained tariff rate in any given circumstance? How would the bargained tariff rate respond to exogenous shocks?

1.2 The modelling approach and the point of departure

As in previous studies, a Ricardo-Viner type two-sector general equilibrium model has described the workings of the economic sphere. In this model of the economic sphere, policies of the government are regarded as exogenous. The economy is assumed to be small and open in relation to the world market. Moreover, by invoking Lerner's symmetry theorem (Lerner, 1936) only one tariff rate is considered instead of two. This makes the rationalized tariff rate the only instrument of income redistribution and sharpens the focus of the study. The model has been employed to predict the economic consequences of a given policy change and derive the implications for the interests of the individuals. These results, in turn, have been employed to determine individual preferences over alternative policies in the political sphere.

One reason why previous studies failed to obtain an existence result is that they did not specify the structure of the general equilibrium model of the economic sphere of the political economy. They worked with general forms of production functions, the properties of the higher-order derivatives of which were not known. Learning from their experience, this study specifies the forms of the production functions. In particular, it is assumed that the production functions can be represented by constant returns to scale CES functions. The choice of this functional form is a pragmatic compromise between simplicity and generality.

Following the contention of the endogenous tariff literature, a government's choice of the tariff rate has been viewed as an outcome of the policy game played in the political sphere. The game is played by the government, which wants to stay in power, and the owners of the specific factors, who behave strategically to maximize their real rental income. The political process has been viewed as an institutional environment in which the conflicts of interests concerning the tariff policy are resolved.

With this stylization of a political economy this study first investigates the existence of an equilibrium in a political economy under the assumption that the political environment is noncooperative. The noncooperative model of the political economy describes the consequences of predatory lobbying to the player themselves, and exposes the rationale for cooperative behaviour. In particular, it is observed that a distinct possibility of saving resources employed in predatory lobbying exists if the players cooperate and agree (i) on some tariff rate, and (ii) not to spend on lobbying the government.

The bargain-theoretic approach has been adopted to study the tariff determination process under a cooperative political environment. The bargaining problem in the tariff game has been solved using the generalized Nash bargaining process in which the players may be endowed with asymmetric bargaining powers. The condition characterizing the bargaining equilibrium has been combined with the model of the economic sphere to derive a policy-endogenous general equilibrium model. The solution of this model yields the level of the politico-economic equilibrium tariff rate that is determined endogenously.

A comparative static (counterfactual experiments) approach has been adopted to derive the endogenous response of the bargained tariff rate to changes in exogenous variables. Unlike previous studies, which studied the endogenous response of the tariff rate to shocks of world price changes only, this study also derives the response of the tariff rate to exogenous changes in the domestic factor endowment.

Two central conclusions emerge out of this analysis. First, the level of the tariff rate depends on the relative bargaining power of the players and the relative fear of ruin (Aumann and Kurz, 1977a, 1977b) held by the players. Provided the distribution of the bargaining power between the players remains unaffected by a shock, consequent changes in the tariff rate do not depend on the distribution of the bargaining power. The extent and direction of change in the bargained tariff rate depends solely on the movement of the relative fear of ruin held by the players, which is completely explained by the condition of the economic sphere. Second, in general, the bargained tariff rate changes to compensate, at least partly, for the relative loss of the loser (compared to that of the other player) that arise from changes in the exogenous environment.

These results have two interesting implications for policy modelling in general equilibrium. First, it is found that the comparative static behaviour of the bargained tariff rate is consistent with the predictions that follow from the maximization of a conservative social welfare function (Corden, 1974). The implication of this similarity is that, if bargaining is accepted as the underlying process that generates the (positive) conservative social welfare function, then the problem of identification of the social welfare function vanishes. Implementation of a social welfare function will not be inconsistent with the self-interested behaviour of the government. The difference between the political economy approach and the welfare function maximizing approach can be eliminated. Second, the results of this study indicate that a bargain-theoretic framework can be adopted to model the policy formation process in a political economy and this is consistent with the self-interested behaviour of all agents.

Choice of the specific-factor model differentiates the present study from Magee, Brock and Young (1989), and imposition of a particular structure on the forms of production functions differentiates it from the other studies of political economy (for example, Findlay and Wellisz, 1982). This study also differs from the endogenous tariff literature in that it allows cooperative behaviour in the political process of tariff determination; and the general equilibrium of the political economy is defined whenever a solution to the bargaining problem is obtained.

1.3   A summary of the chapters and plan of the book

The rest of the book is divided into eight chapters. The purpose and a summary of the main results of the chapter are provided at the beginning of each chapter. A short summary of the book is as follows.

Chapter 2 provides a selective review of endogenous tariff literature. It summarizes the main arguments of previous work holding public-interest and/or self-interest views of the government, and draws some implications for the modelling strategy of this study.

Chapters 3 and 4 describe the economic sphere of a simple open political economy. The structure of a Ricardo-Viner type 2-sector general equilibrium model of the economic sphere is described in Chapter 3, assuming that the policies of the government (tariff rates) are given. The comparative static properties of the endogenous variables are obtained, and on the basis of these results some general properties of the solution functions are deduced. These results are employed in Chapter 4 to derive the properties of the second order derivatives of the real rental functions, the rent transformation frontier and its comparative static properties. The rent transformation frontier summarizes the general equilibrium effects of tariff changes on the sectoral rental incomes.

Chapter 5 describes the political process of tariff determination as a noncooperative game and studies the existence of a Nash equilibrium in a political economy. This chapter establishes that if the government behaves as a Stackleberg leader and the interest groups behave as Nash followers, then there exists at least one non-trivial Nash equilibrium in the political economy. It is also shown that the two strands of the existing political economy approach to endogenous tariff theory, which have either considered support maximizing behaviour of the government without considering the reactions of the lobbyists or considered the lobbying equilibrium for a given pricing function without showing how such a function was obtained, are mutually compatible. They imply the same policy-equilibrium if the political economy admits a unique Nash equilibrium. A formal demonstration of this result, which was previously conjectured by various authors, is also provided in an appendix to this chapter.

In Chapter 6, this study allows the interest groups to search for a cooperative solution to the tariff game. From this chapter onwards activities in the political sphere are viewed as a process of bargaining between the two conflicting interest groups on the level of the redistributive policy - the tariff rate. Moreover, in this chapter, the generalization of a Nash solution in the presence of asymmetric bargaining power is discussed in a considerable detail. A new characterization of the generalized Nash solution is obtained in terms of the players' generalized fear of ruin. It is shown that the equality of players' generalized fear of ruin is an alternative necessary and sufficient condition for the generalized Nash solution to a bargaining problem. This new characterization has been found very useful in providing intuitive explanations of the comparative static results obtained in the subsequent chapters.

The results derived so far are combined in Chapter 7 to obtain the final structure of the general equilibrium model of the political economy. The tariff rate that emerges at the solution of this model guarantees an equilibrium in the economic sphere as well as solving the bargaining problem in the political sphere. This completes the construction of a policy-endogenous general equilibrium model in which the tariff rate (or the redistributive policy) is determined endogenously.

Furthermore, this chapter discusses the problems that arise in identifying the disagreement payoffs and invokes the reference point solution concept to overcome them. To see how the bargained tariff rate would change as the exogenous variables of the model change, the general equilibrium model of the political economy with cooperative behaviour is subjected to comparative static (counter-factual) experiments. Throughout these experiments it is assumed that the relative bargaining powers of the players remain unaffected by the shocks. Intuitive explanations for the comparative static results are also provided.

Chapter 8 implements the policy-endogenous general equilibrium model numerically using hypothetical data sets chosen carefully to cover some extreme cases. The procedure adopted in obtaining the minimum expectation payoffs, and calibration of the model is also discussed in detail. The simulation results show that, in general, the *directions* of the responses of the bargained tariff rate with respect to exogenous shocks are insensitive to the location of the initial equilibrium and to the point of minimum expectation. The magnitudes of responses are, of course, observed to be sensitive to these variations. Some hypotheses that follow from these comparative exercises and which appear to be robust are stated formally. These hypotheses are then checked against the results of previous studies.

Furthermore, the policy-endogenous general equilibrium model has been simulated using one particular data set to predict the consequence of a very large growth in the stock of the specific factor in the import-competing sector. The results showed that the direction of trade in commodities reversed after the shock. The commodity that was imported before the shock is exported and the commodity that was exported is imported after the shock, and the commodity that was being taxed before the shock is subsidized after the shock. This result explains why comparative advantage of a nation may change with the pattern of factor accumulation. Finally, in Chapter 9 this study is concluded, and the limitations of the study are discussed.

Notes

1 For a simple exposition of the logical problems with normative social choice rules see particularly chapters 9 and 10 in Mueller (1979).
2 Shoven and Whalley (1984), Decaluwe and Martens (1988), de Melo (1988) and Robinson (1989) provide comprehensive surveys of the main features of the CGE models.
3 See, for example, Dixon, et al. (1982), Drevis, et al. (1982), Piggott and Whalley (1985), Cassing and Warr (1985); Anderson and Warr (1987); Hertel and Tsigas (1988); and Hertel (1990).
4 Buchanan, Tollison and Tullock (1980), Bhagwati (1982b), Collander (1984), Rowley, Tollison and Tullock (1988) provide a substantial collection of mainly analytical works that are concerned with rent-seeking and the political economy of endogenous tariff determination.

It is useful to note the difference among the three schools - rent-seeking, public choice and the political economy. The rent-seeking literature is primarily concerned with the welfare cost of rent-seeking when the level of rent generating policy is already given. Nevertheless this literature also describes the strategic behaviour of the rent-seekers in seeking rents created by distortionary policies. The public choice school is concerned with the application of economic tools in explaining the nonmarket decision making or simply the application of economics to political science (Mueller, 1979). This school lacks the foundation of general equilibrium in the economic sphere. The political economy school combines the methodologies of the public choice school with that of positive economics to obtain a political economy framework in which both the political and economic markets are considered and the policies are determined endogenously together with the other economic variables.

2 A selective review of endogenous tariff literature

Introduction

This chapter provides a selective review of the literature to outline the evolution of approaches towards modelling the endogenous determination of the tariff rate. More elaborate reviews of the theoretical as well as empirical works in this area can be found in Baldwin (1982, 1984); Magee (1984); Hughes (1986); Nelson (1988); Magee, Brock and Young (1989); Hillman (1989). A summarized version can also be found in Vousden (1990, Chapter 8).

Most of the previous studies have been prompted by the perplexing observation that trade taxes exist in the real world despite the general conclusion that they reduce general 'welfare'. Income redistribution as the sole cause of trade taxes has been dismissed by economists on the ground that, so long as the government is a 'social welfare' maximizer, such taxes do not constitute the first best solutions to the distribution problem (see for example, Bhagwati, 1971).

In trying to explain why trade taxes exist, economists have come up with several possible explanations that trace the evolution of endogenous tariff theory. The analytics of these studies, however, have been geared to predict the response of the tariff rate in the face of increased import competition - that is, when there is a terms of trade gain for whatever reasons. One may be able to use these models to examine the response of tariff rates, when the economy is shocked by any exogenous change.

Previous studies differ considerably in several aspects such as modelling strategies, time horizon, and degrees of refinements. Different reviewers may group them differently depending on the purpose of their review. For example, in a critical survey of the literature Nelson (1988) has classified most of the previous theoretical work into two groups according to their emphasis on the demand side or on the supply side of the political market. This approach treats policies arising solely out of self-interested behaviour of government. Nelson's classification is suitable if one intends to cover only those works that assume self-interested behaviour on the part of government. His classification, however, does not provide enough grounds to evaluate other works that emphasize the social welfare maximizing role of government or the works that have attempted to combine the political market approach with the welfare maximizing behaviour of government in their own perspective.

The fundamental differences among previous studies lie in their assumptions regarding the objective of the government, and there are no clear reasons to accept one or other of these assumptions. Therefore, we will first classify previous studies according to their assumptions on government motivation in taking policy decisions: whether the government is assumed to pursue some kind of 'public interest' or self-interest, or a combination of both.

The studies based on the assumption that government is motivated by self-interested behaviour constitute the core of the political economy approach to endogenous tariff theory. These studies have tried to model the tariff setting process by augmenting the political market with the usual economic market. While these studies differ in assigning a more prominent role either to the demand side or to the supply side of the political market by being explicit about the underlying market fundamentals, they agree on the point that the equilibrium tariff rate should clear the political market. So, these studies are further classified into three groups according to their coverage in explicit modelling of the political market. Thus, ultimately we will classify the endogenous tariff literature in five different groups (see Figure 2.1).

Our purpose in this review is to examine the current state of endogenous tariff theories and their conclusions to obtain some guidelines to make the tariff determination process endogenous in the context of a computable general equilibrium model. In the following sections we will review the endogenous tariff literature with this objective in mind. While doing so, an attempt will be made to summarize the major assumptions and their role in driving the conclusions of each study that are of direct concern to the endogenous tariff literature.

This chapter is divided into five sections. The first section reviews the literature that adopts a public-interest view. The second section reviews the literature that adopts a self-interest view. Section three reviews the literature that adopts a hybrid approach to tariff determination. In particular, this literature maintains that the government responds to political pressure as well as to welfare norms. Section four reviews some works that have addressed the issues of the choice of a specific protective instrument. Finally, section five summarizes the implications to the modelling strategy of the present study.

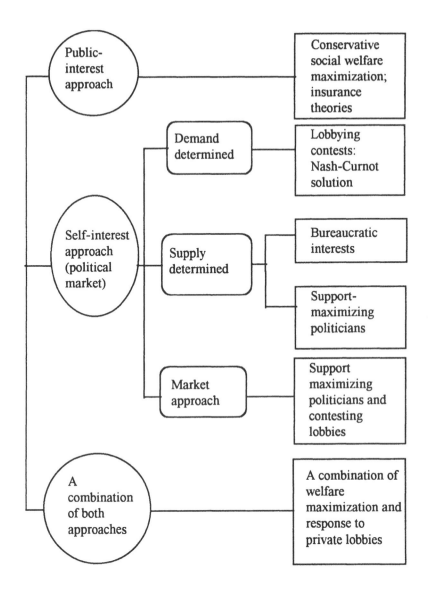

Figure 2.1   The family tree of endogenous tariff literature

2.1 The public-interest approach

In this section we will first review the concept of conservative social welfare function (Corden, 1974) followed by a review of insurance theories of tariff determination (Hillman, 1977; Cassing, 1980; Baldwin, 1982; Eaton and Grossman, 1985; and Cassing, Hillman and Long, 1986; Staiger and Tabellini, 1987). All of these works maintain that the government is a social welfare maximizer.[1] One may also include Findlay and Wellisz (1983 and 1984) in the class of 'public interest' literature, as they assume that the 'prince' is driven to justify his rule by maximizing the output of the composite public good financed by the tariff revenue.

2.1.1 The conservative social welfare function

Corden (1974) introduced the idea of conservative social welfare function (CSWF), describing it as being particularly helpful for understanding actual trade policies of many countries:

> Put in its simplest form it includes the following income distribution target: any significant absolute reductions in real incomes of any significant section of the community should be avoided. This is not quite the same as setting up the existing income distribution as the best, but comes close to it, and so can indeed be described as 'conservative'. In terms of welfare weights, increases in income are given relatively low weights and decreases very high weights (p. 107).

According to Corden, a CSWF expresses the following four ideas.

1. *(Fairness).* Unless there are good reasons or it is unavoidable, it is unfair to allow anyone's real income to be reduced significantly.

2. *(Social Insurance).* Insofar as people are risk averters, everyone's real income is increased when it is known that a government will generally intervene to prevent sudden or large and unexpected income losses. The CSWF is part of the social insurance system.

3. *(Social Peace).* Social peace requires that no significant group's income shall fall if that of others is rising. The reason is that social peace might be regarded as a social good in itself or as a basis for political stability and hence perhaps economic development. Even if social peace does not depend on the maintenance of the incomes of the major classes in the community, the survival of the government may.

4. *(Compensation).* If a policy is directed to a certain target, such as protection of an industry or improving the balance of payments, most governments want to minimize the adverse by-product effects on sectional incomes so as not to be involved in political battles incidental to their main purpose.

The concept of the CSWF, as expressed above, is rather informal. It is also not clear whether the four ideas are sufficient to identify a unique social welfare function or not. It is, however, clear that the CSWF represents a positive concept of social welfare.

It is easy to argue that so far as redistributive policies are concerned idea 1 (fairness) implies idea 3 (social peace), and idea 2 (social insurance) implies idea 4 (compensation). Because, if a government intends to avoid a fall in income of any community in general, then it will also avoid a fall in income of one community when that of others is rising. Similarly, if a government's policies are meant to provide social insurance, then it will compensate the loss in income of any community arising out of the adverse by-product effects of its own policies. Hence, in essence, we can regard CSWF expressing two ideas or principles: fairness, and social insurance.

However, fairness is a subjective concept. Corden views that any *significant absolute reduction* in real income of *any significant section of the community* is unfair. Unless a criterion for significance is explicitly specified, the idea nevertheless remains vague. Moreover, it has not been explained why a government should be concerned with the fairness of its policies at all. In other words, one can always enquire into the motivation that induces a government to remain fair. Moreover, the idea of fairness can be viewed as embodied into the idea of social insurance, because the losers will be compensated unless everyone is a loser. Probably because of this the idea of social insurance has been the one most frequently referred to in the literature.

Corden has made the best use of his CSWF in producing a first best argument for tariffs. He writes

...Yet one can base a first best argument for tariffs on the CWSF. Essentially it depends on the costs or difficulties of obtaining information.

Suppose import prices of particular products fall owing to foreign suppliers becoming more competitive for one reason or another. This will redistribute incomes against producers of import competing goods in favour of consumers or using industries. It may be difficult or even impossible to bring about a redistribution back to the original situation through taxes and subsidies. Quite apart from the institutional difficulties, and collection and disbursement costs, there is the crucial information problem: precisely who gained and lost, and by how much? This is particularly serious if the effects are sudden.

There is only one way of reversing or avoiding the income distribution effects *precisely*, and that is to impose a tariff which will keep the prices facing domestic consumers and producers exactly where they were before import prices fell (p. 109-10).

Corden's first best argument for tariff is somewhat unusual in trade theory. This prompted many others to examine the insurance aspect of the commercial policy more formally.

2.1.2 The insurance theories

Eaton and Grossman (1985) explicitly focused on the role of commercial policy in providing insurance when the insurance market is incomplete. They started with the assumption that there is some uncertainty regarding the international terms of trade. They further assumed that in an equilibrium prior to the terms of trade shock, all individuals are identical in their taste and factor endowments, and each individual owns two factors which earn at competitive market rates. Furthermore, they have also assumed that each individual must engage his capital, which is sector specific in the short-run, entirely in one activity. Finally they assumed that *commercial policy* is the only policy available to a social welfare (Benthamite) maximizing government to allocate the risk of terms of trade change.

With these assumptions Eaton and Grossman have shown that tariff intervention favouring the import competing sector can indeed raise social welfare. Moreover, tariffs may dominate production subsidies or taxes as a means of providing such insurance. Thus, Eaton and Grossman's result not only explains the existence of government intervention on trade but also specifies the exact form of the commercial policy to be adopted.

Cassing (1980), and Cassing, Hillman and Long (1986) have taken a slightly different approach in that these two studies do not explicitly assume that the government intends to maximize a social welfare function of any sort. In the context of a specific factor model of an economy with 2 sectors, where each individual owns one factor only, Cassing, Hillman and Long (1986) have neatly shown, without assuming a social welfare function, that if the insurance market is incomplete, then an ex-ante commitment to a stable domestic price is individually preferred by all agents provided that agents are sufficiently risk averse.

Thus, Cassing, Hillman and Long's study also suggests that if the insurance market is incomplete, then some form of market intervention, for example tariff intervention, can arise through a general consensus of all agents. One can, however, argue that if everybody prefers a stabile domestic price to an uncertain free trade price, then a price stabilizing commercial policy outcome is definitely welfare improving and therefore Cassing, Hillman and Long's result is consistent with the welfare maximizing hypothesis.

It is important, however, to note one difference between Cassing, Hillman and Long's approach and that of other insurance theorists who assume a benevolent government with a social welfare function. A welfare maximizing government may, at times, choose a policy that is not preferred by some individuals in the society. The only requirement for a policy to be selected by a social welfare maximizing government is that it should raise the aggregate welfare of the society irrespective of the levels of individual welfare. In Cassing, Hillman and Long's result, however, a tariff arises as a result of Pareto dominance - that everybody's welfare rises with a government's commitment on terms of trade contingent tariff policy. Thus, in this sense, Cassing, Hillman and Long's result is more powerful than that of other studies concerned with the insurance problem.

All of the above mentioned insurance theories have justified some level of terms-of-trade-contingent tariff protection before the terms of trade changes. This means that people would find their expected welfare increased if the government simply commits to a protective policy in the event that terms of trade change. However, once a government makes some form of commitment it may affect ex-ante allocation of resources and all incentive structures may change accordingly. With this new possibility, how would the government, the producers and the factor owners behave after the shock is actually observed? Once the shock is observed and the uncertainty is resolved, will the social welfare maximizing government behave as expected or committed? Would the same policies still remain optimal? This leads us to the problem of the time-consistency of the optimal policies.

To answer these questions Staiger and Tabellini (1987) took the case of a fall in the price of the home importable and posed the problem in the following way. Suppose that the timing of the decisions after the shock is observed is that, either: (a) first workers relocate and then a tariff is imposed; or (b) the labour relocation and the tariff decisions are made simultaneously.

Staiger and Tabellini have further assumed that (i) the capital incomes and the tariff revenue are distributed to the workers in proportion to their wage incomes, (ii) all workers have identical homothetic utility function, (iii) all workers are endowed with equal amount of labour (iv) there are positive costs of movement for labour, in particular labour will lose a part of its productivity if it has to relocate across the sectors.

With these assumptions they have proved the following three propositions:

1. The optimal tariff policy is either free trade or the imposition of a sufficiently high tariff rate that prevents any sectoral relocation of labour from taking place (p. 831).

2. When free trade is the optimal policy, it is not time-consistent. The time-consistent policy involves a socially excessive level of protection (p. 834).

3. In the time-consistent equilibrium, the production subsidy (rate) is strictly higher than the tariff (rate). If the social gains from redistribution are small enough, the tariff welfare dominates the subsidy (p. 836).

These results are interesting. Therefore, it is worthwhile to see whether they stand when some of the assumptions are relaxed. In particular, we are interested in the validity of the results when labour can move costlessly.

Staiger and Tabellini have argued that if the cost associated with the reallocation of labour is zero, that is if there is no loss in labour productivity when labour moves from one industry to the other, then the time-consistent tariff rate is zero (see their footnote 13). It, therefore, follows that if assumption (iv) is violated then free trade results as the time-consistent policy.

The result that free trade is time-consistent, however, depends critically on the assumption that workers receive capital income and tariff revenue in proportion to their wage income. This assumption implies that initially national income is equally distributed among workers and will remain so after the shock if labour can move costlessly. If, however, capital incomes and tariff revenue are not distributed equally before and after the shock because either the initial distribution rule implies an inequality or the rule itself changes with the shock, then the equilibrium incomes of workers after the price change will not necessarily remain equalized. In this case, a social welfare maximizing government may still obtain a non-zero value for its optimal and time-consistent intervention instrument and free trade may not be obtained as a time-consistent policy. Hence, even if labour movement is costless, Staiger and Tabellini's results may remain valid provided that capital income is not distributed in proportion to wage income.

Hence, what Staiger and Tabellini's work suggest is that if movement of labour is costless, and income is equally distributed, then the optimal and the time-consistent policy is free trade. But, either if there are costs in the inter-sectoral movement of labour and income is equally distributed among the workers, or if there are no costs in the inter-sectoral movement of labour but the capital income is not equally distributed among the workers, then the only optimal and time-consistent policy response to a terms of trade shock is an offsetting change in the tariff rate so that labour does not move across the industries as the terms of trade change.

Thus the insurance school of endogenous tariff, which views commercial policy as a means of sharing risks associated with terms of trade changes, has formally shown that if the insurance market is incomplete, then free trade is sub-optimal and/or time-inconsistent. An optimal and time-consistent policy involves a compensating change in the tariff rate. In particular, when movement of labour is costless and the distribution of capital income is unequal, time-consistency of the optimal policy requires that the tariff rate should change to offset any change in the terms of trade. Surprisingly enough this conclusion, though derived from maximizing a different (Benthamite) social welfare function comes close to what Corden had deduced on the basis of his conservative social welfare function.

The predictions of the public interest approach to the endogenous tariff theory regarding the endogenous behaviour of the tariffs can be summarized as follows.

1. (*insurance*). Given that all people are risk averters, everyone will be better off if the risks associated with the international terms of trade changes are insured

by the government's tariff policy. So, tariffs will change to offset the effects on the domestic relative prices of any change in the international terms of trade. This conclusion is shared by both Corden (1974) and various other authors subscribing to the insurance school.[2]

2. *(fairness)*. In general, if any change occurs in the domestic economy that causes the income of one sector to grow, say due to technological progress or to capital accumulation, causing the income of the other sector to decline, then the theory that maximizes CSWF predicts that the policy (tariff rate) will change to protect the losing sector.

There are two major problems with this approach. First the social welfare approach lacks explanation on how a CSWF or any other social welfare function is derived (existence) and how one can identify the correct form of the CSWF (uniqueness). Second, even if there exists a unique social welfare function one has to show that the government will actually maximize it while choosing policies before this approach can command some positive value. To claim that a government is a social welfare maximizer we require one more assumption that the government is a benevolent agent. Its preference is to see others (citizens) happier.

Once the government is assumed as a benevolent agent we run into a logical problem. Since, in general, a country is governed by a group of elected or selected representatives, who, when not in government, are assumed to be self-interested, then how can one expect the same people to become benevolent once they are elected or selected to run the government?

Both of these problems do not arise if, instead of assuming that there exists a social welfare function, which is maximized by the benevolent government, one assumes that the government will choose policies so as to maximize its chance of remaining in power or maximize side payments or bribes. This shift in the fundamental assumption takes us to the self-interest theory of tariff formation.

2.2   The self-interest approach: political economy of tariff determination

The authors who assume a self-interested behaviour on the part of the government view policies as simply another commodity which is traded in the political market. As Peltzman (1976: 212) puts it

> The essential commodity being transacted in the political market is a transfer of wealth, with constituents on the demand side and their political representatives on the supply side. Viewed in this way, the market here, as elsewhere, will distribute more of the good to those whose effective demand is the highest.

We will review the literature that views policies as the commodities of the political market in three different groups depending on whether they view the quantity of the policies as determined by the supplier or the demanders, or by the market as a whole.

2.2.1 *The supply side literature: Stigler-Peltzman model and its refinements*

Formal politico-economic approach to tariff determination begins with Peltzman's (1976) formalization of Stigler's (1971) theory of economic regulation. The theory is based on the assumption that the government, who supplies the regulation, is a support maximizer. More votes are always desirable because this implies a greater security of tenure, more logrolling possibilities and so on.

The group which benefits from the regulation pays the government with 'votes' and 'dollars' whereas the losers will reduce their support or increase opposition to the government. Not all gainers and losers are fully informed and so there is some scope for manipulating votes by campaigning, lobbying and so on. Therefore, the 'dollar' paid by the beneficiaries is productive to the government.

The Stigler-Peltzman model was initially developed to solve the problem of the regulator confronting a choice of the numerical size of the beneficiary group and was cast in a partial equilibrium setting. The structure of this model is so general that it is possible to express it in a general equilibrium context and use it to address other redistributive policy issues as well. For example, it is possible to use this model to solve the problem faced by a regulator who will transfer the rents in general equilibrium from one sector to the other by means of a change in regulation - the tariff rate.

Assuming that the owners of the specific factors in the two sector are the two active interest groups, following Peltzman (1976) we can write the support function of the government as

$$M = M(\Pi_1(P_1), \Pi_2(P_1))$$

where, the support M is increasing and concave in Π_i - the real rental income of sector $i=1$, 2; and P_1 is the relative price of (the import competing) good 1 such that real rental incomes Π_1 and Π_2 increase and decrease with P_1, respectively.

The maximization of the support function by choosing a tariff rate neatly summarizes the choice problem faced by the government. The government may receive an increased support from sector 1 and a decreased support from sector 2 by increasing the tariff rate, since P_1 increases with the tariff rate.

The first order necessary condition for a maximum support can be written as

$$M_1 \frac{d\Pi_1}{dP_1} + M_2 \frac{d\Pi_2}{dP_2} = 0,$$

and the second order sufficient condition can be written as

$$
\frac{d^2 M}{dP_1^2} = \left\{ \left(M_{11} \frac{d\Pi_1}{dP_1} + M_{12} \frac{d\Pi_2}{dP_1} \right) \frac{d\Pi_1}{dP_1} + M_1 \frac{d^2\Pi_1}{dP_1^2} + \right.
$$
$$
\left. \left(M_{21} \frac{d\Pi_1}{dP_1} + M_{22} \frac{d\Pi_2}{dP_1} \right) \frac{d\Pi_2}{dP_1} + M_2 \frac{d^2\Pi_2}{dP_1^2} \right\} < 0
$$

where the subscripts in M denote partial derivatives of the support function.

Assume that the political support function and the real rental functions are sufficiently well behaved so as to admit a unique support maximizing solution. The unique value of P_1 that satisfies the above condition will solve the support-maximizing problem of the government for a given world price, P_1^*. The relation between the world and the domestic relative price then determines the politically equilibrium level of the tariff rate.

Since the economic equilibrium depends on the values of the exogenous variables, the equilibrium rents will respond to changes in the exogenous variables as well. However, for each configuration of the exogenous variables, the equilibrium level of the policy variable has to satisfy the condition of political equilibrium - support maximization.

Differentiating the first order condition for equilibrium totally we get

$$
\frac{d^2 M}{dP_1^2} \cdot \frac{dP_1}{dP_1^*} = 0 .
$$

Since $d^2 M / dP_1^2 < 0$ by the second order condition, therefore it follows that

$$
\frac{dP_1}{dP_1^*} = 0 .
$$

This result suggests that a support maximizing government will always adjust tariff rates to offset the effect of the terms of trade changes on the domestic relative price.

Thus, the prediction of the Stigler-Peltzman model, which is based on the self-interested behaviour of government, is the same as that of insurance theory or that of Corden (1974). The reason is simple. Essentially, one can view the political support function as the welfare function being maximized by the government choosing a redistributive policy, which benefits one group and harms the other. The two functions may differ in parameters that are irrelevant in determining the optimal choice of the government.[3]

Hillman (1982), however, contested this result. He argued that political support from each interest group depends not on the levels of rents but on the extent to which they differ from their free trade levels. His main argument in this regard is that agents are responsive in their political support only to gains and losses that are due to the authorities acting to cause the domestic price to deviate from the world price via tariff intervention. Political support is not affected by changes in variables that are not due to the authorities' actions. Hence, Hillman (1982) re-specified the political support function and assumed that the government solves the following problem

$$\max_{P_1} M = M(\Pi_1(P_1) - \Pi_1(P_1^*), \Pi_2(P_1) - \Pi_2(P_1^*)).$$

By following the steps as in the Stigler-Peltzman model it can be shown that, for a given world relative price, P_1^*, the first and second order conditions for the maximum of the support function are exactly the same as those in the Stigler-Peltzman model. To see the equilibrium response of the domestic relative price with respect to a small change in the international relative price we differentiate the first order condition totally and obtain

$$\frac{d^2 M}{dP_1^2} \cdot \frac{dP_1}{dP_1^*} = M_{11} \frac{d\Pi_1^*}{dP_1^*} \frac{d\Pi_1}{dP_1} + M_{12} \frac{d\Pi_2^*}{dP_1^*} \frac{d\Pi_1}{dP_1}$$

$$+ M_{21} \frac{d\Pi_1^*}{dP_1^*} \frac{d\Pi_2}{dP_1} + M_{22} \frac{d\Pi_2^*}{dP_1^*} \frac{d\Pi_2}{dP_1}.$$

Given the above properties of the real rental functions and the concavity of the political support function we can deduce, by employing the second order condition, that[4]

$$\frac{dP_1}{dP_1^*} \geq 0$$

provided $M_{12} \geq 0$ and $M_{21} \geq 0$. However, sign ambiguity results if there is envy effect - that is if $M_{12} < 0$ and $M_{21} < 0$.

Hence, without envy effects if the price of home importable in the world market falls then, its price in the home market will also necessarily fall. Thus, Hillman came to the conclusion that 'a declining industry will continue to decline.' Despite the existence of protectionist motives the decline of a declining sector can not be arrested by a politically motivated (support maximizing) government.

If a support maximizing government does not provide a complete protection against import competition then the rate of return in the declining industry will fall below that which can be obtained in the other sector. When sufficient time is allowed for adjustment a part of the capital stock will exit from the declining sector. This will further lower the employment level in the declining industry. By assuming that the capacity to provide political support to the government also depends on the size of its labour employment, Cassing and Hillman (1986) have shown further that the protection to the declining industry will also continue to decline and such industries will eventually reach a stage of catastrophic collapse.

Hillman's (1982) argument that led to the hypothesis that individuals base their political supports on the divergence of rents from the free trade levels was questioned by Long and Vousden (1991). In particular, they raised two pertinent issues. First, if individuals or groups only praise or blame the government for changes directly attributable to the government's actions, then any changes in the tariff revenue and its distribution associated with a fall in the world price should be included in the political calculus. Second, it may be more reasonable to suppose that people care about changes in welfare relative to the situation before the fall in the world price of the home importable good. Moreover, because Hillman's conclusion was based on a partial equilibrium model its validity in the context of general equilibrium was not clear.

Long and Vousden (1991) studied the policy choice of a support maximizing government in the general equilibrium of a 2-sector specific factor model of a small open economy. In their model the government is assumed to maximize the aggregate of the supports from the three different factor groups given by the following function:

$$M(P, P^*) = \sum_i a_i V^i(P, Y_i)$$

where each a_i is a positive constant, which they assumed to have been determined by previous lobbying contests, V^i is the indirect utility function, and Y_i is the total income of the factor group i, which includes respective factor income and its share of the tariff revenue, which is distributed parameterically among the three factor groups.

Under reasonable assumptions they have shown that if all tariff revenue is given to either the mobile factor or the specific factor in the protected sector, a fall in the world price will lead to a fall in the corresponding domestic price. On the other hand, if the revenue is given entirely to the specific factor in the unprotected sector, or if each factor receives the recycled tariff revenue in the same proportion as it receives factor income, then the domestic price may actually rise or fall as the world price falls depending on the relative risk aversion of the three factor groups. However, they have concluded that in the absence of any good reason why the factor groups differ in their relative risk aversion 'the model would appear to offer good support for the proposition that a declining industry will continue to decline.' (p. 100)

In summary, the literature based on the supply side of the political market is still inconclusive in tracking the endogenous behaviour of the tariff rate. It is clear that the authors seem to have agreed on the point that the domestic and world relative prices will not move in the opposite direction. The agreement is not so clear on whether the domestic relative price will move at the same rate as the world price moves or not.

This ambiguity results simply because different authors assumed different reference points to which the interest groups would compare their current outcome to determine whether they need to adjust their support to the government or not. The Stigler-Peltzman model uses the origin, Hillman preferred the free trade point and Long and Vousden employed the recent past as the reference point. One possible solution to this problem could be to model explicitly the demand side of the political market, or to model the behaviour of the interest groups and obtain the reference point empirically.

In terms of modelling difficulties, the assumption that the government is a support maximizer and that the government is a social welfare maximizer are not very different. There are difficulties in defining an appropriate political support function, as well as there are problems in defining an appropriate social welfare function. However, the support maximizing assumption has the advantage that it is internally consistent. It maintains that all agents are self-interested and rational.

2.2.2   The demand side literature: Nash equilibrium in a lobbying economy

Findlay and Wellisz (1982) were the first to study the question of political equilibrium in conjunction with a general economic equilibrium of a political economy. They were mainly interested in demonstrating Tullock's (1967) thesis that the welfare cost of tariffs determined by lobbying contests is much higher than the conventional dead weight loss. Their model of the political process of tariff formation as a noncooperative game between interest groups became more important than their welfare result.

Findlay and Wellisz also used a 2-sector, specific-factor model to describe the general equilibrium of a small open economy producing two goods - food and manufactures - with land and capital as the respective specific factors and labour as the mobile factor. Under free trade the country is assumed to have comparative advantage in the production of manufactures. In this context Findlay and Wellisz conjectured,

> The landed interest would try to introduce a tariff on food at a prohibitive level if they could get away with it, whereas the manufacturing interest would try to preserve free trade. Depending upon the relative strengths and commitments of the two sides it is plausible to think that some tariff between zero and the prohibitive level will emerge. The social value of the resources used up by both sides in this struggle would constitute a welfare cost over and above the familiar deadweight loss associated with whatever tariff level emerges from the political process. (p. 225)

In their model, they represented the supply side of the political market in reduced form by a tariff (supply) function. Specifically, they assumed that a tariff level is determined as a stable function of the resources committed to the political process by each of the two interest groups such that the tariff function is increasing and concave in the resources used in lobbying by the landed interests and decreasing and convex in the resources used in lobbying by the capitalists. They did not specify what sort of government behaviour is implied by this supply function, however.

Given this supply side, the demand side of the political market is described by a noncooperative game between the two interest groups. The landed interest is assumed to maximize its rent, measured in units of food, over and above the free trade level by choosing its lobbying levels. The capitalists were assumed to maximize their rents, measured in units of manufactures, over and above the autarkic level by choosing their levels of lobbying. Findlay and Wellisz then attempted to solve the game for the lobbying levels at its Nash equilibrium. Once this could be obtained, the tariff function would then yield the equilibrium tariff rate.

However, Findlay and Wellisz were unable to show the existence of a Nash equilibrium in the lobbying game. They simply assumed a unique, stable and interior Nash equilibrium to make the point that the welfare costs of the endogenous tariff determined through the political process exceeds the conventional deadweight loss of a tariff rate. For example, they write

> Unfortunately, however, each of these cross-partials is the sum of a long succession of individual terms of conflicting or indeterminate signs. We therefore simply assume that, whatever their slope, the reaction functions have a unique and 'stable' intersection defining a Cournot-Nash equilibrium in the 'political' sphere.... (p. 229).

Findlay and Wellisz (1983 and 1984) illustrated the endogenous determination of the tariff rate in two different regimes - the democratic pluralistic case and the bureaucratic authoritarian case - in two other papers. In the former case they used the same 'tariff formation function' as in their (1982) paper to describe the political process. Their description of the game remained relatively informal. Consequently, they had to make appropriate assumptions on the nature of the reaction curves to obtain an equilibrium and thus their implications.

In the bureaucratic case, however, Findlay and Wellisz have outlined the endogenous determination of the tariff rate by assuming that 'the prince' is driven to justify his rule by maximizing the 'output' of his regime, considered as a composite public good that requires real resources for its production. The resources have to be acquired from the private sector by means of taxation (Findlay and Wellisz, 1983: 476). This model is more or less equivalent to assuming that the government is a maximizer of the tariff revenue which is paid in units of labour. It does not allow interest groups to influence the decision taken

23

by the 'prince' and therefore, comes more closer to the 'public interest' theory of tariff determination.

Similar attempts to analyze the political process of tariff determination as a noncooperative game between the specific factor owners were also made by Wellisz and Wilson (1986) and Hall and Nelson (1992). Wellisz and Wilson have been more explicit in specifying the structure of the 'tariff function'. However, both of these studies failed to establish the existence of a Nash equilibrium formally. For example Wellisz and Wilson (1986: 370) write

Although it is easy to construct examples where this equilibrium exists, a general existence proof does not appear possible because each group's utility-maximizing lobbying effort need not always be a continuous function of the other group's lobbying effort. On the other hand there may exist more than one equilibrium.

Similarly, Hall and Nelson (1992: 72) write

... a long succession of terms involving second derivatives whose signs are not derivable without further assumptions on the model. Whether the reaction functions are positively or negatively sloped we will simply assume that there is a unique, stable solution between the three groups.

The problem of the existence of a Nash equilibrium in a lobbying game between different interest groups was further studied by Coggins, et al., (1991), in the context of a small open exchange economy. Their model had two persons each endowed with a single tradeable commodity. The government's role was to announce the domestic price of the two goods and to take responsibility for clearing the markets by trading in the world market at internationally given prices. While setting domestic prices, the government, in their model, responded to lobbing expenditures of the two agents, which created an incentive to each of the agents to spend resources in lobbying for higher relative price for their commodity.

A 'pricing function' announced by the government summarizes the supply side of the political market in their model. This pricing function is assumed to be common knowledge and is similar to the tariff formation function of previous studies in that it satisfied similar assumptions. It is differentiable in lobby expenditures, yields positive but diminishing returns to lobbying expenditures, and sets some form of bounds on the tariff rate or the domestic relative prices and it transformed the lobbying expenditures of the individuals with conflicting interest into a relative price of the commodities.

With one additional assumption, which they call *own good bias*, that each person consumes more of the good with which he is endowed than of the other good, Coggins, et al. (1991), have shown the existence of a non-trivial Nash equilibrium in a lobbying game in an exchange economy. The assumption of *own good bias* made the indirect utility functions quasiconcave in respective lobby expenditures, which in turn allowed Coggins, et al. to apply Debreu's existence theorem. This assumption, however, also imposed a restriction on the nature of the utility functions of the players. The utility function with own good bias implies that the indifference curves will have either horizontal segments to the right of the 45 degree line if the individual is endowed with the y-commodity or vertical segments to the left of the 45 degree line if the individual is endowed with the x-commodity.[5] Therefore, as they have indicated, the existence result does not hold generally for any pair of arbitrary utility functions. Nevertheless, their study has made a definite contribution to the literature.

In summary, the authors who have tried to explain the endogenous determination of the tariff rate in the context of conflict resolution have had difficulties in simply proving the existence of a Nash equilibrium in the lobbying game. Moreover, these studies have abstracted from the political market by assuming that there exists a 'tariff formation function' or a 'pricing function' that satisfies certain properties. They have neither shown nor explained what sort of government behaviour is consistent with these properties of the pricing function.[6] This approach has remained limited to the analysis of the demand side of a simple political market. To incorporate this approach into a CGE model with production, at this stage, is not a straightforward task.

2.2.3 The political market

Mayer's (1984) approach to the study of endogenous tariff formation is slightly different. He replaced the tariff formation function of Findlay and Wellisz (1982, 1983) by the majority-voting rule. Mayer assumed that the interest groups do not lobby for favourable tariff policy, rather they vote for it. In his framework the conflict of interest is resolved by majority voting.

Mayer's model, in contrast to other models, allows a person to own more than one factor of production. By assuming that factor ownership patterns differ among people he demonstrated, both under Heckscher-Ohlin and the specific factor model, that each factor owner has an optimal tariff rate whose value is uniquely related to the individual's factor ownership. However, in the specific factor model it was necessary to assume that each person possesses at most one type of specific factor in addition to one unit of the mobile factor.

In the special case of majority voting with no voting costs, he showed that it is the median factor owner's optimal tariff rate that will be chosen by the majority. Any shock that changes the position of the median voter would alter the equilibrium tariff rate. By introducing a positive cost of voting, which he assumed to be the same for every voter, Mayer showed that a small minority of big potential gainers had a far greater chance of gaining protection. The large number of losers will find it rational not to vote because the cost of voting exceeds the loss due to increased tariff, thus confirming the hypothesis rigorously of the interest group theories without introducing the lobbying and self-interested behaviour of the government. In fact, in Mayer's model, the government does not play any active role at all. The voters make the decisions themselves.

Magee, Brock and Young (1989) - henceforth MBY - have cited previous studies that provide powerful arguments, particularly relevant when redistributive issues are involved, against the majority voting rule. The major argument against the majority rule is the absence of single peaked preferences.[7] Mayer was aware of this limitation, since he acknowledged this problem somewhat indirectly in his assumption that voting takes place on a single issue - that is, in each case only one industry will be trying to gain tariff protection. When all industries try to get protection there may or may not exist any equilibrium under the majority-voting rule.[8] This has been regarded as the major conceptual flaw in Mayer's approach (Magee, Brock and Young, 1989: 73)

In a major study MBY, on the other hand, used a probabilistic voting model, which was developed previously by Brock and Magee (1978) to analyze the industry structure of protection. In their model of the political market with two lobbies and two political parties each party aims to maximize its chance of being elected by offering either a tariff or a subsidy rate. The lobbies contribute to the parties for favourable policies to maximize the income of their members. Voters are considered rationally ignorant. Each party, however, could affect their level of support positively by spending resources in voters' education and negatively by the distortionary effects of the policies.

Each party can obtain more resources to spend on voters' education from the self-interested lobbies of the two factors, which prefer either tariff protection or export subsidy, by deviating more from free trade. The cost, however, is that an increased deviation will also increase the deadweight loss associated with their policy position and antagonise the general voters.

In MBY's model, a hierarchy in terms of the possession of relevant political and economic information has been assumed. Political parties, who have all the information regarding the reactions of their lobbies and the voters, were at the top level. Therefore, the political parties were assumed to employ Stackelberg strategies against their respective lobbies and the general voters, whereas the parties were assumed to behave as Nash players against each other. The respective lobbies were assumed to have less information than their parties, but better informed than the general voters. So, the lobbies were assumed to follow the parties, but employ Stackelberg strategies against the general voters.

Thus, in MBY's model of the political market each party includes respective lobby's and voters' reactions in its calculus, and each of the lobbies include voters' reactions in their calculus. The parties maximize their probability of election by taking policy positions, lobbies maximize their income by choosing their lobbying contribution, and the general voters, though can be influenced by political campaigns of the lobbies and the parties, generally dislike deviations from free trade. MBY have thus defined a very interesting noncooperative game involving two political parties, two lobbies and the rationally ignorant voters. Their study did not address the question of the existence of an equilibrium in this game. They assumed it.

MBY developed their endogenous tariff theory in general equilibrium (Part II) using a 2-sector Heckscher-Ohlin type general equilibrium model, which assumes perfect factor mobility. Obviously, in such models the conflict of interest arises between labour and capital, not between the industries. Therefore, their politico-economic model did yield a long-run behaviour of the tariff rate that is determined by the political behaviour of the agents holding a long-run view on the economic sphere. Such a model is less suited in explaining the short-run behaviour (or immediate response) of the tariff rates.

Moreover, MBY have studied the endogenous behaviour of the tariff rate under either the Leontief or the Cobb-Douglas production technologies only, and the probabilistic voting model was represented by a logit election function. To a certain extent, their conclusions are shaped by these structures as well. Nevertheless, they have obtained many interesting results some of which are as follows.

1. With a Leontief production function, they obtained a 'compensation effect' in policy changes with respect to exogenous shocks. In particular, the following two results are very interesting in the sense that these results are similar to the predictions of the CSWF or that of the insurance theories.

    (i)   In general, an increase in a country's terms of trade causes the equilibrium level of protection to rise and the export subsidy to fall. Terms of trade are the ratio of the price of a country's exports over that of its imports (p. 157).

    (ii) Endogenous politics is progressive with respect to exogenous changes in prices and technology. When a factor's income falls, ...the injured factor lobbies harder, and the political system provides policies that generate a partial offset to the initial decline in income (p. 18).

2. In a simulation of their model with Leontief production functions, MBY observed that multiple equilibria were pervasive. The equilibria contained cases of either 'Prisoner's Dilemma' equilibrium, where each factor was worse off compared with free trade or 'Dominant Player' equilibrium, where one factor gained and the other lost compared with the free trade outcome. The actual outcome was dependent on the factor endowment ratio of the country. Extreme ratio implied a Dominant Player solution and intermediate ratio implied a Prisoner's Dilemma. For example, higher capital-labour ratio implies, in their model, that capital wins and labour loses and vice versa (p. 171).

3. It is then natural to ask why the lobby groups do not cooperate if they get trapped into Prisoner's Dilemma outcomes? MBY's simulation showed that the cooperation that can make both lobbies better off was not feasible because of enforcement problems. Note that their model does not contain a government that benefits from enforcing cooperative agreements. The political parties, who

are the potential rulers of the country, have an incentive to make the game more noncooperative.

When Cobb-Douglas production and utility functions were used in defining the general equilibrium structure, MBY obtained a change in some of the results.

First, MBY found that domestic politics is independent of international price. That is, even though the terms of trade change had distributive effects, it had no effect on the expenditures on lobbying, probabilities of election and the policies offered by the parties in equilibrium. This is quite different from the previous result.

Second, an increase in the endowment of a factor had the effect of generating policies favouring the factor itself. The main reason is simple: an increase in the endowment of a factor, say capital, will increase the resource base of the capital lobby which then spends more on lobbying for the pro-capital party. This, in turn, increases the success rate of the pro-capital party as well as improves the policy position of the pro-capital party. Both considerations increase the relative price of the capital intensive good, increase the return to capital, and lower wages in their expectational equilibrium. This is what they call increasing return on politics. This result is maintained irrespective to a shift in production technologies.

Third, and more surprising, they observed that if the factors were moderately risk averse (with relative coefficient of risk aversion equal to unity) and the factor intensities (measured by the ratio of physical units of the factors) in the two sectors move together, then an economic black hole could result. That is, all of the economy's factor endowment could be exhausted in predatory lobbying while the equilibrium tariff rate may actually fall (p. 223).

The most important aspect of MBY's approach is that it describes both the supply as well as the demand side of the political market, which has been appended to a general equilibrium model of the economic sphere of the political economy. This is apparently the only study which has analysed the endogenous determination of the tariff rate covering both political and economic markets in detail and in which self-interested behaviour on the part of all agents in the model is maintained.

MBY's model of the political market contains a special assumption that deserves scrutiny. It is the assumption that the labour lobby uses labour only in lobbying for the pro-labour party, whereas the capital lobby uses capital only in lobbying for the pro-capital party. Some of MBY's interesting results are the direct consequences of this assumption. For example, consider the compensation effect or the progressivity of the endogenous politics as referred in point 1 above. MBY explain these results as follows. When capital is harmed by a rise in the world price of the labour-intensive good it becomes cheaper for the capital lobby to be involved in political activity. At the same time, it will be relatively more expensive for the labour lobby to maintain the level of its current lobbying (see Magee, Brock and Young, 1989: 150).

However, they have not explained why the labour lobby, rather than allowing the capital lobby to seek protection through the political process, cannot utilize cheaper capital in lobbying for the pro-labour party and maintain political power when the price of the labour-intensive good, and hence the wage rate, increases. Similar arguments can be made when the relative price of the capital-intensive good increases in the world market and the wage rate falls in the domestic market. Why do the capital lobby and the pro-capital party not utilise cheaper labour in political campaigning to secure a higher subsidy rate or at least block the labour lobby and the pro-labour party in seeking a higher rate of protection on the labour-intensive good? The question whether their result stands with the factors allowed as substitutes in the political activities remains unanswered.

MBY have also assumed that the political market clears faster than economic markets, as if the parties contest an election every now and then, and therefore the economy may alternate between a tariff regime and a subsidy regime. While making decisions, the agents take the expected prices, not the actual prices, in the economic sphere of the model. The expected prices are determined by the equilibrium probabilities of electoral success and the prices that would result in the event of the success of each of the political parties. Thus, the expectational equilibrium, as they call it, is an important property of their model.

Yeldan and Roe (1991) took a slightly different approach to policy modelling. They were mainly interested in the implementation of export subsidy rates in the presence of rent seeking activities holding tariffs and tariff-like instruments exogenously constant. In doing so, they have embedded the political sphere of a political economy with its economic sphere described by a conventional CGE model.

Their CGE model contains four economic sectors - agriculture, industry, commercial service, and the public service - of which the public service is nontraded; and eight households - four worker households, one civil-servant household, and three private-sector capitalists (or the producer) households. Worker households receive sectoral wage bill and civil-servant household receives residual profit from public service operation and the 'bribes'. The three producer households get the sectoral rents. They have further assumed that only the producer households carry out the rent seeking activities by the payments of bribes out of their rental income.

Given this political and economic structure, they have modelled the supply side of the political market as follows. They assume that the public authority (civil-servant household) responds to rent-seeking activities of the private producers by setting the sectoral subsidy rates in an attempt to maximize the following objective function

$$\Omega = \sum_k I_k V_k, \qquad k \in \{\text{producer households}\},$$

subject to the CGE model;
where V_k is the indirect utility level of the producer household k. The *influence weights* I_k are endogenously determined by the rent-seeking process

$$I_k = e^{-(\beta_k/R_k)},$$

where, R_k are the monetized costs of the rent-seeking activity or 'bribes' paid by the producer household k, and β_k are calibration parameters.

The demand side of the political market is described by the utility maximizing behaviour of the producer households. The producer households spend a part of their income in 'bribing' the civil-servant household (the authority) to increase their influence weights in the authority's objective function, which in turn returns with a favourable policy that increases their disposable income, and utilities. The workers' households were assumed to be nonstrategic. The politico-economic system will be in equilibrium at a policy level when no one wants to adjust his rent-seeking activity or bribes.

The model was implemented using Turkish data of 1981. Simulation results with different closure rules, fixed versus flexible exchange rate, with or without government foreign borrowings, etc. provide an innovative application of the model. The results show that different agents gain differently with different closure rules.

The results, however, may imply that the closure rules, for example fixed or flexible exchange rates, limits to government borrowing, etc. themselves could be the targets of rent-seeking activities, a problem which has not been addressed in the study.

In terms of policy modelling in general equilibrium this study has appended a government's objective function, which is simply a weighted average of the welfare of the rent-seekers with weights responding positively to the rent-seeking expenditures of the rent-seeking agents. It does not state clearly whether the government is a welfare function maximizer but with weights being affected by political activities of the agents, or is simply a self-interested agent using the Stackelberg strategy vis a vis the rent seekers.

Yeldan and Roe's study has not addressed the existence issue either, and has not explained how the calibration parameters, β_k, contained in the influence functions are obtained. These parameters, nevertheless, play a critical role in translating the 'bribes' into the influence weights in the 'objective function' of the government.

2.2.4   Summary of the political economy approach

The endogenous tariff literature that adopts the political economy approach to the question of tariff determination is distinguished by its explicit assumption of self-interested behaviour on the part of government. The literature was classified into three groups according to their emphasis on the dimension of the political market.

The supply side literature assumed support-maximizing behaviour of the government and argued that the government would choose a tariff rate, which maximizes its political support. But, it did not analyse explicitly how the individual interest groups would react to the policy choice of the government.

Moreover, they differ considerably on the appropriate specification of the political support function itself.

The demand side literature has made use of the deduction that there are incentives to the rational agents to behave strategically in influencing the policy decision of the government. For a given policy-supply function (tariff function), this literature has attempted to explain the existence of the tariff 'distortion' as an equilibrium outcome of the policy game played by various interest groups. This class of literature has progressed up to the proof of the existence of a Nash equilibrium in a lobbying game in an exchange economy. It has not been explicit in linking the tariff function to particular behaviour of government. Therefore, the supply side of the political market has remained more or less unexplained.

The literature that has considered both the demand and the supply side of the political market is much richer in several aspects than the studies focusing on either the demand side or the supply side. It shows that government policies are the outcome of a complex interaction among interest groups, political parties and general voters in the political market. However, its economic sphere is described by an expectational equilibrium of a long-run model. Therefore, it is not suitable to study the short-run behaviour of the actors in the political market and the short-run outcomes of the political process. Moreover, the simulation results show that the results are highly sensitive to the choice of the production functions. The conditions under which the existence of an equilibrium can be assured are not known.

The following points emerge as the most common ingredient of the political economy approach to endogenous tariff theory. First, all of the existing studies appear to agree on the point that given an institutional process of policy supply, different interest groups lobby for favourable tariff policies. Second, the supplier of the (tariff) policy uses it as an instrument for maximizing its own self-interest - of remaining in power or being (re)elected.

2.3 A hybrid approach: combination of both public-interest and self-interest

There is a third approach to the endogenous tariff theory. It assumes that -

> the actions of the government are determined jointly by its willingness to grant (or perhaps its inability to resist the granting of) tariffs in the face of political pressure and by its desire to maximize social welfare (Feenstra and Bhagwati, 1982: 245).

Feenstra and Bhagwati further explain (p. 246)

> Our underlying assumption that one part of the government responds to the protectionist pressures while another tries to maximize welfare subject to this response suggests, as some conference participants wittily remarked, a 'left-brain, right-brain' or an 'ego versus id' type of approach to the political

economy at hand. It does reflect, however, the classic division and confrontation between the (protrade) executive and the (lobbying dominated) legislature in countries such as the United States.

Feenstra and Bhagwati employed a 2 x 2 Heckscher-Ohlin-Samuelson model to describe the general equilibrium of the economy, which is implicitly assumed to be in free trade equilibrium initially. Furthermore, following Findlay and Wellisz (1982) Fenestra and Bhagwati have assumed that the self-interested 'part' of the government offers a tariff function to each factor group, which is increasing and concave in quantities of labour and capital employed by the factor group in lobbying. Given a group-specific tariff function, Feenstra and Bhagwati assume that a factor group intending to lobby the government for tariff protection faces the following 'reasonable form for the lobbying cost function'

$$C(t,w,r) = \left\{ \frac{t\phi(w,r)}{\max\left\{0,(p_0^* - p^*(1+t)\right\}} \right\}$$

where, t is the tariff rate, w and r are the wage rate and the rental rate respectively, p_0^* and p^* are the international relative prices of the import competing good respectively before and after the shock. The function $\phi(w,r)$ is assumed to be increasing and quasiconcave.

By construction, this cost function has some special properties. First, it implies that only one factor will lobby at a time. This is so because, the expression on the denominator of the lobbying cost function implies that a factor will never engage in lobbying whenever its income is increasing through favourable terms of trade change, because the cost of lobbying remains infinitely large. The factor whose income has fallen, because of an adverse terms of trade change in the international market, will find it rational to engage in lobbying. Second, the injured factor will never lobby for a fully offsetting tariff protection when its income decline is caused by a change in the international terms of trade, because the cost of lobbying will tend to infinity, while the benefits of lobbying will remain finite for every reason. This cost function holds the key to the results obtained by Feenstra and Bhagwati.

With these assumptions Feenstra and Bhagwati obtained some interesting conclusions. For example, take the case of an increased import competition in the context of a specific factor model.[9] The specific factor (or its owner) in the import competing sector will lose as the price of the import competing good falls. To protect its interest it will lobby the government for increased protection.

The government, by assumption, has to respond to the lobbying (political) activity of the injured factor, and may raise the tariff rate on imports. This will, however, create a gap between the world prices and the domestic prices, and for obvious reasons, domestic welfare will fall. The government, by assumption, is

32

also a social welfare maximizer. Therefore, it would prefer not to raise tariff rates if other means are available that can provide protection to the injured sector, and would be interested in keeping the domestic prices as close to the world prices as possible.

Under these circumstances the government will necessarily raise the tariff rate on imports if other nondistortionary (lump-sum) taxes are not available or are not feasible. Nevertheless, the government can utilize the tariff revenue strategically so that the injured sector reduces its lobbying activity and the difference between the domestic price and world price is minimized.

In fact, Feenstra and Bhagwati obtain an *efficient tariff rate* at which the combined effect of the tariff rate and the tariff revenue when transferred fully to the injured factor is just sufficient to make the injured factor indifferent between the reduced level of lobbying, which induces the efficient tariff rate, and its optimal lobbying in the absence of such an income transfer. The government's act of bribing the injured factor with the *efficient* tariff revenue is welfare improving for two reasons. First, the deviation of the domestic price from the world price is reduced with this transfer scheme, and second, the resources absorbed in lobbying for efficient tariff is lower than it would absorb otherwise.

This result accomplishes several things. First, it explains why a tariff exists in the first place. Second, it identifies, in principle, the efficient tariff rate. Third, by virtue of their assumed lobbying cost function, it follows that a declining industry will continue to decline. Fourth, it maintains that the government is basically a benevolent agent.

However, as a guide to policy modelling, this approach is still far from being useful for several reasons. First, it is not clear why the government is supposed to respond to the lobbying effort of the injured factor.[10] Second, the nature and the form of the objective function of the government have not been specified. Third, the lobbying cost-of-tariff function for the injured factor has an ad hoc character. It has not been explained why the cost rises tremendously as the tariff rate approaches to offset the terms of trade change. Fourth, as Baldwin argued in his comments on Feenstra and Bhagwati's paper, it is not clear why the gaining factor does not spend resources in counter lobbying to maintain its gains when the terms of trade change and the injured factor lobbies for an increased tariff protection. Fifth, it is not clear at all whether the hypothesized behaviour of the government has a normative or a positive content. In summary, the approach suggested by Feenstra and Bhagwati, though interesting, does not seem very useful for modelling the process of tariff formation.

2.4 Forms of protection

The studies reviewed so far have assumed that tariff policy is the only instrument available to the government to pursue its objective, whatever it may be. With this assumption these studies have established that the government will change the tariff rate especially when international terms of trade change. Strictly speaking, these studies have shown that it would be in the interest of the government, for political or welfare reason, to insulate the domestic economy from foreign price shocks. They have not determined whether commercial policy interventions will be in the form of a tariff rate, quota, subsidies or something else.

There are situations in which the protective instruments are not equivalent. For example, Warr and Parmenter (1986) have shown that, in a situation with labour market disequilibrium, protection awarded through government procurement policies may dominate tariffs in terms of maintaining employment elsewhere in the economy.

How would a self-interested government choose between the tariff and the competitively auctioned quota as a protective instrument, since a relative-price protection to a 'declining' industry can be provided in either way? Cassing and Hillman (1985) studied this problem in a partial equilibrium setting, but assuming that the industry concerned has a monopoly power in the domestic market.

Cassing and Hillman have shown that the superiority of either instrument depends on the value attached by the government on the tariff revenue. If the government does not value the tariff revenue, and is concerned only with its political support, then tariffs dominate quotas, whereas if the government also values tariff revenue, then the tariff no longer unambiguously dominates the quota as an optimal instrument.

The irrelevance of the welfare comparison of various instruments, when the level of 'distortion' is endogenously determined through the political process, was noted by various authors (for example, Rodrik, 1986). Skirting this limitation, however, Rodrik concluded that tariffs could be welfare superior to production subsidies if the protected sector contains a sufficiently large number of firms. His main argument is that under the tariff regime the free rider problem will lead to 'under-demand' of protection than relative to the subsidy regime and therefore the level of distortion under the tariff regime will be lower. A Similar conclusion can also be found in Hall and Nelson (1992).

Lloyd and Falvey (1986) studied the choice of policy instrument when there is uncertainty in the international terms of trade using a political economy approach. They have shown that, for a given distribution of the international terms of trade, the distribution of the domestic relative price depends upon the nature of the protective instrument employed to provide protection. Given that all interest groups are risk averse the preference orderings of the protective instruments will differ across the interest groups and the choice of a particular instrument therefore determined by the domestic process of conflict resolution. In particular, they argue that such a choice would be determined by the relative political power of the interest groups.

Lloyd and Falvey's study indicates that any of the numerous protective instruments could be observed in place as an outcome of the political process depending on which of the conditions that guarantee the equivalence of the protective instruments is violated. In our study, we will ignore this issue by assuming that the conditions of equivalence between the protective instruments are satisfied.

2.5 Implications to the modelling strategy

We have reviewed the class of endogenous tariff literature which assumes that government is motivated by public-interest and the class of endogenous tariff literature which assumes that government is motivated by its own self-interest. As far as the behaviour of the tariff rate is concerned the predictions of both approaches are similar. Both approaches predict a *compensating* nature of tariff changes. However, they imply different strategies in modelling the endogenous process of tariff determination.

If one follows the public-interest approach in modelling government behaviour, then the implication of this choice to our modelling problem is that a social welfare function has to be specified somehow and the condition(s) that will be satisfied at the maximum of the social welfare function has to be included in the system of equations describing the general equilibrium of the economic sphere. A solution of this augmented system will yield the welfare maximizing tariff rate in general equilibrium.

However, there are conceptual problems in adopting this approach which need to be solved before such a model can be made operational. In particular, the existence and uniqueness of a social welfare function is a very real problem.[11] Moreover, to guarantee that the social welfare function is maximized through policy choices, it is necessary to assume that the policy makers or the politicians are benevolent and they do not pursue their own self-interest while making policy decisions at the cost of the society. Similar problems arise with the hybrid approach as well. Such problems, however, do not arise if we view the government or the politicians as a class of self-interested agents. In this study, therefore, we will assume that the government is guided by its own self-interest - the interest of remaining in power.

This assumption leads the present study into the class of endogenous tariff literature that adopts a political economy approach to tariff formation. On the basis of the experiences of the previous studies we may draw the following guidelines to model the endogenous process of tariff determination.

The first issue is related to the stylization of political economy. Several ways of stylizing the political and economic spheres exist in the literature. However, this study selects a particular stylization of these two spheres based on the following consideration.

Most of the previous studies have agreed on the conclusion that domestic tariffs respond to international terms of trade shocks. Since international market condition may change frequently for different exogenous reasons, it is natural to expect that domestic tariff rates are being reviewed continuously. Therefore, this study explicitly assumes that the marginal changes (adjustments) in domestic tariff rates are essentially short-run phenomenon.

Note, however, that this assumption does not necessarily imply a compensating nature of tariff changes. Tariffs may change in either direction in response to a shock. It simply implies that tariff changes do not involve long-run commitments on the part of the policy maker, and because of time inconsistency, the private sector cannot base its optimal decisions involving long-run commitments, including the capacity adjustments in the production sector, on the levels of the existing tariff rates.

This means that the adjustments in the economic markets triggered by tariff changes will be driven by short-run economic interests. A specific-factor model rather than a model that assumes perfect factor mobility in the economic sphere best describe the economic consequences of tariff changes to the private sector. Because of this reason, in contrast to MBY, this study will employ a specific-factor model to stylize the workings of the economic sphere of the political economy.

On the demand side of the political market this study will allow the players to spend resources in order to obtain favourable tariff policies. In this respect, as in previous studies, it will be assumed that only the owners of the specific factors behave strategically, and the rest behave nonstrategically.[12]

Whether the country is in a pluralistic or in a dictatorial regime, it will be assumed that the government wants to maximize political support while making policy decisions. It is because in a pluralistic setting elections are actually held at an infrequent interval of, say five years, and one party will be ruling in between any two elections. So it would be more relevant to consider the short-run political process under a well-established government's rule. The incumbent party (or the government) would, however, be in constant threat from the opposition and so it will always keep an eye on its re-election prospects.

The relevant description of the political market will, therefore, have a 'certain' government, not an 'expected' one of two or more parties, in place. In contrast to MBY, who studied the politico-economic system based on an expectational equilibrium, this study will be based on the actual (certain) outcomes of the politico-economic process. Thus, the present study differs from MBY in its stylization of the politico-economic environment, and provides an exposition of endogenous determination of tariffs in the short-run. Hence, this study may be regarded as a short-run compliment of MBY's long-run model.

Given this choice of politico-economic environment, this study will attempt to attain its objectives in the following steps:

1. Extend Coggins, et al.'s existence result onto a productive economy for a given pricing function that satisfies the properties stated in previous studies, and
2. Show that the properties satisfied by the pricing function of the government are consistent with the support maximizing behaviour of the government.

These two steps will show that the studies that have focussed on the demand side of the political market and studies that have focussed on the supply side are compatible. Moreover, it will also show that the political economy approach can consistently explain the existence of an 'active' commercial policy, since at least one nontrivial Nash equilibrium exists in the politico-economic system. These results will be obtained in Chapter 5.

The noncooperative approach of the existing literature in modelling the demand side of the political market implicitly assumes that the firms in each industry group cooperate with each other, whereas the industry coalitions do not. Adherence to this assumption in modelling the political process may lead to inefficient policy outcomes. For example, it is well known that in a noncooperative game, unless some arbitrary restrictions are imposed, the existence of multiple and sub-optimal equilibria cannot be ruled out. Such has been the experience of MBY who observed a pervasiveness of multiple equilibria, which also displayed the presence of Prisoner's Dilemma equilibrium, in simulations of models of political economies with endogenous tariff policy.

There is no compelling reason to assume that the political market is characterized by noncooperation only. One can view the political market as an institution which also facilitates communication and negotiation among the interest groups and the political activities as a bargaining process through which the conflicting interest groups reach in an agreement that is individually rational.[13] Such a view of the political sphere, however, does not rule out the possibility of noncooperation. The players may play the game noncooperatively if they choose to do so.

However, in MBY cooperation did not arise as a viable solution in a tariff-setting game, which they attributed to the presence of multiple equilibria, and the absence of an enforcement mechanism. In the presence of multiple equilibria a double cross in a cooperative solution could lead at least one player to an even worse noncooperative outcome. This result is possible in their model because they had taken a very long-run view in modelling the political economy in which there were two political parties contesting to govern the country. As a result, they had no government in place to enforce a cooperative solution. The problem of enforcement does not arise if one takes a short-run view in modelling the political economy because one can always observe a government in the short-run, which is interested in maximizing political support to remain in power. Enforcement of the cooperative agreement eliminates opposition that would otherwise arise from a policy choice and thus a government will have incentives to enforce cooperative agreements. More importantly, the tariff rate thus obtained at a cooperative solution will be Pareto efficient.

Therefore, in the third step we will extend the scope of the tariff-setting game by permitting cooperation to be in the strategy sets of the players. The policy making process will be defined in the framework of a Nash bargaining problem in which players will explicitly bargain over the appropriate level of the tariff rate, and also agree on not to be engaged in predatory lobbying activities. We will obtain the condition that will be satisfied by a Nash bargaining solution, and combine it with the conditions of general equilibrium in the economic sphere to obtain a general equilibrium model of the political economy. This model will allow us to study the comparative static behaviour of the bargained tariff rate with respect to the exogenous variables of the model. Chapters 6 to 8 will be devoted to this exercise, which will, in totality, represent the major departure of this study from the existing literature.

However, as it was observed in the previous sections, the predictions of the political economy approach are surprisingly close to that of the approach that maintains 'public interest' hypothesis in characterizing the government behaviour. Hence, the conclusion of our study can not be expected to be very different from that of these studies. In the event of agreement, the bargain-theoretic approach of the political economy may provide a political economy foundation for the CSWF. The two contending schools can thus be reconciled.

Notes

1   Yunker (1989) has provided some 'empirical' support to the social welfare maximizing approach to policy determination. Using a general equilibrium model of the US Yunker evaluated different forms of social welfare functions over a range of income tax rates to see whether the actual income tax rate in the US confirms to some welfare maximizing notion or not. He found that the income tax rates that maximize Benthamite (sum of utilities) or Nash (product of utilities) social welfare function are very close to the actual average income tax rate in the US. So, he concluded that the 'empirical result is consistent with society (or its government) unconsciously maximizing a social welfare function - suggesting that the concept of social welfare maximization may indeed possess positive as well as normative content' (p.111).

2   See Vousden (1990: 73-4) for arguments against the use of tariffs as a form of social insurance. He has argued that this form of insurance is not free from the problems of moral hazard and adverse selection, and therefore it will impose another cost on to the society. This raises a question that whether the welfare maximizing government will really choose to provide this kind of insurance at all. For rigorous demonstrations of the result see also Dixit (1987a, 1987b, 1989a, 1989b).

3   See also Baldwin (1987) for a similar result.

4   See also Long and Vousden (1991) for this result.

5   A question of noncommensurability of units of different commodities may arise, which Coggins et al. claim to have solved by their price normalization rule. That is, the units of commodities were chosen so that the prices of the two commodities add up to unity.

6   It is, however, claimed in Coggins, et al. (1991), that the pricing function 'could be considered a component of a more general model in which the government chooses the pricing function as a Stackelberg leader, with individuals in the economy reacting to the pricing function in an associated lobbying game. Any number of postulates regarding the government behaviour could be consistent with this approach.' (p. 535)

7   Let us consider n proposals, and arrange them in any arbitrary order. If there exists any one voter whose preference over these n proposals first declines and then rises, then his preference over these n alternatives is not single peaked. Majority voting rule can produce an equilibrium outcome if voters' preferences are all single peaked. Note that voters' preferences on a single issue are always single peaked. For details see Mueller (1979: 40-44) and references therein.

8   See footnote 19 in Mayer (1984).

9   Strictly speaking, the basic conflict runs along the factor lines in Feenstra and Bhagwati's model, however, the essential ideas of their model can be captured by a specific factor model as well.

10   The reason why the government in their model responds to lobbying by the injured factor is not clear. In the text Feenstra and Bhagwati use a 'tariff function' of Findlay and Wellisz (1982) and say that 'this lobbying function should be interpreted as derived from given political behaviour and institutions, such as the desire of politicians to maximize their probability of reelection' (p. 247), and later on in footnote 10 they write, 'the government's desire to maximize social welfare is consistent with its willingness to grant tariff protection, in that the latter can represent its reaction to distributive equity whereas the former corresponds to allocative efficiency' (p. 257). If the government is prepared to grant protection on equity grounds, then to invoke a 'lobbying function' and a reference to Brock and Magee (1978) is not justified. The social welfare function used by the government should be sufficient enough to generate the optimal tariff rate. On the other hand, if the government is assumed to maximize political support while granting tariff protection to the injured sector, then to claim that it represents the government's reaction to distributive equity is not justified. Thus, the position of Feenstra and Bhagwati is not easily understandable.

11   For a critical view on welfare economics as such see Sen (1979).

12   See for example Findlay and Wellisz (1982, 1983, 1984), Rodrik (1986), Yeldan and Roe (1991), and Hall and Nelson (1992).

13   For applications of cooperative game-theoretic approach in addressing the question of policy determination see Zusman (1976), Zusman and Amiad (1977), Beghin (1990), and Beghin and Karp (1991). Zusman's approach provides a game-theoretic basis for a policy preference function of the government, which is the sum of the government's own objective function and the interest group's objective functions weighted by their respective marginal strength of power over the government. He had also suggested a programming technique to estimate the marginal strengths of the interest groups. Zusman's approach was subsequently applied to explain the price polices, and estimate the marginal social powers of different producers and consumers of diary products under the Israeli Diary Program. Beghin (1990), and Beghin and Karp (1991) also adopted a bargain-theoretic approach in explaining the food pricing policy in Senegal. Their approach differs from that of Zusman in that they have attempted to estimate the game

econometrically. However, their specification of the estimating equations is rather ad hoc.

All of the above studies have described the game in general terms in which the government, just like any other player, has interest in policies that are in conflict with the interest of the other private players. Since they have not described a theory of government it is not possible to identify what the objective of the government is. However, in the application of their model to the pricing problem of a particular regulated commodity or a commodity group they have assumed that the government is a revenue maximizer, which could be a reasonable assumption because the game being studied is a small part of the overall policy game in which the government is involved. An application of their approach in a CGE framework does not seem straightforward. However, these studies may provide alternative methods of implementing a bargain-theoretic approach to study the problems of policy formation that could be a matter for future research.

3 An equilibrium model of the economic sphere of a small open political economy

Introduction

The purpose of this chapter is to describe the workings of the *economic* sphere of a small open political economy treating the policies of the government as given. This chapter is set out in three steps. First we specify a simple structure of the economic sphere of the political economy in neo-classical terms in which government policies, factor endowment, production technologies, and tastes are treated as exogenous. This structure defines a unique equilibrium of the economic sphere that is characterized by a set of necessary and sufficient conditions. In the second step, these conditions are linearized in terms of percentage changes of the model variables around the equilibrium point, and solved to obtain comparative static responses of the endogenous variables to exogenous shocks. Finally, the properties of the shares and elasticity parameters involved in determining the comparative static responses are employed to deduce the general properties of the equilibrium solution functions that hold at all equilibrium points of the model.

Because government policies are considered exogenous, the model described in this chapter belongs to the class of policy-exogenous general equilibrium models. Moreover, it belongs to a specific sub-class of policy-exogenous models, called specific-factor models, because the structure assumes that capital is specific to industries. Therefore, most of the results of this chapter are fairly well-known in the literature (see for example Jones, 1971; Mussa, 1974; Neary, 1978). We, derive, nevertheless, them because these results form the building blocks for the subsequent chapters.

The choice of the specific-factor model is motivated by the following three reasons. First, the problem of tariff determination, the specific modelling issue of this study, has already been studied extensively by Magee, Brock and Young (1989) in the context of a Heckscher-Ohlin-Samuelson type general equilibrium model of the economic sphere. Second, tariffs and other redistributive policy changes can be viewed as short-run phenomena in the sense that they can, in principle, be adjusted quite frequently by the incumbent government. The optimal responses of the producers to the tariff and other policy changes would be constrained by the specificity of some of the productive factors.

Third, unless there are reasons, such as credible commitments by the government, to believe that the government's policies will not change over a long period a small variation in policies is unlikely to affect the allocation, within the private sector, of factors that are relatively immobile in the short-run.

This chapter is divided into four sections. The first section outlines the main assumptions of the model. The second section develops the structure of the general equilibrium system. The comparative static results and the properties of the solution functions are studied in the third section. A short summary of the chapter is provided in the fourth section.

3.1 The economy

In building the model of the economic sphere we start with the following assumptions. The economy has two single-product sectors, each one with many identical firms. The firms in each sector employ capital and labour according to constant returns to scale CES technology to produce a homogenous good. The existence of intermediate inputs is ignored. All firms are price takers in all commodity, factor and foreign exchange markets, and all firms in both production sectors are profit maximizers. These assumptions allow us to aggregate all firms producing each of the homogenous commodities into an industry-sector, which is simply a scalar multiple of a single firm.

In the short run, capital is (firm) sector-specific, whereas (homogenous) labour is perfectly mobile. The endowment of all factors is exogenously given.

Both goods are internationally traded. The economy is small and open relative to the world market of the two goods. Transportation costs and other margins on trade are ignored. As a result, the relative price of commodities in the domestic market is exogenously determined by the international relative price and government intervention, which can be expressed in equivalent nominal tariff rate.

To simplify further it is also assumed that all factor owners have identical homothetic preferences, and each one is a price taker in goods, factor and foreign exchange markets. The implication of this assumption is that the personal distribution of income plays no role in determining the aggregate demand for commodities, and aggregation of preferences across individuals is valid. More specifically, it is assumed that the economy has a single national (or a representative) consumer with a preference structure that can be represented by a Cobb-Douglas utility function defined on the two commodities, and all final demand is treated as consumption of the national consumer. The consumer receives all factor incomes and the tariff revenue. The consumer is a utility maximizer.

Furthermore, it is assumed that all prices are fully flexible, and all markets clear instantly. All factors are internationally immobile. With these assumptions we proceed to derive the general equilibrium structure of the economic sphere of a small open political economy.

3.2 The structure of the policy-exogenous general equilibrium model

This section specifies the basic structure of the policy-exogenous general equilibrium model (PXGEM). First, under the above assumptions, we analyze a producer's behaviour facing a quantity constraint on the stock of capital. Given the wage rate and the output price, we derive an expression for the virtual rental rate of capital such that the existing stock of capital is optimal to produce a given level of output. We then derive the virtual cost of production at each output level by paying the fixed capital its virtual rental rate and labour its market wage rate. It is then shown that a unique profit maximizing output level can be determined by requiring that average virtual cost be equal to the given output price.

The 'zero-profit' condition and the rental function are then solved to obtain the equilibrium output level and the virtual rental rate in terms of the wage rate and commodity prices. These results are then used to derive conditional labour demand functions in terms of given commodity prices and the wage rate. These equations represent solutions to producer's problem of determining profit maximizing output levels and yield equilibrium rental rates and labour demand of each sector at given prices of commodities and the wage rate.

A simple labour market has been specified in which the supply of labour is exogenous. Sectoral labour demand functions are aggregated to obtain the market demand for labour, at given commodity prices. The wage rate adjusts to clear the labour market. The equilibrium wage rate, thus, can be regarded as a function of commodity prices, quantity of labour supplied, and other technological parameters.

Consumer demands are generated by maximizing a Cobb-Douglas utility function.[1] Goods market, and the foreign exchange market-clearing conditions simultaneously determine the quantities of net trade on the two goods and the exchange rate at the equilibrium of goods and the foreign exchange markets. This yields a system of 14 equations in 14 endogenous variables. One of the market-clearing conditions, however, is redundant by Walras' law. We, therefore, delete the market-clearing condition for foreign exchange, and end up with 13 equations in 14 variables. The system is closed by choosing commodity 2 as the numeraire. This choice sets the price of commodity 2 at unity and thus the number of unknowns is reduced to thirteen, the same as the number of equations in the system.

Furthermore, trade taxes have been rationalized into a single import tariff rate using the Lerner symmetry theorem. Since the domestic and the foreign price of the numeraire commodity are equal to unity, this rationalization forces the value of the nominal exchange rate to unity, and effectively reduces the number of endogenous variables and the number of equations in the system by one. Thus, we finally obtain a system of twelve equations in twelve endogenous variables that describes the general equilibrium structure of the 'real' economic sphere of a small open economy. The following sections derive these relations formally.

3.2.1 The production sectors

For each sector j=1, 2 the production function can be described by the CES function:

$$Y_j = \left(\alpha_j L_j^{-\rho_j} + \beta_j K_j^{-\rho_j} \right)^{-1/\rho_j} ; \tag{3.1}$$

where, Y_j is the quantity of output, L_j is the number of labour units, K_j is the number of capital unit employed; α_j and β_j are distribution parameters, which are strictly positive and add up to unity; ρ_j is a CES parameter which can take any value such greater than -1. It is straightforward to verify that the production function represented by equation (3.1) implies constant returns to scale.

Let W be the market wage rate of labour and let R denote the rental rate of capital. Given R and W, the problem of a price taking, profit-maximizing producer is to choose the levels of L and K so that the cost of producing a given level of output is minimized. Formally, the problem may be stated as:

$$\min_{L_j, K_j} \quad (WL_j + RK_j) \tag{3.2}$$

subject to $\quad Y_j = \left(\alpha_j L_j^{-\rho_j} + \beta_j K_j^{-\rho_j} \right)^{-1/\rho_j} .$

The solution to this minimization problem yields conditional factor demand functions. The conditional demand function for capital stock can be obtained as

$$K_j = \beta_j^{1/(1+\rho_j)} R^{-1/(1+\rho_j)}$$
$$\left[\alpha_j^{1/(1+\rho_j)} W^{\rho_j/(1+\rho_j)} + \beta_j^{1/(1+\rho_j)} R^{\rho_j/(1+\rho_j)} \right]^{1/\rho_j} Y_j ; \tag{3.3}$$

and the conditional demand function for labour can be obtained as

$$L_j = \alpha_j^{1/(1+\rho_j)} W^{-1/(1+\rho_j)}$$

$$\left[\alpha_j^{1/(1+\rho_j)} W^{\rho_j/(1+\rho_j)} + \beta_j^{1/(1+\rho_j)} R^{\rho_j/(1+\rho_j)} \right]^{1/\rho_j} Y_j . \tag{3.4}$$

Upon substitution, the minimum cost function is given by

$$C_j\left(Y_j\right) = \left[\alpha_j^{1/(1+\rho_j)} W^{\rho_j/(1+\rho_j)} + \beta_j^{1/(1+\rho_j)} R^{\rho_j/(1+\rho_j)} \right]^{(1+\rho_j)/\rho_j} Y_j . \tag{3.5}$$

Equations (3.3) - (3.5) represent a straightforward solution to the cost minimization problem which assumes perfect mobility of factors, both capital and labour, across the sectors in response to higher rewards. Since it is well understood that production sectors are unable to adjust their existing stock of some factors to their desired level in the short-run, the assumption of perfect factor mobility is more reasonable for the longer run than for the short run.

As long as the main modelling issue is one concerned with the short-run producers' behaviour, for example rent seeking, the ideal framework should treat some factors as inter-sectorally immobile. Therefore, this study closely follows the specific-factor model (Mussa, 1974; Neary, 1978; and references therein) in modelling the economic sphere.[2] In what follows, the term 'capital' represents all factors that are given and sector-specific in the short-run and the term 'labour' represents all factors that are perfectly mobile.

Thus, with the assumption that the capital stock is given for each sector, equation (3.3) can be solved for the sector-specific rental rate that would make the existing stock of sector-specific capital optimal for given wage rate and given level of activity. Solving equation (3.3) we get:

$$R_j = \left[\left(K_j / Y_j \right)^{\rho_j} - \beta_j \right]^{-\left(1+\rho_j\right)/\rho_j} \alpha_j^{1/\rho_j} \beta_j W . \tag{3.6}$$

The rental rate R_j obtained from equation (3.6) is the maximum rental rate that a firm would be willing to pay if it had to hire its stock of the specific-factor from the rental market to produce the output level Y_j under the CES production function (3.1) and a given wage rate W. In other words, at the rental rate R_j and the wage rate W, the producer will find the existing stock of capital K_j optimal for the production of Y_j. In line with the literature (for example, Neary and Roberts, 1980) that address the issue of valuation when the choice is quantity constrained, we distinguish this rental rate from the market-clearing (long-run) rate of return to capital by stating the following definition:

Definition 3.1 (*virtual rental rate*). *For a given level of output and price of the mobile factor, an endogenously determined rental rate that makes the given stock of the specific factor optimal is defined as the virtual rental rate of the specific factor.*[3]

Substituting the virtual rental rate, R_j, from equation (3.6) into equation (3.4) and solving for L_j, the labour demand, we get:

$$L_j = \alpha_j^{1/\rho_j}\left[K_j^{\rho_j} / \left(K_j^{\rho_j} - \beta_j Y_j^{\rho_j} \right) \right]^{1/\rho_j} Y_j . \tag{3.7}$$

Equation (3.7) shows that given the technological parameters, the short run conditional demand for labour depends on the level of output and the stock of fixed factor but not directly on any price including the wage rate. The reason is very simple - if output is to be increased in the short run the only way is to employ more labour as dictated directly by the production function. Therefore, the conditional demand for labour can alternatively be derived directly from the production function without going through the process of cost minimization.

Definition 3.2 (*virtual cost*). *The minimum cost of producing a given level of output when the mobile factor is paid its market rate and the specific factor is paid its virtual rental rate is defined as the **virtual cost** of production; the corresponding cost function is defined as the **virtual cost function**.*

Substitution of the virtual rental function from equation (3.6) into the minimum cost function given by equation (3.5) yields

$$C_j^*(Y_j) = \alpha_j^{1/\sigma_j}\left[K_j^{\rho_j} / \left(K_j^{\rho} - \beta_j Y_j^{\rho} \right) \right]^{(1+\rho_j)/\rho_j} W Y_j \tag{3.8}$$

where, $C_j^*(Y_j)$ is the virtual total cost of producing Y_j.

Given a wage rate W and the capital stock K_j, equation (3.8) describes the short run total minimum cost of producing the output level Y_j when sector-specific factors are paid at their virtual prices. In order to distinguish this virtual cost function from the conventional minimum cost function, in which the specific-factors are valued at their opportunity cost of zero, we make the following definitions:

Definition 3.3 (*variable cost*). *Given a stock of the specific factor, and price of the mobile factor(s), the minimum cost of employing the mobile factor so that a* *given level of output can be produced is defined as the total variable cost of the given level of output. The function that yields the **variable cost** of production for each level of output is defined as the **variable cost function**.*

In the long-run when all factors are mobile and command a market price virtual cost becomes equal to the variable cost. However in the short run, when there is at least one sector-specific or fixed factor of production, the virtual cost and the variable cost diverge. Virtual cost exceeds variable cost when the virtual rental rate is positive. The cost $C_j^*(Y_j)$, defined in equation (3.8), is an example of virtual cost of producing the output level Y_j. The wage bill is an example of the variable cost when labour is the only mobile factor of production.

3.2.2 Determination of profit maximizing output: zero pure profit condition

A simple manipulation of equation (3.8), using the production function (3.1), yields[4]

$$C_j^*(Y_j)/Y_j = W / \left[\alpha_j (Y_j / L_j)^{1+\rho_j} \right] \tag{3.9}$$

It can be easily seen that $W / \alpha_j (Y_j / L_j)^{1+\rho_j}$, the expression on the right-hand side of equation (3.9), represents the marginal cost (wage rate divided by marginal product of labour) of producing Y_j, when labour is the only variable factor of production. This is the derivative of variable cost function. The expression on the left-hand side, however, is the average virtual cost, $C_j^*(Y_j)/Y_j$, of producing Y_j. *This means that the average virtual cost of production (when capital is paid its virtual price) is exactly equal to the (conventional) marginal variable cost of production for each value of Y_j.*

Since profit maximization under competitive conditions requires that the output level be chosen so that marginal cost equals price, equation (3.9) implies that under similar conditions profit maximization requires that output level be chosen so that average virtual cost be equal to the price.[5] This means that when we are dealing with virtual cost functions profit maximization requires zero profit conditions to hold. So long as the production function implies a falling marginal product the average virtual cost curve is upward sloping for given price of mobile factors, and 'zero pure profit' also becomes a sufficient condition for profit maximization.

For given output price, P, and wage rate W, Figure 3.1 shows the determination of the profit maximizing output level. The horizontal axis measures output level and the vertical axis measures virtual cost and price. The average virtual cost curve is drawn sloping upwards, which is implied by the derivative of the average virtual cost function. We know from equation (3.6) that as output level rises the virtual price of capital also rises. It is precisely so because the marginal productivity of the specific-factor, capital, increases and the marginal productivity of labour falls with more employment of labour.

Equation (3.6) can also be written as

$$R_j = P_j\beta_j\left(\frac{Y_j}{K_j}\right)^{1+\rho_j}\left(\frac{W}{P_j\alpha_j\left(Y_j/L_j\right)^{1+\rho_j}}\right).$$
(3.6)

This equation represents nothing more than what can be seen from the first order conditions of cost minimization: that the price paid to each factor be proportional to the corresponding value of its marginal product. However, the way it is expressed in equation (3.6) helps us to understand the nature of the virtual cost function.

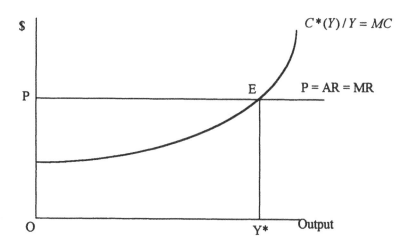

Figure 3.1 Average virtual cost, the marginal variable cost and the zero profit condition

The right hand side of equation (3.6) contains two parts: the first is the value of marginal product of capital and the second is the ratio of wage to the value of marginal product of labour. It shows that if labour is paid less than the value of its marginal product, then the virtual price of a given stock of capital will also be proportionately less than the value of its marginal product. This means that if producers want to produce less than the profit maximizing level of output at a given wage rate, capital stock and output price, they can hire labour at the market wage rate which will be less than the value of the marginal product. Hence the virtual price of capital will also be less than the value of its marginal product. Therefore, for all output less than that which maximizes profit, it follows that, the virtual cost of production will be less than the value of output and the average virtual cost will be less than the output price.[6]

This explains why in Figure 3.1 for all $Y < Y^*$ we have $C^*(Y)/Y$ less than the output price P. Similarly, to the right of Y^* labour has to be paid more than its value of marginal product and so the virtual price of capital will also be more than its value of marginal product. Linear homogeneity of the production function implies that the value of output will be short of the virtual cost of production and hence the curve depicting $C^*(Y)/Y$ lies above the revenue line. At point E average virtual cost equals price, so the value of output is just sufficient to pay for the factors. This means that at E 'zero-pure-profit condition' holds and the given stock of capital obtains its maximum feasible virtual-rental rate.

It is also clear that the output level at which the zero-profit condition holds is unique so long as the production function admits a unique profit maximizing output for any configuration of factor and product prices. The implication of this discussion is that combining a 'zero pure profit' condition with the virtual cost function is sufficient to identify the profit maximizing output level. The average virtual cost function can serve as a short-run output supply function.

Therefore, using equation (3.8) we can write the zero pure profit condition as

$$P_j = \alpha_j^{1/\rho_j} \left[K_j^\rho / \left(K_j^\rho - \beta_j Y_j^\rho \right) \right]^{(1+\rho_j)/\rho_j} W . \qquad (3.10)$$

Solving equation (3.10) for Y_j one can obtain the output supply function as

$$Y_j = K_j \beta_j^{-1/\rho_j} \left[1 - \alpha_j^{1/(1+\rho_j)} \left(W/P_j \right)^{\rho_j/(1+\rho_j)} \right]^{1/\rho_j} . \qquad (3.11)$$

It can be seen from equation (3.11) that the supply of output increases with output price and falls with the wage rate. An increase in the stock of specific factor raises output level at unchanged prices.

For each wage and product price combination, the value of the output given by equation (3.11) maximizes the virtual rent (or the quasi-rent). Substitution of the value of Y from (3.11) into equations (3.6) and (3.7) yields the equilibrium rental rate and the equilibrium labour demand functions respectively for given wage rate and the product price.

The equilibrium *rental function* can, therefore, be written as

$$R_j = \beta_j^{-1/\rho_j} \left(P_j^{\rho_j/(1+\rho_j)} - \alpha_j^{1/(1+\rho_j)} W^{\rho_j/(1+\rho_j)} \right)^{(1+\rho_j)/\rho_j} .$$

(3.12)

Thus, equation (3.12) yields the virtual rental rate of the sector-specific capital for given output price and the price of the mobile factor. It shows that in equilibrium the virtual rental rate rises with output price, P, and falls with the price of the mobile factor, W. Making use of equation (3.11) it can also be seen from equation (3.12) that the equilibrium rental rate is equal to the value of marginal product of the sector-specific factor - capital.

The equilibrium labour demand function can be obtained as

$$L_j = K_j \alpha_j^{1/(1+\rho_j)} \beta_j^{-1/\rho_j}$$

$$\left[\left(P_j / W \right)^{\rho_j/(1+\rho_j)} - \alpha_j^{1/(1+\rho_j)} \right]^{1/\rho_j} \qquad j = 1,2.$$

(3.13)

Equation (3.13) shows that equilibrium demand for labour increases with output price and falls with wage rate. Furthermore, at given prices, an increase in the stock of the specific-factor raises the equilibrium demand for the mobile factor.

Thus, the equilibrium behaviour of the production sectors in terms of output supply, labour demand and the payment to their specific factors can be obtained from equations (3.11)-(3.13).

3.2.3 The labour market

A simple form of labour (mobile factor) market is assumed. The supply of labour is assumed to be exogenous. For given output prices, production sectors determine their profit maximizing level of output and employment at each wage rate, which determine the aggregate demand for labour. Since, the aggregate demand for labour has to match the exogenous supply of labour, the labour market is cleared and labour is allocated to various sectors by a flexible wage rate.

Let L be the total stock of labour in the economy, then equilibrium in the labour market requires that

$$L = \sum_{j=1}^{2} L_j .$$

(3.15)

It is clear from (3.13) that the sectoral-labour demand is unaffected by a given change its output price if the wage rate also changes in the same proportion. It follows from (3.15) that the wage rate moves in proportion to a uniform change in all output prices. Therefore, the nominal wage rate is homogenous of degree one in output prices.

50

3.2.4   Demand for goods

All domestic final demanders are merged into a single national consumer. The consumer encompasses all households, the government, and all investors. This national consumer is assumed to receive all payments to the primary factors, and the tariff revenue. In this framework, lending, borrowing and tax payments cancel out within the group and the aggregate budget constraint holds. The purpose of this assumption is to abstract from the distributional issues.[7]

The preference ordering of this national consumer over the two goods is assumed to be represented by a Cobb-Douglas utility function. The objective of the consumer is to maximize utility, which depends on (C_1, C_2) the quantities of the two goods consumed. In particular, the problem of the consumer can be written as:

$$\max_{c_1, c_2} U(C_1, C_2) = C_1^{\delta_1} C_2^{\delta_2}; \qquad \delta_1 + \delta_2 = 1; \quad \delta_1, \delta_2 > 0; \qquad (3.16)$$

subject to

$$P_1 C_1 + P_2 C_2 = I. \qquad (3.17)$$

The income, I, of the consumer is given by

$$I = P_1 Y_1 + P_2 Y_2 + Z. \qquad (3.18)$$

where, Z is the total tariff revenue to be defined below.

Solution to this maximization problem leads to the following demand functions:

$$C_i = \delta_i I / P_i; \qquad\qquad i = 1, 2. \qquad (3.19)$$

The demand functions expressed in equation (3.19) imply that the income elasticities of consumer demand are unity, own price elasticities are -1, and cross price elasticities are zero for both goods. Furthermore, they also imply a constant share of each good in the consumer's budget. These restrictions are the consequences of assuming a Cobb-Douglas utility function.[8]

3.2.5   Price determination

The country under study is assumed to satisfy the small country assumption. This implies that the country is a price taker in the international market. It can affect domestic prices through various policies, but not international prices. Let Φ

denote the nominal exchange rate, P_i^* denote the international price of good i, and T_i denote the proportional ad valorem tax rate on the international trade (positive entry for tax on imports and negative entry for tax on exports) of good i. Now we can write the domestic price of good i as

$$P_i = \Phi P_i^* (1 + T_i); \qquad i = 1,2. \tag{3.20}$$

In writing equation (3.19) it is implicitly assumed that no other taxes and/or controls are used to affect the domestic price of commodity i, and there are no transportation or other margins cost.

3.2.6   Equilibrium in goods and the foreign exchange markets

Let M_i denote the volume of net imports (exports, if negative) of commodity i at a given domestic relative price, then domestic market-clearing conditions for commodities $i = 1, 2$ can be written as

$$C_i = Y_i + M_i. \tag{3.21}$$

The tariff revenue collection is given by

$$Z = \sum_{i=1}^{2} \Phi P_i^* T_i M_i. \tag{3.22}$$

The value of exports at world price represents the supply of, and the value of imports at world price represents the demand for foreign exchange in the domestic economy. Equilibrium in the foreign exchange market requires these two quantities be equal. Therefore we have,

$$P_1^* M_1 + P_2^* M_2 = 0. \tag{3.23}$$

This equation implies that for all domestic prices the value of domestic exports has to be equal to the value of imports at world price. In other words, trade account at the world price should remain balanced in equilibrium. The implicit assumption here is that there are no capital flows in and out of the country. Of course, this is another simplification.

Equations (3.11)-(3.23) fully describe the real sector of the economy. Y eliminating defining equations, the set of minimum equations reflecting the equilibrium of the economic sphere is given in Table 3.1.

The model consists of 14 equations in 14 variables: the two domestic outputs, the two consumer demands, the two net imports of commodities, the two domestic commodity prices, the two sectoral labour demands, the two sectoral rental rates, the wage rate and the exchange rate. The system contains seven exogenous variables: the two world prices, the two tax rates, the two quantities of sector-specific factors, and the total supply of labour.

The story that is told by this system of equations is the following. For given domestic prices, the three equations of the labour market determine the three variables: wage rate, and sectoral allocation of labour. The sectoral output levels can be determined from the two sectoral supply functions, since the market-clearing wage rate and the commodity prices are already determined. Similarly, sectoral rental rates are determined from the two rental functions.

Once commodity prices are given, the production side of the economy is completely determined without any reference to the structure and the level of consumer demand. This independence of the supply side from the demand side of the economy occurs because the model describes a small open economy that does not produce any non-tradable commodity. This feature of a small open economy simplifies the modelling problem considerably, and will be used extensively in the subsequent sections and chapters.

The five variables - the two consumer demands, the two net imports of commodities and the consumer's income (that is, the tariff revenue part of the consumer's income), are simultaneously determined by the five equations, the two consumer demand functions and the three market-clearing conditions, at given product prices. The domestic prices of the two commodities will be determined by the pricing equations (3.20), if the nominal exchange rate is known.

Multiplying both sides of equation (3.21), the market-clearing conditions for commodities, by P_i and using equations (3.17), (3.18), (3.20), and (3.22) we can obtain equation (3.23). This means that equilibrium in the commodity markets (equation 3.21) implies an equilibrium in the foreign exchange market. This, in other words, is an instance of Walras' Law. Therefore, one of the three market-clearing conditions is redundant. We have chosen to delete the trade balance constraint.

The Goods Market:

The supply functions of domestic production sectors:

$$Y_j = K_j \beta_j^{-1/\rho_j} \left[1 - \alpha_j^{1/(1+\rho_j)} \left(W / P_j \right)^{\rho_j/(1+\rho_j)} \right]^{1/\rho_j} ; \qquad j = 1,2. \qquad (3.11)$$

Consumer demand functions:

$$C_i = (\delta_i / P_i) \sum_{j=1}^{2} (P_j Y_j + \Phi T_j P_j^* M_j) ; \qquad i = 1,2. \qquad (3.19)$$

Goods market equilibrium:
$$C_i = Y_i + M_i; \qquad i = 1, 2. \qquad (3.21)$$

Domestic Price Determination:

$$P_i = \Phi P_i^* (1 + T_i); \qquad i = 1,2. \qquad (3.20)$$

The Labour Market:

Sectoral labour demand:

$$L_j = K_j \alpha_j^{1/(1+\rho_j)} \beta_j^{-1/\rho_j} \left[\left(P_j / W \right)^{\rho_j/(1+\rho_j)} - \alpha_j^{1/(1+\rho_j)} \right]^{1/\rho_j} ; \qquad j = 1,2. \quad (3.13)$$

Labour market equilibrium:

$$L = \sum_{j=1}^{2} L_j . \qquad (3.15)$$

Rental Rates:

$$R_j = \beta_j^{-1/\rho_j} \left(P_j^{\rho_j/(1+\rho_j)} - \alpha_j^{1/(1+\rho_j)} W^{\rho_j/(1+\rho_j)} \right)^{(1+\rho_j)/\rho_j} ; \qquad j = 1,2. \quad (3.12)$$

The Foreign Exchange Market:

Equilibrium in the Foreign exchange market:
$$P_1^* M_1 + P_2^* M_2 = 0. \qquad (3.23)$$

However, once equation (3.23) is dropped out, the system contains only thirteen independent equations in fourteen variables. We are left with two pricing equations (3.20), and three price variables: the exchange rate and two commodity prices. Therefore, one price (or any one nominal quantity) has to be exogenously determined (that is, one more price relation has to be added into the system). This is precisely the point where the money market of the macro economic system becomes quite useful for a model of the present type.

A feature of all Walrasian general equilibrium models, including the present one, is that the functions determining the demand for and supply of real quantities are all homogenous of degree zero in all prices (commodity and factor prices and the exchange rate); the nominal quantities, such as income, are homogenous of degree one in all prices. Equilibrium levels of real quantities - outputs, consumption, net trade, and employment - will, therefore, be unaffected by proportionate change in all prices; only the nominal quantities will change proportionately which are of no significance. This property of the model has been used to isolate one of the price variable (or any nominal quantity) to be determined outside the system of 'general' equilibrium.[9]

3.2.8   Price normalization rule[10]

To eliminate these uninteresting cases of pure nominal changes, commodity prices are normalized and the tariff rates are rationalized in the following way.

First, we invoke the Lerner symmetry theorem (Lerner, 1936) and replace export tax by its equivalent import tax. Since, the economy exports good 2, and imports good 1, let

$$T_1^R = [(T_1 - T_2) / (1 + T_2)].$$
(3.24)

Then, the Lerner symmetry theorem implies that in terms of revenue and relative price effects the imposition of a single tariff rate T_1^R on the imports of good 1 and no tax on exports of good 2 is equivalent to the joint imposition of export tax rate T_2 on good 2, and a import tariff rate T_1 on good 1. We will call T_1^R the *rationalized tariff rate.*

Note that, T_1^R is invariant of pure scalar change in both export and import tax rates.[11] Therefore, for given world relative price, T_1^R is in one-to-one correspondence with the domestic relative price P_1. The sign of T_1^R indicates whether the economy is subsidizing or taxing foreign trade. In particular, $T_1^R > 0$ implies a net tax and $T_1^R < 0$ implies a net subsidy on foreign trade.[12]

Table 3.2
A policy exogenous general equilibrium model of the real economic sphere

The Goods Market:
The supply functions of domestic production sectors:

$$Y_j = K_j \beta_j^{-1/\rho_j} \left[1 - \alpha_j^{1/(1+\rho_j)} \left(W / P_j \right)^{\rho_j/(1+\rho_j)} \right]^{1/\rho_j} ; \qquad\qquad j = 1,2. \qquad (3.11)$$

Consumer demand functions:

$$C_j = (\delta_j / P_j) \sum_{i=1}^{2} (P_i Y_i + \Phi T_i P_i^* M_i) ; \qquad\qquad j = 1,2. \qquad (3.19)$$

Goods market equilibrium:

$$C_i(P) = Y_i(P) + M_i(P); \qquad\qquad i = 1, 2. \qquad (3.21)$$

The Labour Market:
Sectoral labour demand:

$$L_j = K_j \alpha_j^{1/(1+\rho_j)} \beta_j^{-1/\rho_j} \left[\left(P_j / W \right)^{\rho_j/(1+\rho_j)} - \alpha_j^{1/(1+\rho_j)} \right]^{1/\rho_j} ; \qquad j = 1,2. \qquad (3.13)$$

Labour market equilibrium:

$$L = \sum_{j=1}^{2} L_j . \qquad\qquad (3.15)$$

Domestic price determination:

$$P_1 = P_1^* (1 + T_1^R). \qquad\qquad (3.26)$$

Rental Rates:

$$R_j = \beta_j^{-1/\rho_j} \left(P_j^{\rho_j/(1+\rho_j)} - \alpha_j^{1/(1+\rho_j)} W^{\rho_j/(1+\rho_j)} \right)^{(1+\rho_j)/\rho_j} ; \quad j = 1,2. \qquad (3.12)$$

Price Normalization Rule:

$$P_2 \equiv 1 . \qquad\qquad (3.25)$$

List of 12 Endogenous Variables:

Y_j	$j = 1,2.$	: 2 Sectoral outputs
C_j	$j = 1,2.$	: 2 Domestic demands
M_i	$i = 1,2.$	: 2 Net import quantities
L_j	$j = 1,2.$	: 2 Sectoral employment of labour
R_j	$j = 1,2.$	: 2 Sectoral rental rates in units of commodity 2
W		: 1 Wage rate in units of commodity 2
P_1		: 1 Price of commodity 1 in units of commodity 2

Second, we choose good 2 as the *numeraire*, and express all prices and nominal quantities in units of good 2. In other words, by the choice of unit we set

$$P_2 = P_2^* = 1. \tag{3.25}$$

Now, with the imposition of the rationalized tariff rate on imports of good 1 and no tax on exports of good 2, which is also the numeraire, we can see from pricing rule (3.20) that the nominal exchange rate, Φ, is always unity. The domestic price of good 1 is given by

$$P_1 = P_1^* (1 + T_1^R). \tag{3.26}$$

Clearly, equations (3.25) and (3.26) replace the original pricing equation (3.20) in the system of equations described in Table 3.1.

3.2.9   A model of the real economic sphere

Now, we obtain a general equilibrium model of the real sectors of the economic sphere by applying the normalization rules of the previous section. This concludes the construction of a simple policy-exogenous general equilibrium model of the economic sphere of a small open economy. By deleting the trade balance constraint, writing unity for the nominal exchange rate, and replacing the pricing equation (3.20) by equations (3.25) and (3.26) the system of equation describing the general equilibrium can be written as in Table 3.2.

The model of the real sector organized into Table 3.2 contains 12 equations in 12 endogenous variables (excluding the price normalization rule), which are listed at the bottom of the same Table. The exogenous variables are domestic factor endowments K_1, K_2, L, the rationalized tariff rate T_1^R, and the international relative price of commodity 1, P_1^*. This model of the real economic sphere is a stylized example of policy exogenous general equilibrium models (PXGEM), because the tariff rate is being treated as an exogenous variable. The model is of the standard textbook type; the existence of a solution to this model is not a problem at all (see, for example, Shoven, 1974).

3.2.10   Factor and employment shares

Let S_{Lj} and S_{Kj} denote respectively the share of labour and the share of the sector-specific factor in the value of output (which equals total cost) of sector j. Then, by making use of equations (3.11) and (3.13), and keeping in mind that $P_2^* = 1$ we can write:

$$S_{Lj} = \frac{WL_j}{P_j Y_j} = \alpha^{1/(1+\rho)} \left(P_j / W \right)^{-\rho/(1+\rho)}; \qquad\qquad j = 1,2. \qquad (3.28)$$

Using equations (3.11) and (3.12) the share of the specific factor in sector j can be obtained as:

$$S_{Kj} = \frac{K_j R_j}{P_j Y_j} = 1 - \alpha^{1/(1+\rho)} \left(P_j / W \right)^{-\rho/(1+\rho)}; \qquad\qquad j = 1,2. \qquad (3.29)$$

Equations (3.28) and (3.29) show that in equilibrium the distributive shares add up to one.

Let us further define

$$\lambda_j = L_j / L; \qquad\qquad j = 1,2; \qquad\qquad (3.30)$$

$$\sigma_j = 1 / (1 + \rho_j); \qquad\qquad j = 1,2; \qquad\qquad (3.31)$$

and,

$$\tau = 1 / (1 + T_1^R) \qquad\qquad (3.32)$$

then, λ_j represents the employment share of sector j in total employment of labour, σ_j is the elasticity of factor substitution, which is a constant; and τ represents the rationalized tariff coefficient.

Equations (3.28) to (3.32) describe the structure of the share and other parameters which will be used in the following sections to derive the comparative static properties of the model.

3.3   Comparative static results and the properties of the solution functions

For use in subsequent chapters, we will derive the comparative static responses of the endogenous variables under three different tariff regimes: free trade, autarkic and a tariff regime which is intermediate between the two. The derivation of comparative static responses under a free trade regime is provided in Appendix-3A, and that under autarkic regime is provided in Appendix-3B. This section derives the comparative static responses of the endogenous variables under the intermediate tariff regime. These responses are further analyzed to deduce some general properties of the solution functions. We have called the equilibrium under the intermediate tariff regime as the 'observed' equilibrium because the intermediate tariff regime is the one that is observable in the real world. In subsequent chapters we will, therefore, be analyzing the behaviour of a political economy that has a positive rationalized tariff rate in place.

Values of endogenous variables and their shares that are specific to a particular equilibrium point are distinguished by superscripts. Superscript 'o' refers to the observed equilibrium, whereas '*' and 'a' refer to the free trade equilibrium and the autarkic equilibrium respectively.

Let $E \equiv (Y_1, Y_2, C_1, C_2, L_1, L_2, R_1, R_2, W, P_1)$ be the solution vector of the relevant endogenous variables at the general equilibrium of the economic sphere. Let E^o, E^* and E^a be the general equilibrium solution vectors in the three different tariff regimes but with the same factor endowment and the world relative price. Then the solution vector in observed equilibrium can be written as:

$$E^o = E^o (K_1, K_2, L, T_1^R, P_1^*);$$ \hfill (3.33)

since tariffs do not exist in a freely trading environment, the solution vector in free trade equilibrium can be written as

$$E^* = E^* (K_1, K_2, L, P_1^*);$$ \hfill (3.34)

the economy does not trade with the rest of the world and therefore changes in foreign prices do not matter in autarky in an autarkic environment, the autarkic solution vector can be written as

$$E^a = E^a (K_1, K_2, L);$$ \hfill (3.35)

where, the E's on the right hand side of the above equations represent the appropriate vectors of the solution functions.

3.3.1   Linearization of the model around the observed equilibrium

The model described in the previous section (Table 3.2) contains non linear functions making its analytical solution impossible. Comparative statics, however, can be performed with ease, if equations are linearized around an equilibrium point. In this subsection, the model will be linearized in terms of percentage changes in the variables around the observed equilibrium point. This technique was initially introduced by Johansen (1960) as a method of solving multi-sectoral models.

The variables of all equations in Table 3.2 are in levels, and they have been written in upper case letters. Let the percentage change of the variables be denoted by corresponding lower case letters with one exception. The exception is that the variable 't' represents change in percentage point of variable T_1^R rather than percentage change in T_1^R. This will allow T_1^R to take any value, positive, negative or zero. Once it is understood that t represents a change in the percentage point of the rationalized tariff rate the superscript becomes redundant, and as it applies to only one sector the subscript is also unnecessary. So, in what follows the superscript and subscript on t are suppressed.

As mentioned in section 3.2.7, the domestic demand system plays no role in determining domestic output, employment, and prices in this small open economy. Therefore, changes in consumer demand are of no consequence for changes in the variables of interest - the variables related to the supply side. Changes in consumer demand affect the quantity of net imports only. Linearization of consumer demand equations, and goods market equilibrium conditions have been deferred until we are ready to perform comparative statics around the autarkic equilibrium where the consumer demands matter.

With these definitions and preliminaries, let us consider E^o - the observed equilibrium of the economy for a given set of values of the exogenous variables - and perturb it by changing the exogenous variables infinitesimally. By taking logarithmic total differentials around E^o most of the model equations can be linearized and the variables can be expressed in their percentage changes. Making use of the defining equations (3.28)-(3.32), the linearized expressions for the model equations can be obtained as follows.

Output supply functions: Taking logarithmic total differential of equation (3.11) and evaluating the shares around the 'observed' equilibrium we get

$$y_j^o = k_j + \sigma_j \left(\frac{S_{Lj}^o}{S_{Kj}^o} \right) (p_j^o - w^o); \qquad j = 1, 2 \qquad (3.36)$$

where, y_j^o is the percentage change in the supply of output of sector j; w^o is the percentage change in the normalized wage rate; p_j^o is the percentage change in the normalized price of commodity j and k_j is the percentage change in the stock of sector-specific factor (physical capital) in sector j.

Equation (3.36) shows that the supply of sectoral-output increases with the increase in the stock of the sector-specific capital and the relative price of the product, and decreases with increase in the equilibrium wage rate. The magnitudes of the effects depend on cost share of factors and the degree of 'ease' in factor substitution.

The labour market: By linearizing the labour demand functions given by equation (3.13) and the labour market equilibrium condition (3.15) around the 'observed' equilibrium and simplifying the resulting expressions by making use of equations (3.28) - (3.31) we can obtain

Labour demand functions:

$$l_j^o = k_j + \frac{\sigma_j}{S_{Kj}^o}(p_j^o - w^o); \qquad\qquad j = 1, 2 \qquad\qquad (3.37)$$

and,

$$l = \sum_{j=1}^{2} \lambda_j^o l_j^o. \qquad\qquad\qquad (3.38)$$

where, l is the percentage change in the total endowment of labour in the economy, and l_j^o is the percentage change in the employment of labour in sector j.

Equation (3.37) shows that the change in the sectoral-demand for labour, in equilibrium, is governed by change in the quantity of the sector-specific factor, change in the product price, change in the equilibrium wage rate, cost share of capital and the 'ease' of factor substitution. Increased product price or increased stock of the sector-specific factor would increase sectoral-demand for labour, and an increase in the wage rate would depress it. The equation also shows that the real-wage elasticity of sectoral-demand for labour is equal to $-\sigma_j / S_{Kj}$.

Equation (3.38) means that any change in the national endowment of labour has to be accommodated by changes in the sectoral employment of labour. Other things remaining the same, equation (3.37) and (3.38) imply that this is possible only through an adjustment in the wage rate.

Sectoral rental rates: The equilibrium rental function (3.12) can, similarly, be linearized by logarithmic differentiation. Simplifying the expression by using equations (3.28) and (3.29) and the fact that the factor shares add up to unity we get

$$r_j^o = \frac{1}{S_{Kj}^o}(p_j^o - S_{Lj}^o w^o); \qquad\qquad j = 1, 2 \qquad\qquad (3.39)$$

where, r_j^o is the percentage change in the virtual rental rate in sector j. Equation (3.39) shows that the virtual rental rate in each sector rises with relative price of own output and falls with the wage rate.

Price equations: Similarly, linearizing the price equations (3.25) and (3.26) we get

$$p_1^o = p_1^* + \tau^o \, t, \tag{3.40}$$

and

$$p_2^o = 0 \tag{3.41}$$

where, τ^o is defined in equation (3.32), and t, as indicated above, is 100 x $d\,T_1^R$ the change in the percentage point of the rationalized tariff rate.

Table 3.3
The PXGEM: linearized around the observed equilibrium

Output supply functions:

$$y_j^o = k_j + \sigma_j \left(\frac{S_{Lj}^o}{S_{Kj}^o} \right)(p_j^o - w^o) ; \qquad\qquad j = 1, 2. \tag{3.36}$$

Labour demand functions:

$$l_j^o = k_j + \frac{\sigma_j}{S_{Kj}^o}(p_j^o - w^o) ; \qquad\qquad j = 1, 2. \tag{3.37}$$

The labour market equilibrium condition:

$$l = \sum_{j=1}^{2} \lambda_j^o l_j^o . \tag{3.38}$$

Sectoral rental rates:

$$r_j^o = \frac{1}{S_{Kj}^o}(p_j^o - S_{Lj}^o w^o) ; \qquad\qquad j = 1, 2. \tag{3.39}$$

Price equations:

$$p_1^o = p_1^* + \tau^o \, t . \tag{3.40}$$

and

$$p_2^o = 0 . \tag{3.41}$$

Equation (3.40) shows that any change in the international relative price or the tariff rate results in a change in the domestic relative price. Equation (3.41) simply restates that the price of good 2 does not change, because it is the numeraire commodity.

The system of the linearized equations is brought together in Table 3.3. The exclusion of the demand sides of the goods markets has left the linearized system with only eight variables in eight equations. This system will be used in the following section to derive comparative static results around the observed equilibrium.

3.3.2   Comparative statics around the observed equilibrium

Wage effects: Substituting the equilibrium labour demand functions from equation (3.37) into the market-clearing equation (3.38) and solving for the wage rate, w^o, we get:

$$w^o = A^{-1} [\lambda_1^o k_1 + \lambda_2^o k_2 + (\lambda_1^o \sigma_1 / S_{K1}^o) p_1^o - l] , \qquad (3.42)$$

where, $A = \lambda_1^o \sigma_1 / S_{K1}^o + \lambda_2^o \sigma_2 / S_{K2}^o > 0$ is the magnitude of the real wage elasticity of the aggregate labour demand.

Equation (3.42) fully describes the behaviour of the equilibrium wage rate with respect to changes in exogenous variables of the model. Since p_1^o is completely and independently explained by exogenous variables - foreign price and tariff rate, it can be regarded as a given datum. By setting all exogenous variables equal to zero except one at a time we can obtain the elasticity of wage rate with respect to each of the exogenous variables.

In particular, by setting changes in all endowment variables equal to zero, the elasticity of the wage rate with respect to the relative price of commodity 1 can be obtained as

$$\eta^o \equiv \frac{w^o}{p_1^o} = A^{-1} (\lambda_1^o \sigma_1 / S_{K1}^o) . \qquad (3.43)$$

Both the numerator and the denominator of the right hand side of the expression (3.43) are positive, because all the share parameters and the elasticities of factor substitution are positive. Since the numerator of the term is less than the denominator, it follows that $0 < \eta < 1$. That is, as the relative price of good 1 increases the wage rate will increase, but by less than in proportion.

Similarly, it can be inferred from equation (3.42) that the equilibrium wage rate will increase with an increase in the stock of the sector-specific factor in either sector but will fall with an increase in the stock of labour in the economy.

Employment effects: Substituting back the response of the equilibrium wage rate from equation (3.42) into equation (3.37) we can obtain the changes in the sectoral-employment of labour as

$$l_1^o = A^{-1}\left[\frac{\lambda_2^o \sigma_2}{S_{K2}^o}\left(\frac{\sigma_1}{S_{K1}^o}p_1^o + k_1\right) + \frac{\sigma_1}{S_{K1}^o}\left(l - \lambda_2^o k_2\right)\right], \tag{3.44}$$

and,

$$l_2^o = A^{-1}\left[\frac{\lambda_1^o \sigma_1}{S_{K1}^o}k_2 - \frac{\sigma_2}{S_{K2}^o}\left(\lambda_1^o k_1 + \frac{\lambda_1^o \sigma_1}{S_{K1}^o}p_1^o - l\right)\right]. \tag{3.45}$$

From these two equations (3.44) and (3.45) we can obtain the extent and direction of changes in sectoral-employment with respect to given changes in the exogenous variables. For example, the equilibrium employment of labour in sector 1 expands if (1) the relative price of commodity 1 increases, (2) the stock of capital in sector 1 increases, (3) the stock of labour in the economy increases, and (4) the stock of capital in sector 2 decreases.

Similarly, in equilibrium, the employment of labour in sector 2 increases if (1) the capital stock in sector 2 expands, (2) the stock of labour in the economy expands, (3) the stock of capital in sector 1 decreases, and (4) the relative price of commodity 1 falls (that is the relative price of good 2 rises). The elasticity of sectoral-employment with respect to each of the exogenous variables can be obtained as in the case of the wage rate.

Some properties of labour demand functions follow from equation (3.44). These properties are very general and remain valid irrespective of the location of the point of equilibrium. Since the equilibrium level of employment of labour in sector 1, ceteris paribus, is a strictly increasing function of the relative price of good 1 (equation 3.44), it follows form labour market equilibrium condition that if the tariff rate (that is, the relative price of good 1) is increased in steps, then λ_1^o, the employment share of sector 1, will increase at successive equilibrium points. Hence, we write the following proposition for future reference.

Proposition 3.1 *Ceteris paribus, the employment share of sector 1, $\lambda_1(P_1)$, is a strictly increasing function of the relative price P_1. That is, $d\lambda_1 / dP_1 > 0$. In other words, increased protection of the import competing sector increases the share of the import competing sector in total employment of labour in the economy.*

Non-specialization in production implies $0 < \lambda_1 < 1$, and $\lambda_1 = 1$ when the economy specializes in the production of good 1. In a non-specialization case, it can be seen from equation (3.43) using (3.42) that the relative price elasticity of the wage rate is an increasing function of the employment share of sector 1 and cost share of capital in sector 2 and a decreasing function of the cost share of capital in sector 1. Equations (3.28) and (3.29) can further be analysed to see that the cost share of capital in sector 1 is a decreasing function and the cost share of capital in sector 2 is an increasing function of P_1, provided the elasticity of factor substitution in both sectors are at least unity. Hence, we have the following proposition:

Proposition 3.2 *The relative-price elasticity of the wage rate (measured in units of commodity 2) is an increasing function of the relative price of good 1, that is $d\eta / dP_1 > 0$, provided the elasticity of factor substitution in both sectors are at least unity.*

Propositions 3.1 and 3.2 capture the second order effect of a relative price change. In particular, Proposition 3.2 means that the relative price elasticity of the wage rate depends upon the size of the price change. The larger the price change the larger the elasticity of the wage rate will be. However, equation (3.43) also shows that the relative-price elasticity of the wage rate will never exceed unity. Hence, we can state the following proposition:

Proposition 3.3 *Protection of the import competing sector **always** lowers the real wage faced by the import competing sector, and raises the real wage faced by the exporting sector.*

Effects on the sectoral-rental rates: The wage rate can be eliminated from the rental equation (3.39) by using equation (3.42). This yields expressions for percentage changes in sectoral-rental rates in terms of percentage changes in the exogenous variables. After simplification, sectoral-rental rates can be expressed as

$$r_1^o = \frac{1}{AS_{K1}^o}\left[\left(\frac{\lambda_2^o \sigma_2}{S_{K2}^o} + \lambda_1^o \sigma_1\right)p_1^o - S_{L1}^o\left(\lambda_1^o k_1 + \lambda_2^o k_2 - l\right)\right] \qquad (3.46)$$

and,

$$r_2^o = -\frac{S_{L2}^o}{AS_{K2}^o}\left(\frac{\lambda_1^o \sigma_1}{S_{K1}^o}p_1^o + \lambda_1^o k_1 + \lambda_2^o k_2 - l\right) \qquad (3.47)$$

Equations (3.46) and (3.47) show that rental rates in both sectors increase as the supply of labour in the economy increases; and rental rates in both sectors fall if the stock of capital increases in either sector. In other words, an increase in the stock of capital in sector 1 not only lowers the rental rate in sector 1 but also

65

lowers the rental rate in sector 2 as well. It is because an exogenous increase in the stock of capital in sector 1 increases the demand for labour, which bids the wage rate up causing the rental rate in sector 2 to fall. Similar reasoning holds if the stock of capital in sector 2 increases exogenously.

Elasticities of sectoral rental rates with respective to each exogenous variable can be computed from equations (3.46) and (3.47). In particular, by setting all endowment changes to zero the elasticities of rental rates with respect to the relative price of good 1 can be obtained as

$$\frac{r_1^o}{p_1^o} = A^{-1}\left(\frac{\lambda_1^o \sigma_1}{S_{K1}^o} + \frac{\lambda_2^o \sigma_2}{S_{K1}^o S_{K2}^o}\right) > 1, \tag{3.48}$$

and

$$\frac{r_2^o}{p_1^o} = -\frac{S_{L2}^o}{S_{K2}^o A}\left(\frac{\lambda_1^o \sigma_1}{S_{K1}^o}\right) < 0. \tag{3.49}$$

Equation (3.48) shows that the elasticity of the rental rate in sector 1 with respect to the relative price of commodity 1 is greater than unity. Mussa (1974) has provided the following interpretation of this result. As the price of commodity 1 rises, the value of the share of initial output of sector 1 that went to fixed capital also rises proportionately. Since the wage rate does not rise in proportion to the output price, some surplus arises from part of the initial output, which went to the payment of wages, but that will now accrue to the capital. Moreover, there will be an increase in output, which means a part of the incremental output will again go to the given stock of capital. Hence the rental rate in each sector will rise more than proportionately as the relative price of its output rises.

Equation (3.49) shows that the elasticity of the rental rate in sector 2 with respective to the relative price of good 1 is negative. The magnitude of the elasticity depends on the elasticity of the wage with respect to the relative price of good 1, and the labour intensity in sector 2. The absolute value of the elasticity will be higher, the higher the distributive share of labour in sector 2, and the higher the relative price elasticity of the wage rate.

From these results we can state the following proposition regarding the property of the rental functions:

Proposition 3.4 *The rental rate in sector 1, R_1, is a strictly increasing, and the rental rate in sector 2, R_2, is a strictly decreasing function of the relative price of commodity 1, P_1. That is $dR_1 / dP_1 > 0$, and $dR_2 / dP_1 < 0$.*

Output effects: Using the wage equation (3.42) the output supply functions given by equation (3.36) can be rewritten as

$$y_1^o = A^{-1}\left[\left(\frac{\lambda_2^o \sigma_2}{S_{K2}^o} + \lambda_1^o \sigma_1\right)k_1 + \frac{\sigma_1 S_{L1}^o}{S_{K1}^o}\left(\frac{\lambda_2^o \sigma_2}{S_{K2}^o}p_1^o - \lambda_2^o k_2 + l\right)\right], \qquad (3.50)$$

and

$$y_2^o = A^{-1}\left[\left(\frac{\lambda_1^o \sigma_1}{S_{K1}^o} + \lambda_2^o \sigma_2\right)k_2 - \frac{\sigma_2 S_{L2}^o}{S_{K2}^o}\left(\lambda_1^o k_1 + \frac{\lambda_1^o \sigma_1}{S_{K1}^o}p_1^o - l\right)\right]. \qquad (3.51)$$

From these two equations it is clear that an increase in the relative price of good 1 results in an increase in the output of sector 1 and a fall in the output of sector 2; and an increase in the stock of labour in the economy leads to an increase in the output of both sectors. These effects are quite intuitive. What is interesting is that an increase in the stock of capital in sector 1 leads to an increase in the output of sector 1 and a fall in the output of sector 2. Similarly, an increase in the stock of capital in sector 2 leads to an increase in the output of sector 2 and a fall in the output of sector 1. In other words, irrespective of the capital intensity of the sectors, an increase in the capital stock in one sector leads to a fall in the output of the other sector. This effect is quite different from the Rybczynski Theorem, which predicts that increase in the stock of capital will lead to an increase in the output of capital intensive good and a fall in the output of labour intensive good.

The reason is quite simple. An increase in the stock of capital (or the sector-specific factor) in sector 1 raises the productivity of labour (the mobile factor) in sector 1 and therefore, at unchanged prices, the demand for labour goes up. Consequently, the wage rate will go up. The result is, as can be seen from equation (3.37), that the equilibrium employment for labour in sector 2 falls, and hence the output of sector 2 falls.

3.4 Summary

A simple model of the economic sphere of a small open political economy has been described in this chapter. The model assumed that the tariff rate that creates a wedge between domestic and foreign relative price is exogenously determined.

Comparative static results have shown that the rental income of each sector is a strictly increasing function of the relative price of own commodity and a strictly decreasing function of the relative price of other's commodity. This remains valid whether the rental income is measured in units of own commodity or in units of the numeraire commodity.

This result clearly demonstrates that changes in tariff rates are capable of redistributing rents from one sector to the other. The mechanism behind this transfer is the difference in the real wage rates faced by the two sectors, which induces a reallocation of labour between the two sectors, and hence the outputs and the rents.

Therefore, for given endowment of factors, technologies of production and the international prices, it can be inferred that the choice of a particular tariff rate by the government determines a particular combination of sectoral rental incomes at the equilibrium of the economic sphere. In the next chapter we will obtain the analytical relationship between the sectoral rental incomes that summarizes the mechanism and redistributive effects of tariff changes in the economic sphere of a political economy.

Appendix-3A: Comparative statics around the free trade equilibrium

The purpose of this Appendix is to re-model the 'observed' economic sphere under free trade environment and derive some comparative static results. An economic sphere that is freely trading can be mimicked from the model of the real sector listed in Table 3.3 by setting the tariff rate to zero and replacing P_i by P_i^*. This means nothing more than requiring that the domestic relative price be equal to the international relative price.

Since, at the observed level of other exogenous variables, E^* denotes the vector of the equilibrium levels of the endogenous variables in the free trade environment, a linearized version of the model around E^* can be obtained by following the same procedure as was done in linearizing the model around the observed equilibrium. The linearized system of equations is listed in Table 3A.1.

The set of equations listed in Table 3A.1 contain three different changes compared to equations listed in Table 3.3 of the text. First, the domestic relative price has been replaced by the international relative price. Second, all shares have been evaluated at the free trade equilibrium point. Third, the endogenous variables now represent a percentage change over their free trade equilibrium levels. However, the values of the exogenous variables are assumed to be the same in all the three states hence they represent a percentage change over their observed levels.

The comparative static results will be similar to that described by equations (3.42) - (3.51) except that the shares correspond to free trade equilibrium and the percentage change in the domestic relative price p_1^o has been replaced by the percentage change in the international price ratio p_1^*.

68

The PXGEM: linearized around the free trade equilibrium

The output supply functions:

$$y_j^* = k_j + \sigma_j \left(\frac{S_{Lj}^*}{S_{Kj}^*} \right) (p_j^* - w^*) ; \qquad\qquad j = 1, 2. \qquad (3A.1)$$

Labour demand functions:

$$l_j^* = k_j + \frac{\sigma_j}{S_{Kj}^*} (p_j^* - w^*) ; \qquad\qquad j = 1, 2 . \qquad (3A.2)$$

Labour market equilibrium condition:

$$l = \sum_{j=1}^{2} \lambda_j^* l_j^* . \qquad\qquad (3A.3)$$

The rental rates:

$$r_j^* = \frac{1}{S_{Kj}^*} (p_j^* - S_{Lj}^* w^*) ; \qquad\qquad j = 1, 2. \qquad (3A.4)$$

The price normalization rule:

$$p_2^* = 0 . \qquad\qquad (3A.5)$$

In particular, the response of the rental rates around free trade equilibrium will be given by

$$r_1^* = (1 / S_{K1}^*)(\lambda_1^* \sigma_1 / S_{K1}^* + \lambda_2^* \sigma_2 / S_{K2}^*)$$
$$\{[(\lambda_2^* \sigma_2 / S_{K2}^*) + \lambda_1^* \sigma_1 \} p_1^* - S_{L1}^* (\lambda_1^* k_1 + \lambda_2^* k_2 - l)], \qquad (3A.6)$$

and

$$r_2^* = -\frac{S_{L2}^*}{S_{K2}^*} \left(\frac{\lambda_1^* \sigma_1}{S_{K1}^*} + \frac{\lambda_2^* \sigma_2}{S_{K2}^*} \right)^{-1} \left(\frac{\lambda_1^* \sigma_1}{S_{K1}^*} p_1^* + \lambda_1^* k_1 + \lambda_2^* k_2 - l \right) \qquad (3A.7)$$

The natures of these rental response functions are similar to those of the rental response functions (3.46) and (3.47). The difference is in the magnitudes of their elasticities. These equations have been derived for future reference.

Appendix-3B: Comparative statics around the autarkic equilibrium

The other extreme of free trade is the autarky in which the economy does not trade with the rest of the world. An equilibrium under autarky requires that the domestic demand for and supply of each commodity be equal. Thus, an economy under autarky can be described by the presence of domestic market-clearing conditions.

Table 3B.1
Description of an autarkic PXGEM

The goods market:
The supply functions of domestic production sectors:

$$Y_j = K_j \beta_j^{-1/\rho_j} \left[1 - \alpha_j^{1/(1+\rho_j)} \left(W / P_j \right)^{\rho_j/(1+\rho_j)} \right]^{1/\rho_j} \qquad j = 1,2 \qquad (3.11)$$

Consumer demand functions:

$$C_j = (\delta_j / P_j) \sum_{i=1}^{2} P_i Y_i ; \qquad\qquad j = 1,2 \qquad (3.19)$$

Goods market equilibrium:

$$C_1 = Y_1 . \qquad\qquad (3.21)$$

The labour market:
Sectoral labour demand:

$$L_j = K_j \alpha_j^{1/(1+\rho_j)} \beta_j^{-1/\rho_j} \left[\left(P_j / W \right)^{\rho_j/(1+\rho_j)} - \alpha_j^{1/(1+\rho_j)} \right]^{1/\rho_j} ; \qquad j = 1,2 . \qquad (3.13)$$

Labour market equilibrium:

$$L = \sum_{j=1}^{2} L_j . \qquad\qquad (3.15)$$

Rental rates:

$$R_j = \beta_j^{-1/\rho_j} \left(P_j^{\rho_j/(1+\rho_j)} - \alpha_j^{1/(1+\rho_j)} W^{\rho_j/(1+\rho_j)} \right)^{(1+\rho_j)/\rho_j} ; \qquad j = 1,2 . \qquad (3.12)$$

Price normalization rule:

$$P_2 \equiv 1 . \qquad\qquad (3.25)$$

Assume that E^a represents the vector of the level of endogenous variables at autarky equilibrium. Then the model can be linearized around E^a. The linearized version of the model is listed in Table 3B.2.

Table 3B.2
The PXGEM: linearized around the autarkic equilibrium

The output supply functions:

$$y_j^a = k_j + \sigma_j \left(\frac{S_{Lj}^a}{S_{Kj}^a} \right) (p_j^a - w^a);. \qquad j=1, 2. \qquad (3B.2)$$

Commodity demand functions:

$$c_j^a = -p_j^a + \sum_{i=1}^{2} H_i^a (p_i^a + y_i^a); \qquad j=1, 2. \qquad (3B.3)$$

where, $H_i^a = P_i^a Y_i^a / \sum_{j=1}^{2} P_j^a Y_j^a$.

Labour demand functions:

$$l_j^a = k_j + \frac{\sigma_j}{S_{Kj}^a} (p_j^a - w^a); \qquad j=1, 2. \qquad (3B.4)$$

Labour market equilibrium condition:

$$l = \sum_{j=1}^{2} \lambda_j^a l_j^a. \qquad (3B.5)$$

The rental rates:

$$r_j^a = \frac{1}{S_{Kj}^a} (p_j^a - S_{Lj}^a w^a); \qquad j=1, 2. \qquad (3B.6)$$

Market-clearing condition:

$$c_1 = y_1. \qquad (3B.7)$$

Price normalization rule:

$$p_2^a = 0. \qquad (3B.8)$$

One of the important features of the set of equations presented in Table 3B.2 is the presence of demand functions, which were absent in other models. Demand functions play an important role in determining the relative commodity price in autarky whereas in the observed state of the economy foreign prices and the tariff rate determine the relative price.

Substituting the demand function for commodity 1 from equation (3B.3) into the market-clearing condition (3B.7) and solving for the relative price, noting that $p_2^a = 0$ and that $\sum_i H_i^a = 1$, yields

$$p_1^a = y_2^a - y_1^a. \tag{3B.9}$$

Equation (3B.9) has a strong rule of price change.[13] It shows that *the relative price of the commodity, whose supply grows at the relatively faster rate falls. The rate of fall is equal to the differential in the growth rate of outputs in the two sectors.* For future reference we call it **the autarky rule of price.**

Substituting the output supply function (3B.2) into equation (3B.9) and solving for price we get

$$p_1^a = \mu_0 \left(k_2 - k_1 + \mu_1 w^a \right), \tag{3B.10}$$

where,

$$\mu_0 \equiv 1 / \left(1 + \sigma_1 S_{L1}^a / S_{K1}^a \right) > 0 \tag{3B.11}$$

and

$$\mu_1 \equiv \frac{\sigma_1 S_{L1}^a}{S_{K1}^a} - \frac{\sigma_2 S_{L2}^a}{S_{K2}^a}. \tag{3B.12}$$

Solving the labour market equilibrium condition (3B.5) for the wage response using the demand functions given by equation (3B.4) yields

$$w^a = \psi_0 \left(\lambda_1^a k_1 + \lambda_2^a k_2 - l \right) + \psi_1 p_1^a, \tag{3B.13}$$

where,

$$\psi_0 \equiv 1 / [\lambda_1^a \sigma_1 / S_{K1}^a + \lambda_2^a \sigma_2 / S_{K2}^a] > 0, \tag{3B.14}$$

and

$$\psi_1 \equiv \psi_0 \lambda_1^a \sigma_1 / S_{K1}^a > 0. \tag{3B.15}$$

Equations (3B.10) and (3B.13) can be solved for the two variables p_1^a and w^a. The solution yields

$$w^a = \frac{1}{1-\psi_1\mu_0\mu_1} \times$$
$$\left[(\psi_0\lambda_1^a - \psi_1\mu_0)k_1 + (\psi_1\mu_0 + \lambda_2^a\psi_0)k_2 - \psi_0l\right],$$

(3B.16)

and

$$p_1^a = \frac{\mu_0}{1-\psi_1\mu_0\mu_1} \times$$
$$\left[(1+\mu_1\lambda_2^a\psi_0)k_2 - \left(1 - \mu_1\lambda_1^a\psi_0\right)k_1 - \mu_1\psi_0l\right].$$

(3B.17)

The effects of changes in endowment variables on the equilibrium wage rate and the relative price of commodity 1 are given by equations (3B.16) and (3B.17). Substitution of the values of p_1^a and w^a into equations (3B.2), (3B.4) and (3B.6) yield the effects on sectoral outputs, employment and the rental rates respectively. The elasticities of the endogenous variables with respect to the change in endowment variables can be evaluated in turn by changing one endowment variable at a time. In particular, response of the rental rate in sector 2 can be obtained from equation (3B.6) as

$$r_2^a = -\frac{S_{L2}^a}{S_{K2}^a\left(1-\psi_1\mu_0\mu_1\right)} \times$$
$$\left[(\psi_0\lambda_1^a - \psi_1\mu_0)k_1 + (\psi_1\mu_0 + \lambda_2^a\psi_0)k_2 - \psi_0l\right].$$

(3B.18)

Since the price of commodity 2 is held fixed (as it is the numeraire), it is obvious that the channel through which changes in exogenous variables affect the rent in sector 2 is the wage rate. If a shock leads to an increase in the wage rate, then the rental rate will fall, and if it leads to a decrease in the wage rate the rental rate in sector 2 will rise.

The mechanism through which exogenous shocks affect the wage rate is as follows. Ceteris paribus an increase in the stock of capital in sector 2 produces effects on the wage rate in two rounds. In the first round, the productivity and hence the demand for labour is increased in sector 2. Therefore, the aggregate demand for labour increases and the wage rate will go up to clear the labour market. As a result the employment of labour and the level of output rise in sector 2 and fall in sector 1. It will produce the second round effect - the relative price effect. The positive relative growth of output in sector 2 will raise the relative price of good 1 (equation 3B.9) which, in turn, raises the demand for labour in sector 1 and the wage rate will rise further.

Similar arguments can be provided to explain the effects of an increase in the stock of capital in sector 1. The first round effect on the wage rate of an increase in the stock of capital in sector 1 is quite similar - it will lead to an increase in the wage rate. However, the relative price effect is different. As the stock of capital in sector 1 increases, employment and output in sector 1 increase while they fall in sector 2. The relative decline in the output of sector 2 lowers the price of commodity 1 at constant price of commodity 2. The real wage rate faced by sector 1 increases and the labour demand schedule shifts back producing a fall in the wage rate.

The net effect of a change in K_1 on the wage rate, therefore, depends on the relative size of the productivity effect and the relative price effect. It can be shown that the productivity effect dominates the relative price effect if the elasticity of factor substitution in sector 1 is less than unity and vice versa.[14] That is, the wage rate rises with an increase in K_1 if the capital stock in sector 1 cannot easily substitute labour.

It thus follows clearly from equation (3B.18) that the rental rate in sector 2 will increase in autarky either if (1) the supply of labour in the economy increases, or if (2) stock of capital in sector 2 declines, or if (3) stock of capital in sector 1 increases (decreases) with $\sigma_1 > 1$ ($\sigma_1 < 1$). A change in the stock of capital in sector 1, however, will have no impact on the rental rate of sector 2 if $\sigma_1 = 1$.

Notes

1   Cobb-Douglas utility function has been chosen to reduce parametric information, since the demand side is of not much importance to the main purpose of the study.

2   For a long run view on this issue see Magee, Brock and Young (1989).

3   Note that this virtual rental rate is quite different from the contractual rental rate if the production sector has entered into any such contract with respect to some of its fixed factors. This is because the virtual rental rate changes with changes in output price while the contractual rate does not. The gap between the two rates will accrue to that part of the specific-factor for which no contractual price has been determined.

4   It follows from the CES production function (3.1) that

$$\alpha^{1/\rho}\left[K^\rho / \left(K^\rho - \beta Y^\rho\right)\right]^{(1+\rho)/\rho} = 1/[\alpha(Y/L)^{1+\rho}].$$

5   The problem of a profit maximizing sector when the stock of specific factor is fixed at K, can be written as $max \, \Pi = \underset{L}{max} \, \{P(\alpha L^{-\rho} + \beta K^{-\rho})^{-1/\rho} - WL\}$. The condition for profit

maximization under competitive conditions then becomes $W = P\alpha (Y / L)^{(1+\rho)}$ that is, in equilibrium, the mobile factor should be paid the value of its marginal product. Or alternately, the condition may be stated as $P = W / [\alpha (Y / L)^{(1+\rho)}]$ which means that, in equilibrium, the marginal cost should be equal to the price of output.

6 To see clearly that the above assertion holds, let us take any linearly homogenous production function $Y = f(L, K)$ and hold K at certain level. Then by Euler's theorem we have $PY = Pf_L + Pf_K K$, and the virtual cost is given by $C(Y) = WL + RK$. For output levels less than the profit maximizing level we have $W < Pf_L$ and $R < Pf_K$; which implies $C(Y) < PY$.

7 For a model that distinguishes between households that own different factors see Long and Vousden (1991).

8 A rigorous justification of Cobb-Douglas utility function, however, can be found in Willig (1976)

9 For a discussion on closure rules in a CGE model see Robinson (1989). Robinson has concluded that 'a macro model is needed to determine any two, but no more than two, of the following variables: the domestic aggregate price level, the balance of trade, and the nominal exchange rate.' (p. 921). In our case, we have both tradable goods, and the trade balance holds by Walras law, the exogenous determination of the nominal exchange rate is sufficient to close the model. For the consistency of an exogenously specified exchange rate, and the trade balance constraint see Dervis, et al. (1982: 184-87).

10 A good discussion of price normalization rule and its implication can be found in Chapter 6 of Dervis, et al. (1982).

11 For any positive number λ, the relative price neutral tariff rates, T_i', are given by
$$T_i' = \lambda T_i + \lambda - 1, \qquad \text{for } i = 1, 2. \tag{3.27}$$

12 For more discussions on the Lerner symmetry theorem, see Chapter 2 in Vousden (1990).

13 The above assertion is based on the underlying assumptions that the economy does not trade, and that the preferences of the consumer can be represented by a Cobb-Douglas utility function. It is shown by Willig (1976) that if the price elasticities of demand are locally constant, then the only form of utility function that is consistent with neo-classical utility maximization is the Cobb-Douglas. In a two good case it can be easily seen that the direction of price change (not the magnitude) implied by equation (2B.9) is valid with any utility function that yields demand functions with income elasticity equal to unity. Finally, if the economy trades with the rest of the world, then the autarky model could be applied to the world economy. The market-clearing condition that will be applicable at a global level will imply a similar

conclusion at global level. But the conclusion will not necessarily hold at a national level.

14   Using the defining equations (2B.11), (2B.14) and (2B.15) it can be shown that

$$\psi_0 \lambda_1^a - \psi_1 \mu_0 = \frac{\lambda_1^a}{[\lambda_1^a \sigma_1 / S_{K1}^a + \lambda_2^a \sigma_2 / S_{K2}^a]} \cdot \frac{S_{K1}^a (1 - \sigma_1)}{(S_{K1}^a + \sigma_1 S_{L1}^a)}.$$

Therefore, the sign of the coefficient of k_1 in equation (3.B16) depends on the size of σ_1.

4 The rent transformation frontier

Introduction

It was shown in the previous chapter that, as far as the owners of the sector-specific factors are concerned, any change in the rationalized tariff rate means a reduction in the rental income of one sector and a gain in the rental income of the other. An increase in the rationalized tariff rate increases the rent to the specific factor in the import competing sector, and decreases the rent to the specific factor in the exporting sector. In other words, a change in the tariff rate, ceteris paribus, effects a transfer of rents between the owners of the sector-specific factors. The purpose of this chapter is to derive a rent transformation frontier that describes the combinations of Pareto-efficient distribution of rental incomes, and to study its nature and comparative static properties. This chapter together with Chapter 3 completes the description of the economic sphere of a small open political economy. More importantly, this chapter provides an interface between the economic and the political spheres of the political economy.

A study of the nature and comparative static properties of the rent transformation frontier is important for two reasons. First, it shows the condition under which the rent possibility set is compact and convex, which is a sufficient condition for a unique bargaining solution. This, in turn, provides a preview of the applicability of the bargain-theoretic approach in endogenizing the tariff formation process. Second, it also describes the way the rent possibility set responds to the changes in the exogenous variables. A clear understanding of this feature of the rent possibility set is necessary in understanding the comparative static behaviour of the bargaining solution that will be derived in the later chapters.

This chapter is divided into five sections. The first section analyzes the second-order properties of the rental functions and derives the rent transformation frontier. The second section discusses the shape of the frontier. The third section compares the rent transformation frontier with the product transformation frontier. The fourth section derives the comparative static properties of the frontier. The chapter is concluded in section five.

4.1 Derivation of the rent transformation function

Given the world relative price, domestic factor endowments, technologies and tastes, a general economic equilibrium can be defined for each level of the tariff rate. A vector of levels of endogenous variables that solves the system of equations (model) listed in Table 3.2 constitutes the economic equilibrium. Since the rental incomes to the sector-specific factors are among the endogenous variables of the model, a particular combination of the rental incomes is associated with each tariff rate. Using the fact that the domestic relative price is in one-to-one correspondence with the tariff rate a one-to-one correspondence can be defined between the domestic relative price and the combination of sectoral-rental rates.

Let us define, for each sector i

$$\widetilde{R}_i \equiv R_i / P_i \tag{4.1}$$

where R_1 and R_2 measure the equilibrium rental rates in units of the numeraire, the commodity 2. It is clear from the defining equation (4.1) that $\widetilde{R}_i$ simply measures the (virtual) rental rate of the specific factor in each sector in units of the respective commodity - that is commodity i. We will call $\widetilde{R}_i$ the *real rental rate* of the specific factor.

From equations (3.6), (3.11) and (3.12) we obtain

$$\widetilde{R}_i = \beta_i \left(\frac{Y_i}{K_i} \right)^{1+\rho_i}. \tag{4.2}$$

Equation (4.2) simply restates that the real rental rate in each sector is equal to the marginal physical product of the specific factor. Differentiating both sides of equation (4.2) totally with respect to P_i yields

$$\frac{d\widetilde{R}_i}{dP_i} = \beta_i K_i^{-(1+\rho_i)} (1 + \rho_i) Y_i^{\rho_i} \frac{dY_i}{dP_i} \tag{4.3}$$

As we know that Y_i is an increasing function of P_i, equation (4.3) confirms the first-order property of the sectoral rental function that, *ceteris paribus*, $\widetilde{R}_i$ is an increasing function of P_i. Since total rental income can not exceed sectoral output the following proposition is stated for future reference.

Proposition 4.1 *The equilibrium real rental rate (and hence rental income) in each sector is a real-valued, bounded and increasing function of the relative price of own-output, and decreasing function of the relative price of the output of the other sector.*

Differentiating both sides of equation (4.3) again with respective to P_i we get

$$\frac{d^2 \tilde{R}_i}{dP_i^2} = \beta_i K_i^{-(1+\rho_i)} (1+\rho_i) Y_i^{\rho_i} \left[\rho_i Y_i^{-1} \left(\frac{dY_i}{dP_i} \right)^2 + \frac{d^2 Y_i}{dP_i^2} \right]. \tag{4.4}$$

We know that for each sector i,

$$\beta_i K_i^{-(1+\rho_i)} (1+\rho_i) Y_i^{\rho_i} > 0 \text{, and}$$

$$Y_i^{-1} \left(\frac{dY_i}{dP_i} \right)^2 > 0 .$$

Therefore, for each sector i, the sufficient conditions for

$$\frac{d^2 \tilde{R}_i}{dP_i^2} < 0 \tag{4.5}$$

are that

(i) $-1 < \rho_i \le 0$; and

(ii) $\dfrac{d^2 Y_i}{dP_i^2} < 0 .$

    The first of the above two conditions requires that in both sectors the long run elasticities of factor substitution, σ_i, be finite and be greater than or equal to unity. The second condition requires that, in general equilibrium, the supply of output of each sector grow at a decreasing rate as its relative price (in terms of units of the other commodity) increases.[1] Whether condition (ii) is met generally or not when condition (i) is satisfied, is a pertinent question. Instead of evaluating

79

the second-order property of the supply functions we make the following assumptions on the production technologies (and, hence on output supply functions). In what follows we will assume that the above conditions (i) and (ii) hold.

Assumption 4.1 We assume that the elasticities of factor substitution in both sectors are at least unity; and that in each sector the output supply is a concave function of its own relative price.

It follows from condition (4.4) that if Assumption 4.1 holds, then the real rental function of each sector is not only increasing but also concave in the relative price of own commodity.

Now, clearly the combination of the equilibrium rental rates of the two sectors, when the domestic relative price is P_1, is given by the pair $(\widetilde{R}_1(P_1), \widetilde{R}_2(P_1))$. Various combinations of equilibrium rental rates can thus be obtained by varying the domestic relative price of commodity 1 and a rent transformation frontier analogous to the surplus transformation curve described in Gardner (1983, 1987) can be obtained.[2]

Definition 4.1   The locus of combinations of equilibrium rental incomes (or rates) in units of own-output corresponding to each tariff rate (or domestic relative price), with all other exogenous variables held fixed, is defined as the Rent Transformation Frontier (RTF). A function that describes the locus is the Rent Transformation Function.

Given a relative price of commodity 1, the equilibrium real rental rates for the two sectors, $(\widetilde{R}_1(P_1), \widetilde{R}_2(P_1))$, can be obtained from equation (3.12) as functions of the wage rate and the relative price of commodity 1. Since both sectors face the same wage rate, the rental function for sector 2 can be used to eliminate wage rate from the rental function for sector 1. As a result we can obtain the Rental Transformation Function as

$$\widetilde{R}_1 = P_1^{-1}\beta_1^{-\frac{\sigma_1}{1-\sigma_1}}\left[P_1^{1-\sigma_1} - \alpha_1^{\sigma_1}\alpha_2^{-\frac{\sigma_2(1-\sigma_1)}{1-\sigma_2}}\left(1-\beta_2^{\sigma_2}\widetilde{R}_2^{1-\sigma_2}\right)^{\frac{1-\sigma_1}{1-\sigma_2}}\right]^{\frac{1}{1-\sigma_1}}. \qquad (4.6)$$

Equation (4.6) expresses the rental rate to the specific factor in sector 1 as a function of the rental rate to the specific factor in sector 2. It is a condition that will be satisfied by the rental rates at all equilibrium points and defines a locus in $\widetilde{R}_1 \times \widetilde{R}_2$ plane which coincides with the sectoral output plane.[3]

Noting that $P_2 = 1$, the slope of the rental transformation function can be obtained from the properties of the rental functions as follows. Since,

$$\frac{d\tilde{R}_1}{dR_2} = \frac{d\tilde{R}_1 / dP_1}{d\tilde{R}_2 / dP_1}$$

$$= \frac{d(R_1 / P_1) / dP_1}{dR_2 / dP_1}$$

$$= \left(\frac{R_1 / P_1}{R_2}\right)\left(\frac{r_1 / p_1 - 1}{r_2 / p_1}\right)$$

and from equation (3.48) we have $r_1 / p_1 > 1$, and from equation (3.49) we have $r_2 / p_1 < 0$, it follows that

$$\frac{d\tilde{R}_1}{d\tilde{R}_2} = \left(\frac{\tilde{R}_1}{\tilde{R}_2}\right)\left(\frac{r_1 / p_1 - 1}{r_2 / p_1}\right) < 0. \tag{4.7}$$

Thus, the rental transformation frontier slopes downward to the right. This result holds at any arbitrary equilibrium of the economic sphere, and does not depend on the values of the share parameters specific to a particular point. Hence, a proposition follows:

Proposition 4.2 *At every equilibrium of the economic sphere, a tariff change benefits the owner of the specific factor in one sector and hurts the owner of the specific factor in the other sector. Therefore, the owners of sector-specific factors will have a conflict of interest with respect to tariff changes.*

4.2   The shape of the rent transformation frontier

Substituting the expressions for r_1 / p_1 and r_2 / p_1 from equations (3.48) and (3.49) into equation (4.7) and simplifying the expression making use of equation (3.43), which gives the price elasticity of the wage rate, yields

$$\frac{d\tilde{R}_1}{d\tilde{R}_2} = -\frac{\tilde{R}_1}{\tilde{R}_2}\left(\frac{\lambda_2 \sigma_2 S_{L1}}{\lambda_1 \sigma_1 S_{L2}}\right). \tag{4.8}$$

Differentiating both sides of equation (4.8) with respect to $\tilde{R}_2$ yields, on further simplification,

$$\frac{d^2\widetilde{R}_1}{d\widetilde{R}_2^2} = -\left(\frac{\sigma_2\lambda_2 S_{L1}}{\sigma_1\lambda_1 S_{L2}}\right)\left(\frac{\widetilde{R}_1}{\widetilde{R}_2^2}\right)\times\left[\left(\frac{\widetilde{R}_2 d\widetilde{R}_1}{\widetilde{R}_1 d\widetilde{R}_2}-1\right)\right.$$

$$\left.+\widetilde{R}_2\left\{\left(\frac{d\lambda_2}{\lambda_2 d\widetilde{R}_2}-\frac{d\lambda_1}{\lambda_1 d\widetilde{R}_2}\right)+\left(\frac{dS_{L1}}{S_{L1} d\widetilde{R}_2}-\frac{dS_{L2}}{S_{L2} d\widetilde{R}_2}\right)\right\}\right].\qquad (4.9)$$

Since $\lambda_i = L_i / L$, and since the motive variable for change in this general equilibrium system is the domestic relative price, then

$$\frac{dS_{Lj}}{d\widetilde{R}_2} = \frac{dS_{Lj}/dP_1}{d\widetilde{R}_2/dP_1}, \qquad\qquad j=1,2\,; \qquad (4.10)$$

and $\dfrac{dL_i}{d\widetilde{R}_2} = \dfrac{dL_i/dP_1}{d\widetilde{R}_2/dP_1}, \qquad\qquad j=1,2\,. \qquad (4.11)$

Using equation (4.8), equation (4.9) can be rewritten as

$$\frac{d^2\widetilde{R}_1}{d\widetilde{R}_2^2} = -\left(\frac{\sigma_2\lambda_2 S_{L1}}{\sigma_1\lambda_1 S_{L2}}\right)\left(\frac{\widetilde{R}_1}{\widetilde{R}_2^2}\right)\times\left[\left(-\frac{\sigma_2\lambda_2 S_{L1}}{\sigma_1\lambda_1 S_{L2}}-1\right)\right.$$

$$\left.+\frac{(l_2/p_1-l_1/p_1)+(s_{L1}/p_1-s_{L2}/p_1)}{r_2/p_1}\right] \qquad (4.12)$$

Making use of equations (3.28), (3.44) and (3.45) around any arbitrary equilibrium equation (4.12), after a simplification, can be rewritten as

$$\frac{d^2\widetilde{R}_1}{d\widetilde{R}_2^2} = -\left(\frac{\sigma_2\lambda_2 S_{L1}}{(\sigma_1\lambda_1 S_{L2})^2}\right)\left(\frac{\widetilde{R}_1}{\widetilde{R}_2^2}\right)\times\left[-\left(\sigma_2\lambda_2 S_{L1}+\sigma_1\lambda_1 S_{L2}\right)+\sigma_1\sigma_2\right.$$

$$\left.+(1-\sigma_1)(\lambda_2\sigma_2-\sigma_2\lambda_2 S_{L1})+(1-\sigma_2)(\lambda_1\sigma_1-\sigma_1\lambda_1 S_{L2})\right]. \qquad (4.13)$$

On a further simplification using the adding up property of the distributive and employment shares equation (4.13) can be rewritten as

$$\frac{d^2\tilde{R}_1}{d\tilde{R}_2^2} = -\left(\frac{\sigma_2\lambda_2 S_{L1}}{(\sigma_1\lambda_1 S_{L2})^2}\right)\left(\frac{\tilde{R}_1}{\tilde{R}_2^2}\right) \times \left[\sigma_2\lambda_2 S_{L1}(\sigma_1 - 1)\right.$$

$$\left. + \sigma_1\lambda_1 S_{L2}(\sigma_2 - 1) + \sigma_1\lambda_1 S_{K2} + \sigma_2\lambda_2 S_{K1}\right] \tag{4.14}$$

Now, it can clearly be seen from the right hand side of equation (4.14) that the condition $\sigma_i \geq 1$ for each i is sufficient but not necessary for $d^2\tilde{R}_1 / d\tilde{R}_2^2 < 0$. This condition holds under Assumption 4.1, and thus we have the following proposition:

Proposition 4.2 *If rental rates are measured in units of own-output; and if long-run elasticity of factor substitution is unity in both sectors, then the rental transformation function is concave and negatively sloped. That is, the rental transformation frontier slopes downward to the right and is concave to the origin in the rental plane, and the set of feasible combinations of rental rates (and rental income) is convex.*

4.3   The product and rent transformation frontiers

On the basis of the results derived so far, the nature of the rent transformation frontier can be illustrated geometrically. Figure 4.1 shows the rental and product transformation frontiers for given technologies, endowment of sector-specific factors, and the economy wide supply of the mobile factor.

The second and the fourth quadrants in Figure 4.1 show the production functions of sector 1 and sector 2 respectively. The total endowment of labour in the economy is OL (or OL'). The line LL' in the third quadrant represents this labour constraint faced by the economy. The x-axis in the first quadrant measures the output of commodity 2, and the y-axis measures the output of commodity 1. The curve AB represents the usual product transformation frontier - it shows the combination of maximum attainable output of one sector given the output level of the other sector. For example, if all labour is employed in sector 2, OB units of commodity 2 will be produced. Alternately, if all labour is employed in sector 1, OA units of commodity 1 will be produced, while the output of commodity 2 will be zero.[4] The curve AB shows the transformation possibilities of commodity 2 into commodity 1 and vice versa.

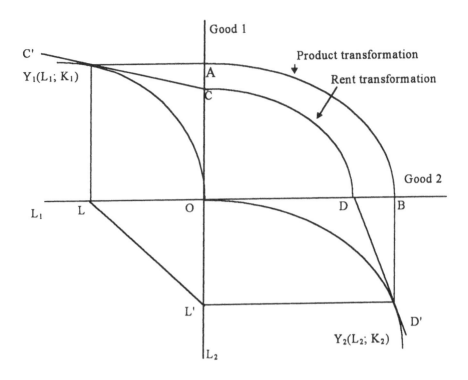

Figure 4.1   The rent and product transformation frontiers

A product transformation, in equilibrium, under the maintained hypothesis that production sectors are profit maximizers, can always be induced by a change in the domestic relative price of commodities. The mechanism behind this transformation is that a change in the relative price of commodities alters the equilibrium wage rate, which will induce a reallocation of the mobile factor - labour, between the sectors.   Thus each point on the curve AB is a point of production equilibrium that corresponds to a particular domestic relative price of commodities.

Consider first a case in which all mobile factor is employed in sector 1. Since the mobile factor would be paid its marginal product, AC represents the wage bill and OC represents the rent to the specific factor in sector 1. Rent to the specific factor in sector 2 is zero. Similarly, when all labour is employed in sector 2, DB represents the wage bill and OD represents the rent to the specific factor in sector 2, while the rent to the specific factor in sector 1 is zero. The curve CD traces out the combination of the real rents to the two sector-specific factors at different possible relative price of commodities.

The product transformation frontier and domestic price ratios are well known tools of economists that help to locate the equilibrium product mix. It is natural to enquire about the location of equilibrium rents for given commodity prices.

We know from equation (3.12) that the specific factors, in equilibrium, are paid their corresponding value of marginal product. Therefore, using equation (3.6) and noting that commodity 2 is the numeraire, we can write

$$\frac{R_1}{R_2} = \frac{P_1 \beta_1 (Y_1 / K_1)^{1+\rho_1}}{\beta_2 (Y_2 / K_2)^{1+\rho_2}} . \tag{4.15}$$

Hence, by expressing the rents in units of own-output equation (4.15) can be rewritten as

$$\frac{K_1 \tilde{R}_1}{K_2 \tilde{R}_2} = \frac{\beta_1 K_2^{\rho_2}}{\beta_2 K_1^{\rho_1}} \left(\frac{Y_1^{1+\rho_1}}{Y_2^{1+\rho_2}} \right) . \tag{4.16}$$

Equation (4.16) provides the translation from output levels to the ratio of sectoral rental incomes. However, it can be seen from equation (4.16) that the relation between rental mix and output mix, in general, is non-linear.

In particular, if production functions in both sectors are Cobb-Douglas, then both ρ_1 and ρ_2 tend to zero and equation (4.16) reduces to

$$\frac{K_1 \tilde{R}_1}{K_2 \tilde{R}_2} = \frac{\beta_1}{\beta_2} \left(\frac{Y_1}{Y_2} \right) . \tag{4.17}$$

Now it is easy to see that the rental mix (ratio of rental incomes) is proportional to the output mix (ratio of sectoral outputs). This relationship can be illustrated graphically.

As in Figure 4.1, AB and CD in Figure 4.2 represent the product transformation frontier and the rent transformation frontier respectively. Given that the relative price of commodity 1 is P_1, the optimal output mix is determined by the point E where the absolute value of the slope of the product transformation frontier is $1/P_1$. Sectoral outputs of the two sectors are respectively Y_1 and Y_2. The slope of the ray OE shows the equilibrium output mix.

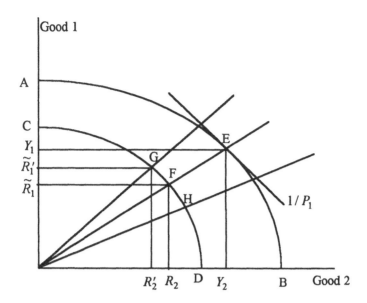

Figure 4.2   Location of equilibrium rental incomes

If both sectors have the same cost shares of capital (as if they have identical Cobb-Douglas production functions) then it follows from equation (4.17) that the rental mix will also be given by the slope of the same ray OE. The rental equilibrium will be at point F on the rental transformation frontier.[5] If the cost-share of capital in sector 1 is greater than the cost-share of capital in sector 2, (that is, if $\beta_1 > \beta_2$) the equilibrium rental mix will be given by the slope of the ray, such as OG, which lies to the left of the ray OE. If $\beta_1 < \beta_2$ then the rental mix will be given by the slope of the ray such as OH which lies to the right of the ray OE. In general, there is no reason to assume that the production technologies of the two sectors are identical and Cobb-Douglas and therefore, the value of the rent transformation frontier in locating distributive equilibrium geometrically is quite limited. Nevertheless, with sufficient structure imposed, it can be a useful illustrative device.

4.4   Comparative static properties of the RTF

This section identifies the variables that bring shifts in and movements along the rent transformation frontier. It then describes the nature of the effects on the RTF of changes in the exogenous variables.

Changes in the endowment of factors in the economy bring about changes in the capacity of the economy to produce. In general, these changes are responsible for the shifts in the RTF. For example, an increase in the stock of capital in sector 1 will increase the level of output that it can produce. If the consequent increase in the marginal product of labour is not very high, so as not to raise wage rates prohibitively high, then the rental income of sector 1 will also increase. However, the rental income of sector 2 under complete specialization will be unaffected by change in the stock of capital in sector 1. Therefore, the RTF will shift in favour of sector 1. A similar argument applies to the case in which the stock of capital in sector 2 increases. It will induce a shift in the RTF in favour of sector 2.

Similarly, an increase in the stock of labour in the economy, *ceteris paribus*, lowers the wage rate which, in turn, contributes to an increase in the rental income of both sector. The extent of shift in the rental income under complete specialization, as will be indicated below, depends on the distributive shares of labour and the elasticity of factor substitution in the two sectors. The intuitive mechanism can be tracked from equation (3.42) which yields the response of the wage rate as labour supply changes, and from equation (3.39), which yields the response of rental rate as the wage rate changes.

Analytically, the effects of the endowment changes in the sectoral rental rate can be observed from equations (3.46) and (3.47). The extreme points of the RTF can be observed by creating situations of complete specialization in the employment of the mobile factor, which can be ensured by setting $\lambda_1 = 1$ and $\lambda_2 = 1$ respectively.

When $\lambda_1 = 1$, the effect of an endowment change in the rental rate of sector 1, at constant commodity prices, can be obtained from equation (3.46) and is rewritten as

$$r_1 = -\frac{S_{L1}}{\sigma_1}(k_1 - l).$$

(4.18)

Therefore, *ceteris paribus*, for $k_1 > 0$, the percentage change in the maximal rental income of sector 1 can be written as $k_1 + r_1 = (1 - S_{L1}/\sigma_1)k_1$ that is positive for $\sigma_1 \geq 1$ and; for $l > 0$, we have $r_1 = (S_{L1}/\sigma_1)l$ which is always positive. That is, the rental income of sector 1 will increase under specialization as the national endowment of labour and/or the stock of capital in sector 1 increases, and the elasticities of factor substitution are not very small.

Similarly, by setting $\lambda_2 = 1$ we can obtain the effect of endowment changes on the rental income of sector 2. For $k_2 > 0$, ceteris paribus, we can obtain from equation (3.47) that $k_2 + r_2 = (1 - S_{L2} / \sigma_2)k_2$ which is positive for $\sigma_2 \geq 1$, and for $l > 0$, we get $r_2 = (S_{L2} / \sigma_2)l$ which is always positive. These results show that the maximal rental income of sector 2 will increase with an increase in the endowment of labour and/or with an increase in the stock of capital in sector 2, provided the elasticity of factor substitution is not very small.

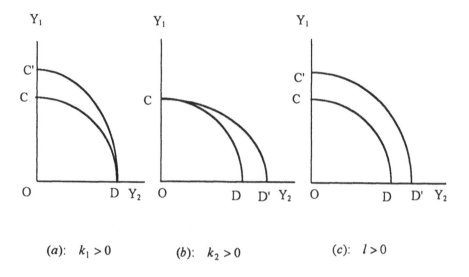

(a): $k_1 > 0$ (b): $k_2 > 0$ (c): $l > 0$

Figure 4.3   Effects of endowment change on the RTF

Figure 4.3 illustrates typical patterns of shifts on the RTF as endowments change. Panel (a) shows the effect of an increase in the stock of capital in sector 1, panel (b) shows the effect of an increase in the stock of capital in sector 2, and panel (c) shows the effect of an increase in the endowment of the mobile factor on the RTF. The axes measure the rental incomes in units of own-output.

4.4.2   Effects of price change

Any change in the domestic relative price, by definition of the RTF, causes a movement along the RTF. Therefore, changes in the world price and the tariff rate cause a movement along the frontier.

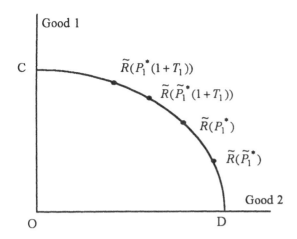

Figure 4.4   Price changes: movement along the RTF

To illustrate, let P_1^* be the initial world price ratio and T_1 be the tariff rate. It can be seen from Figure 4.4 that the imposition of T_1 raises the rental income of sector 1 and lowers the rental income of sector 2 compared to the free trade situation. Suppose the world relative price of commodity 1 falls, from P_1^* to $\tilde{P}_1^*$. Then, at an unchanged tariff rate the domestic relative price of commodity 1 also falls and consequently, the point $\tilde{R}(\tilde{P}_1^*(1+T_1))$ gives the combination of equilibrium rental incomes.   If the tariff rate is sufficiently increased to compensate for the fall in the world price then the combination of rental incomes will can be maintained at its pre-shock level, as given by the point $\tilde{R}(P_1^*(1+T_1))$.

Thus, if the source of the shock is the tariff rate or the international relative price, then the effect will be a movement along the RTF.   If the source of the shock is a change in one of the factor endowments, then the effect will be a shift on the RTF.

4.5   Summary

Basing on a simple general equilibrium model of a small open economy described in the previous chapter a rent transformation function was derived in this chapter. A corresponding rent transformation *frontier* was defined which traces the equilibrium combinations of the sectoral rental incomes as the tariff rate changes. Along the frontier an increase in the rental income of one sector necessarily implies a reduction of the rental income of the other sector.   The mechanism behind this transfer is the induced difference in the real wages faced by the two sectors, which further induces a reallocation of labour between the two sectors and hence the outputs and the rents.

It has been shown that if the long run elasticity of factor substitution is at least unity in both sectors and rents are measured in units of own-output, then the rental transformation frontier is concave to the origin and lies inside the product transformation frontier. *This shows that the sectoral-rental functions, that yield rental income at each relative price, are bounded, and the real-rent possibility set is convex.*

Any change in the endowment of factors causes a shift in the frontier and a change in the tariff rate or the international price ratio will cause a movement along the frontier. Since, tariff rates are such powerful instruments of income redistribution an obvious question that follows is how the tariff rates are determined. An attempt to answer this question using a political economy approach will be made in the next chapter. As we will see, the results presented here are quite useful in finding an answer to this question.

Notes

1 For simplicity, we can interpret the second-order property of the rental function of each sector by taking the commodity of the other sector as the numeraire in turn. In other words, while evaluating the second-order property of the rental function (and also the output supply function) of sector 1, we will consider commodity 2 as the numeraire and express the price of commodity 1 in units of commodity 2, and while evaluating the second-order property of the rental function (and the output supply function) of sector 2, we will consider commodity 1 as the numeraire.

2 See also Bullock (1992) for an application of Gardner's concept of surplus transformation curve.

3 We note that, an expression describing the transformation of the real rental-incomes as the relative price change can be obtained as follows.

Let $\Pi_i = \tilde{R}_i K_i$. Then Π_i measures the real rental income in sector i. By following the same procedures we can obtain the rent transformation frontier as

$$\frac{\Pi_1}{K_1} = P_1^{-1} \beta_1^{-\frac{\sigma_1}{1-\sigma_1}} \times$$

$$\left[P_1^{1-\sigma_1} - \alpha_1^{\sigma_1} \alpha_2^{-\frac{\sigma_2(1-\sigma_1)}{1-\sigma_2}} \left(1 - \beta_2^{\sigma_2} \left(\frac{\Pi_2}{K_2} \right)^{1-\sigma_2} \right)^{\frac{1-\sigma_1}{1-\sigma_2}} \right]^{\frac{1}{1-\sigma_1}}$$

(4.6')

It is clear that equation (4.6') can be obtained from equation (4.6) simply by dividing and multiplying the rental rate terms in (4.6) by the respective values of the sectoral capital stocks. The properties of the two forms of expression are essentially the same. The frontier described by equation (4.6) will be referred as the rental transformation frontier, and that by equation (4.6') will be referred as the rent transformation frontier.

4   Note that if the production functions are not characterized by unitary elasticity of factor substitution, then the output of sector 2 will not be zero even if all of the mobile factor is employed in sector 1. Similarly, the output of sector 1 will not be zero even if all of the mobile factor is employed in sector 2. Each sector can produce a minimum quantity of its output by employing the sector-specific factor only. In this case both product and the rent transformation frontiers will have some linear segments on both ends. However, the above properties of the frontiers will remain unchanged. In what follows we will ignore this possibility until Chapter 7, since at this level of aggregation corner solutions are rare possibilities.

5   In fact, using the definition of cost share of labour from equation (3.28), employment share from (3.30), and noting that rental mix is given by equation (4.17), it can be seen from equation (4.8), by normalizing the sectoral stock of capital to unity, that the slope of the rental transformation function under Cobb-Douglas technologies is given by

$$d\widetilde{R}_1 / d\widetilde{R}_2 = -\beta_1 / P_1\beta_2.$$

Therefore, if the share of capital in the two sectors are equal then in equilibrium the slope of the rental transformation frontier will be equal to the slope of the product transformation frontier. That is, the product transformation frontier is a proportionate blow out of the rent transformation frontier.

5 Nash equilibrium of a political economy and the tariff rate

Introduction

In Chapters 3 and 4 we have analysed the economic sphere of a political economy and have seen that some agents gain and some agents loose as a government changes the tariff rate. There we assumed that agents take policies as given by the government; they do not attempt to influence the government's policy choice even if the cost of doing so is less than its benefit to them.

From this chapter onwards we will relax this assumption. We will assume that policies of the government are determined in the political sphere, where agents, who are price-takers in the economic sphere, behave strategically to influence policy choices of the government, and consequently, determine prices they face in the economic sphere. With this change in assumption it now becomes possible to determine the tariff rate that will emerge at the simultaneous equilibrium of the political and the economic spheres of the political economy. The very nature of this political economy, however, violates the assumptions of Arrow-Debreu model that all agents are price takers. As a result, the existence of an equilibrium in such a political economy becomes a non-trivial question. The main purpose of this chapter is to address this question.

Coggins (1989) and Coggins, et al. (1991) have studied this problem in the context of a 2-person exchange economy in which the government's policy (the relative price of the two goods) was determined by a lobbying contest between the two players. An equilibrium was shown to exist for such a political economy under certain conditions some of which, as noted in Chapter 2, are rather restrictive. More importantly, it is not clear whether their existence result can be extended onto a productive economy or not. In particular, when a lobbying process is grafted onto the model of a productive economic sphere, such as described in Chapters 3 and 4, whether we can be certain of the existence of an equilibrium of the resulting political economy will be the main issue of this chapter.

In proving the existence of an equilibrium in a lobbying exchange economy, Coggins, et al., assumed a lobbying sensitive pricing function satisfying certain properties that summarized the strategic behaviour of the government. We will begin this chapter by employing a *similar* pricing function to establish the existence of an equilibrium in a productive political economy. We will further show that the pricing function satisfying the assumed properties is consistent with the government's maximization of a Peltzman-type political support function. The later result demonstrates that the studies that examined the behaviour of the tariff rate from the supply side of the political market by simply maximizing a political support function, and the studies that examined the tariff formation process from the demand side of the political market assuming a stable tariff (or pricing) function are mutually consistent. The conclusion of the two approaches would be the same if the tariff game admits a unique Nash equilibrium.

This chapter is divided into six sections. The first section provides an intuitive link between the economic and the political spheres which provides a motivation for the construction of a tariff setting game. The second section specifies the properties of the government's pricing function as in previous studies.

Given a pricing function of the government, the problem of the lobbies (or the interest groups) is specified in section three. Here, we differ from Coggins, et al., in (the form of) one assumption. Coggins, et al., have assumed that the players are utility maximizers, whereas we follow Findlay and Wellisz (1982) and assume that the players, the owners of sector-specific factors, are payoff - real rental income less lobbying expenditure - maximizers.

In section four, the tariff game is specified in strategic form. The existence theorem and related lemmas are proved in section five. In addition to the existence results, this section also shows that in all Nash equilibria of the tariff game each player spends a nonzero amount of its real rental-income in predatory lobbying. Moreover, it is also shown that under a reasonable assumption, the conjecture of Findlay and Wellisz (1982) that a positive tariff rate will result at the Nash equilibrium of the game is correct. Section six concludes the chapter. Finally, it is shown in the Appendix that the support maximizing behaviour of the government, which is a Stackelberg leader in the game, leads to a pricing function that satisfies the properties used in proving the existence result.

The result that each player spends a non-zero amount of rental income in lobbying at every Nash equilibria is critical. This result clearly shows that in this tariff game, players, therefore, have an incentive to cooperate; they both can save the income spent in lobbying. It is because of this result that we do not regard a noncooperative Nash equilibrium as a stable equilibrium of the game. We, instead, consider the possibility of cooperation between the players in the next chapter and study the comparative-static behaviour of the tariff rate at the cooperative equilibrium of the game.

5.1 The political sphere

Given that the economic sphere of a political economy can be described by a specific-factor model, as in Chapter 3, it was shown in Chapter 4 that the owners of specific-factors have conflicting interests over the tariff rate, which is determined in the political sphere. The government, which is based on political support from the general public, is assumed to use the tariff rate as an instrument to muster the required political support. In this environment, other interest groups, such as the owners of the specific factors, find it reasonable to link political support to the benefits they finally derive from the government's choice of the tariff rate. It is easy to see that this political environment inter-locks the government and the owners of specific-factors in a lobbying game, which can be described intuitively as follows.

An increase in the tariff rate will raise the domestic relative price of the import competing good and hence will increase the rent to the specific factor employed in the import competing sector. The import competing sector, therefore, always has an incentive to spend resources in lobbying the government for an imposition of or an increase in the tariff rate on the imports of the import-competing good (good 1). But, a tariff on the imports of good 1 also means a lower relative price of the export good (good 2) and a higher price for the mobile factor, which, in turn, means a lower rent to the specific factor employed in the exporting sector. Thus, the owners of the specific factor in the exporting sector will have an incentive to spend resources in counter-lobbying the government not to raise the price of import competing good, that is not to increase tariffs on imports of good 1. Conversely, if the exporting sector starts to spend resources in lobbying the government to lower the tariff rate there will be an incentive to the import competing sector to spend resources on counter-lobbying to maintain the tariff level and the level of its rents.

If the tariff policy (or the pricing policy) of the government responds to the lobbying efforts of the two sectors, a sector may be able to increase its rental income by increasing its lobbying activities. However, if the other sector increases its counter-lobbying activities in response then it is possible that the equilibrium tariff rate may not change at all. Hence, the relative price and the distribution of rents may remain unchanged despite an increase in the intensities of the lobbying activities of both sectors.

What a sector obtains from lobbying, therefore, depends not only on how it behaves but also on how the other sector(s) behaves. While taking decisions on whether to lobby or not to lobby the government, each sector has to consider the possible reaction from the other sector(s). Therefore, the lobbying contest between the two sectors can be viewed as a 2-person game with lobbying expenditures as their strategies. The objective of the game is to obtain a favourable tariff rate which, in turn, means a favourable domestic price ratio and higher net rental income.

Since for each price ratio there is a unique equilibrium in the economic sphere (which has been described by a GE model of the economic sphere), we will obtain a full equilibrium of the political economy if there is also an equilibrium in the political sphere. The lobbying contest in the tariff game has been assumed as the only set of strategic interactions that take place in the political sphere of the political economy. Therefore, the immediate question is whether there exists any equilibrium in such a lobbying contest of the tariff game? If so, how can we characterize it? These questions will be answered formally in the following sections.

5.2 The pricing function

Let the strategic response of the government to the lobbying efforts of the interest groups be summarized by a pricing function

$$P_i = P_i(\eta_i, \eta_{-i}); \qquad\qquad i = 1,2 \qquad\qquad (5.1)$$

where, η_i and η_{-i} are non-negative real numbers that represent the lobbying expenditures[1] of sector i and sector(s) $-i$ (all other sectors but not i) respectively,[2] and P_i is the normalized relative price of good i in terms of the other good.[3] It is assumed that the pricing function of the government is common knowledge.

As in previous studies (in particular, Findlay and Wellisz, 1982; Wellisz and Wilson, 1986; and Coggins, et al., 1991), we assume that the pricing function satisfies the following properties:[4]

(P1) The function $P_i = P_i(\eta_i, \eta_{-i})$ is continuous and differentiable in η_i and η_{-i}.

(P2) $P_i(0,0) = P_i^*$.

Property (P2) guarantees that if no one chooses to lobby then the world price prevails. This assumption presupposes that the government has no reason of its own to deviate from the world price, and if we observe a deviation it is because at least one agent in the economy wants the domestic price to be different from the world price.

(P3) (*Productive Lobbying*) $P_i = P_i(\eta_i, \eta_{-i})$ is strictly increasing and concave in η_i and strictly decreasing and convex in η_{-i}.

Satisfaction of property (P3) guarantees that, for a given lobbying effort of player 2, if player 1 increases its lobbying effort, then the domestic price of good 1 will increase relative to the price of good 2 (monotonicity). But successive increases in lobbying efforts will bring increasingly smaller increase in the relative price of good 1 (concavity).

(P4) (*Bounded Pricing*) There exist two finite and positive real numbers P_i' and P_i'' such that for all η_i and η_{-i}, $P_i(\eta_i, \eta_{-i}) \in [P_i', P_i'']$.

Property (P4) means that the government will choose tariffs in such a way that, for each i, the induced domestic relative price of good i will be within the bounds regardless of the level of lobbying expenditure of the private agents. The bounds include world relative prices in the feasible set by property (P2). The rationale behind such limiting prices may be that if the domestic relative price is too far off from the world price and/or autarky price the overall dead weight loss may be sufficiently high to invite a successful political opposition.[5]

Many pricing functions can satisfy properties (P1) - (P4). A set of such functions can be defined as follows. Let,

$$\aleph = \{P_i : R_+^2 \to [P_i', P_i''] \mid P_i(\eta_i, \eta_{-i}) \text{ satisfies } (P1) \text{ through } (P4)\}.$$

Then elements of $\aleph$ are admissible pricing functions.

To fix the idea let us consider a specific example of an admissible pricing function. Since it is easier to construct examples of pricing functions that map lobbying expenditures into the unit interval (simplex), for the sake of this example, let us assume that prices of the two commodities satisfy $P_1 + P_2 = 1$. Then, the price ratio can be identified from the two normalized prices. For nonzero lobbying expenditures let us specify a pricing function as follows:

$$P_i(\eta_i, \eta_{-i}) = P_i' + (P_i'' - P_i')[\eta_i^\alpha / (\eta_i^\alpha + \eta_{-i}^\beta)] \tag{5.2}$$

where $0 < \alpha < 1$ and $0 < \beta < 1$ are constants. If we take normalized free trade and autarky prices as the bounds, then equation (5.2) can display a family of price - lobbying expenditure relationship satisfying the properties (P1) through (P4). The parameters α, and β reflect the asymmetric costs to the two players of obtaining a given change in the relative price.

It is clear that, in a 2-player case, when player 2 spends sufficiently large amount of resources in lobbying for a given lobbying expenditure of player 1 then $P_1(\eta_1, \eta_2) = P_1'$, that is the relative price of good 1 takes its lower bound, and when player 1 spends sufficiently large amount of resource in lobbying for a given lobbying expenditure of player 2 then $P_1(\eta_1, \eta_2) = P_1''$, that is the distorted price of good 1 will take its upper bound.

The pricing function (5.2) is very sensitive to small lobbying expenditures around the origin in the lobbying space. For example, if player 2 does not lobby at all, then player 1 can obtain its upper bound price just by spending a cent in lobbying. Will the government announce such a pricing function? Herein lies the strategic behaviour of the government. It is because, when no one is lobbying, it costs less to obtain a large favour from the government, every player will be lured to spend some resources in lobbying. When one player starts lobbying with a very small sum and is able to obtain a good deal in price changes then it becomes almost a necessity to the other player to spend resources in counter-lobbying. The dynamics of competitive lobbying will be set into motion. The government then can rely on the pricing function to induce competitive lobbying involving larger sums. So, a government may offer such a very sensitive pricing function if it wants to induce more competitive lobbying from the interest groups.

Properties (P1)-(P3) may be found in Coggins, et al. (1991). In addition to these three assumptions they have one more assumption, which they call *Bounded Lobbying*. This means that, given the lobbying expenditure(s) of the other agent(s), there exists a finite maximum lobbying expenditure for each agent that exhausts all of his resources. This implies that the agent is incapable of increasing lobbying expenditure beyond that bound. Evaluation of the bound for agent i when others are not lobbying at all gives the greatest upper bound for agent i's lobbying expenditure. The price that is obtained with this greatest upper bound lobbying expenditure yields the ceiling for the price that agent i can ever obtain. Thus *Bounded Lobbying* implies *Bounded Pricing* - (P4). As will be argued below, while describing the nature (compactness) of the strategy set of payoff maximizing players, that bounded pricing assumption implies bounded lobbying.

Instead of taking this indirect route of arriving at bounded pricing via bounded lobbying, we have directly assumed that the pricing function is bounded. As will become clear at various points that it is handy to have the pricing function satisfy bounded lobbying as well, we will have this because we will be maintaining throughout that agents are payoff maximizers. The implication of this assumption together with bounded pricing property is that lobbying expenditures will remain bounded. As will be seen below, this shift in the assumption has been very helpful in proving the existence of an equilibrium in the lobbying economy.

5.3   The problem of the lobbies

Let us recall that the stock of sector-specific capital in sector i is K_i and the equilibrium real rental rate (measured in units of own output) at given price

$P_i(\eta_i, \eta_{-i})$ is $\widetilde{R}_i(P_i(\eta_i, \eta_{-i}))$. The payoff to player i, when all players are behaving strategically, at any strategy combination (η_i, η_{-i}) can be written as

$$\Pi_i(\eta_i, \eta_{-i}) \equiv K_i \widetilde{R}_i(P_i(\eta_i, \eta_{-i})) - \eta_i .$$ (5.3)

Given the pricing rule of the government and lobbying expenditure η_{-i}, of the other player(s), the problem of each player i is to choose a level of lobbying expenditure η_i such that the problem

$$\max_{\eta_i} \Pi_i(\eta_i, \eta_{-i}) \equiv \max_{\eta_i} [(K_i \widetilde{R}_i(P_i(\eta_i, \eta_{-i})) - \eta_i]$$ (5.4)

is solved.

Recall that, for each player i, $\widetilde{R}_i$ is real-valued, bounded, continuous and strictly increasing function of P_i (Proposition 4.1). Since P_i is increasing in lobbying expenditure of player i and decreasing in lobbying expenditure of the other player, player $-i$, each player can raise its rental income by increasing expenditure on lobbying. Concavity of the pricing function implies that each player needs to spend increasing amounts on lobbying in order to obtain constant increases in the relative price of his commodity, given the lobbying expenditure of the other player.

Under the assumption that each player shows Nash behaviour, i.e. takes the lobbying expenditure of the other player as given, the optimization problem of each player, represented by (5.3), is to determine the level of lobbying expenditure that maximizes his payoff (the total rent net of lobbying expenditure). The constraints in this problem are implicit in the nature of the equilibrium rental functions and in the nature of the pricing function.

5.4 The game in strategic form

With these preliminaries we can proceed to describe a tariff setting game in strategic form. For each player i, and for given η_{-i} of other player(s), let us define

$$\hat{\eta}_i(\eta_{-i}) = K_i \widetilde{R}_i(P_i(\hat{\eta}_i, \eta_{-i})) , \text{ and}$$ (5.5)

$$\overline{\eta}_i = \max_{\eta_{-i}} \hat{\eta}_i(\eta_{-i})$$ (5.6)

then, $\hat{\eta}_i$ represents the maximum lobbying expenditure that agent i can incur if he is a payoff maximizer and player $-i$ is spending η_{-i}, and $\overline{\eta}_i$ represents the level of lobbying expenditure which will never be exceeded by the payoff maximizing agent i, whatever be the lobbying expenditure of the other player. Thus, $H_i = [0, \overline{\eta}_i]$ defines the strategy set of player i.

From the defining equations (5.5) and (5.6) it is clear that $\hat{\eta}_i \leq \overline{\eta}_i$ for each player i. This implies that for any given η_{-i} the choice set of player i is limited to a subset of the strategy set H_i. Let φ_i be a correspondence defined on the strategy space such that $\varphi_i(\eta_{-i}) \equiv [0, \hat{\eta}_i]$, then $\varphi_i(\eta_{-i}) \subset H_i$ and $\varphi_i(\eta_{-i})$ represents player i's constraint correspondence - a mapping - that determines the choice set of player i given the strategy choice of other players.

Let I={1,2} be the player set, then $H = \times_{i \in I} H_i$ is the set of ordered pairs that describes all possible strategy combinations of the two players, and Π_i is the associated payoff function for each player i.

Definition 5.1. *Any* $\Gamma = \left\{ (H_i, \Pi_i, \varphi_i)_{i \in I} \right\}$ *is a collection of tariff games in strategic form.*

Definition 5.2. *A pair* (η_i^*, η_{-i}^*) *is a noncooperative Nash equilibrium of the tariff game if* η_i^* *solves*

$$\max_{\eta_i \in \varphi_i(\eta_{-i}^*)} \Pi_i(\eta_i, \eta_{-i}^*); \qquad\qquad i \in I \qquad\qquad (5.7)$$

In other words, Definition 5.2 means that if, for each player i, the knowledge that player $-i$ spends η_{-i}^* in lobbying implies that player i finds it optimal to spend η_i^* in lobbying the government, then the strategy combination (η_i^*, η_{-i}^*) is optimal for each player. It represents a Nash equilibrium of the game.

5.5   The existence result

The sufficient conditions for the existence of an equilibrium of a game in Γ are listed in the following theorem.

Theorem 5.1 (Debreu, 1982: 702-3). *If, for every* $i \in I$, *the set* H_i *is a non-empty, compact, convex subset of a Euclidean Space,* Π_i *is a continuous real-valued function on* $H = \times_{i \in I} H_i$ *that is quasiconcave in its* i^{th} *variable, and* φ_i *is* *a continuous, convex-valued correspondence from H to H_i, then the social system $(H_i, \Pi_i, \varphi_i)_{i \in I}$ has an equilibrium.*

Given the properties of $\widetilde{R}_i$, it is easy to see that the payoff function Π_i is real-valued and continuous on $H = \times_{i \in I} H_i$, the immediate problem is to check whether the remaining conditions of the theorem are satisfied by a tariff-setting game in Γ. We will check these conditions for an arbitrary player i. If the conditions of the theorem are satisfied for the player i, then it will be valid for all players, and the theorem will be applicable to our problem. We will accomplish that by a series of lemmas.

Lemma 5.1   *Let $X \subset R$, $Y \subset R$, and let $g: X \to Y$ be differentiable, then g is quasiconcave if and only if for every pair of elements x_1, x_2 of X $[g'(x_1) < 0$ and $x_2 > x_1]$ together imply $g'(x_2) < 0$.*

Proof: See Coggins, et al. (1991).

Lemma 5.2. *If the pricing function satisfies (P1) through (P4), then for given η_{-i}, the payoff function*

$$\Pi_i(\eta_i, \eta_{-i}) \equiv K_i \widetilde{R}_i(P_i(\eta_i, \eta_{-i})) - \eta_i \qquad (5.8)$$

is quasiconcave in η_i ; $\eta_i \in R_+$.

Proof: First note that $\Pi_i(0, \eta_{-i}) > 0$ for, the price has a lower bound, and the rental rate is positive at this price. Even though the rental rate increases with P_i, and P_i increases with the lobbying expenditure, the payoff $\Pi_i(\eta_i, \eta_{-i})$ eventually becomes negative as η_i increases. The arguments run as follows. Since, the pricing function satisfies (P4), P_i has its upper bound P_i^*. Now, let $\eta_i' = K_i \widetilde{R}_i(P_i'')$, then for all $\eta_i > \eta_i'$, it follows from equation (5.8) that we must have $\Pi_i(\eta_i, \eta_{-i}) < 0$.

The payoff becomes negative from positive also suggests that there must be a $\eta_i'' \in [0, \eta_i']$ such that $\partial \Pi_i / \partial \eta_i < 0$ for $\eta_i = \eta_i''$.

Differentiation of equation (5.8) partially with respect to η_i yields

$$\partial \Pi_i / \partial \eta_i = K_i(d\widetilde{R}_i / dP_i)(\partial P_i / \partial \eta_i) - 1. \qquad (5.9)$$

100

Since, $\partial \Pi_i / \partial \eta_i < 0$ for $\eta_i = \eta_i"$ and $\widetilde{R}_i(P_i)$ is strictly increasing in P_i, equation (5.9) implies that at $\eta_i = \eta_i"$ we have $(\partial P_i / \partial \eta_i) < 1/[K_i(d\widetilde{R}_i / dP_i)]$.

Property (P3), the concavity of P_i implies that the slope of P_i falls as η_i increases. Therefore, for all $\eta_i > \eta_i"$ we must have

$$(\partial P_i / \partial \eta_i) < (\partial P_i / \partial \eta_i)\Big|_{\eta_i=\eta_i"} < 1/[K_i(d\widetilde{R}_i / dP_i)] \qquad (5.10)$$

Therefore, it follows from conditions (5.9) and (5.10) that for all $\eta_i > \eta_i"$, we have $\partial \Pi_i / \partial \eta_i < 0$. Hence by Lemma 5.1 the payoff function $\Pi_i(\eta_i, \eta_{-i})$ is quasiconcave in η_i. Q. E. D.

The argument used in the proof of Lemma 5.2 asserts that if the payoff function declines some level of lobbying expenditure then it continues to decline for all higher levels of lobbying expenditures. This effectively precludes nonconvexities in the choice set and the constraint correspondence remains convex valued which is shown in the following lemma.

Lemma 5.3. *If the pricing function satisfies properties (P1) to (P4) then the strategy set of player i, H_i, is nonempty, compact and convex subset of R, the real line, and further, the constraint correspondence $\varphi_i(\eta_{-i})$ is convex-valued and continuous.*

Proof: By definition the strategy set of player i is $H_i = [0, \overline{\eta}_i]$. The player can always choose not to lobby, implying that $0 \in H_i$, therefore, $H_i \neq \varnothing$. The set is obviously closed for it also includes boundary points. Compactness requires that the set be bounded.

Since P_i is bounded from above by $P_i"$ [Property (P4)], and $\widetilde{R}_i$ is increasing in P_i, we have by definition that $\widetilde{R}_i(P_i") < +\infty$. Since $0 < K_i < +\infty$, it follows from equations (5.5) and (5.6) that for all non-negative values of η_{-i} we must have $\overline{\eta}_i \leq K_i \widetilde{R}_i(P_i")$. Therefore, H_i is compact. Convexity of H_i is automatically satisfied because it is a closed interval of a real line.

To show that the choice set is convex or the constraint correspondence is convex valued let us consider the definition of $\varphi_i(\eta_{-i})$. Since $\varphi_i(\eta_{-i})$ is a collection of strategies (lobbying levels) available to player i when player $-i$ has chosen to spend η_{-i} amount of resources in lobbying $\varphi_i(\eta_{-i})$ can also be defined by

$$\varphi_i(\eta_{-i}) \equiv \{\eta_i \in H_i \mid \Pi_i(\eta_i, \eta_{-i}) \geq 0\} \qquad (5.11)$$

But this means $\varphi_i(\eta_{-i})$ is a better set defined by the payoff function $\Pi_i(\eta_i, \eta_{-i})$, which is quasiconcave by Lemma 5.2. Therefore, $\varphi_i(\eta_{-i})$ is a convex set.

Lastly, it remains to be shown that the constraint correspondence $\varphi_i(\eta_{-i})$ is continuous. Continuity of $\varphi_i(\eta_{-i})$ has been shown in Coggins, et al. (1991), which is restated here for the sake of completeness.

It suffices to show that $\varphi_i(\eta_{-i})$ is upper and lower hemicontinuous.[6] Since P_i is continuous in H_i, and $\tilde{R}_i$ is continuous in P_i, it follows from equation (5.5) that $\hat{\eta}_i(\eta_{-i})$ is continuous in $[0, \overline{\eta}_{-i}]$. Thus the graph of $\varphi_i(\eta_{-i})$ is closed. As $\varphi_i(\eta_{-i})$ is also compact valued by the above argument, it is upper hemicontinuous. To show lower hemicontinuity, consider a sequence $\{\eta_{-i}^n\}$ converging to η_{-i}^o, and take any arbitrary $\eta_i^o \in \varphi(\eta_{-i}^o)$. If $\eta_i^o < \hat{\eta}_i(\eta_{-i}^o)$ then, for sufficiently large N and n > N, we may set $\eta_i^n = \eta_i^o$. Then clearly $\eta_i^n \to \eta_i^o$, and the conditions for lower hemicontinuity are satisfied. If $\eta_i^o = \hat{\eta}_i(\eta_{-i}^o)$ then, let $\eta_i^n = \hat{\eta}_i(\eta_{-i}^n)$. As $\hat{\eta}_i(\eta_{-i})$ is continuous, the conditions for lower hemicontinuity are again satisfied. It is concluded that $\varphi_i(\eta_{-i})$ is lower hemicontinuous. Thus, it is continuous.

Q. E. D.

Theorem 5.2. *(Existence of an equilibrium in a tariff game). Given a Tariff Game in* $\Gamma = (H_i, \Pi_i, \varphi_i)_{i \in I}$ *as defined above, if the pricing function* $P_i(\eta_i, \eta_{-i})$ *satisfies properties (P1) to (P4), then there exists at least one noncooperative Nash equilibrium.*

Proof: First we note that under the conditions of the theorem, Lemma 5.2 and Lemma 5.3 hold. We know that the pricing function is continuous in lobbying expenditures η_i and η_{-i}, and $\tilde{R}_i$ is continuous and real valued in P_i, the payoff function of any arbitrary player i defined by equation (5.3) is continuous and real valued in H. The payoff function is quasiconcave in its ith variable by Lemma 5.2 and the constraint correspondence is convex-valued and continuous by Lemma 5.3. Hence, the theorem is proved by virtue of Theorem 5.1. Q. E. D.

Theorem 5.2 has guaranteed that at least a Nash equilibrium exists in an economy where tariff policy responds to the lobbying efforts of the interest groups. Since $0 \in H$, no lobbying is always a feasible strategy to both players; it is a candidate for an equilibrium. It is natural to ask, at this point, whether

$(\eta_i, \eta_{-i}) = (0,0)$ can be a Nash equilibrium of the game. The following lemma answers this question in negative.

Lemma 5.4. *In addition to the conditions of Theorem 5.2, if the pricing function is such that the partial elasticities of price with respect to the lobbying expenditures are locally constant, then $(\eta_i, \eta_{-i}) = (0,0)$ cannot be a Nash equilibrium.*

Proof: Let us consider the behaviour of player i when player $-i$ chooses not to spend in lobbying, that is $\eta_{-i} = 0$. The payoff to player i is given by

$$\Pi_i(\eta_i, 0) = K_i \widetilde{R}_i(P_i(\eta_i, 0)) - \eta_i, \qquad\qquad \eta_i \in \varphi_i(0).$$

The first order condition for the maximum requires that player i choose lobbying expenditure satisfying

$$K_i(\partial \widetilde{R}_i / \partial P_i)(\partial P_i / \partial \eta_i) \le 1 \text{ and } \eta_i(\partial \Pi_i / \partial \eta_i) = 0.$$

For $K_i \ge 1$, these conditions will yield a solution of $\eta_i = 0$ if and only if $(\partial \widetilde{R}_i / \partial P_i)(\partial P_i / \partial \eta_i) < 1$ for all $\eta_i \in \varphi_i(0)$. But

$$\left(\frac{\partial \widetilde{R}_i}{\partial P_i}\right)\left(\frac{\partial P_i}{\partial \eta_i}\right) = \left(\frac{P_i}{\widetilde{R}_i}\frac{\partial \widetilde{R}_i}{\partial P_i}\right)\left(\frac{\eta_i}{P_i}\frac{\partial P_i}{\partial \eta_i}\right)\left(\frac{\widetilde{R}_i}{\eta_i}\right).$$

We now note that under the conditions of the Lemma, the first two terms on the right (the elasticities) are always positive and locally constant around the origin of the lobbying space and the real rental income is positive at all feasible prices. Therefore, in the neighbourhood of the origin, we have

$$\lim_{\eta_i \to 0}\left(\frac{\partial \widetilde{R}_i}{\partial P_i}\right)\left(\frac{\partial P_i}{\partial \eta_i}\right) = \lim_{\eta_i \to 0}\left(\frac{P_i}{R_i}\frac{\partial \widetilde{R}_i}{\partial P_i}\right)\left(\frac{\eta_i}{P_i}\frac{\partial P_i}{\partial \eta_i}\right)\left(\frac{\widetilde{R}_i}{\eta_i}\right) = +\infty.$$

That is, $(\partial \widetilde{R}_i / \partial P_i)(\partial P_i / \partial \eta_i) > 1$ in the neighbourhood of $\eta_i = 0$, and the first order necessary condition for a maximum is not satisfied. Therefore, $\eta_i = 0$ cannot be a best reply of player i to the strategy $\eta_{-i} = 0$ of player $-i$. Since choice of i is arbitrary, we find that $(\eta_i, \eta_{-i}) = (0,0)$ cannot be a Nash equilibrium (see Definition 5.2) in the tariff game. Q. E. D.

Thus, given the properties of the pricing function, Lemma 5.4 asserts that at all Nash equilibria players will spend positive amounts in lobbying the government. It just shows that so long as the government responds to lobbying, spending a non-zero amount in lobbying is a dominant strategy of each player. It is tempting to conclude that all prices determined at Nash equilibria are, therefore, necessarily different from free trade prices. This may not be the case, however. In fact, as Coggins, et al. (1991) also have shown, if the lobbying expenditure of one player is matched appropriately by another player in equilibrium then the free trade price may result. The argument runs as follows:

Let η_i and η_{-i} be any combination of feasible lobbying expenditures of the two players. Then by the assumption of productive lobbying, (P3), we have

$$P_i(\eta_i, 0) > P_i(0,0) = P_i^* > P_i(0, \eta_{-i}).$$

By the mean value theorem, there exist feasible expenditures $\tilde{\eta}_i \in [0, \eta_i]$ and $\tilde{\eta}_{-i} \in [0, \eta_{-i}]$ such that $P_i(\tilde{\eta}_i, \tilde{\eta}_{-i}) = P_i^*$.

Thus, the result that non-zero lobbying expenditures may generate the free trade price ratio is still a possibility provided that the government has no interest of its own in deviating from the free trade. It is not yet known whether such combination of lobbying expenditures can constitute an equilibrium of the game. What has been shown so far is insufficient to rule out the possibility that at least one Nash equilibrium outcome of the game will yield the free trade price ratio.

Definition 5.3. *Given a small open Walrasian economic sphere, a domestic relative price, induced by the government's tariff policy, is* **self-financing** *if the total collection of tariff revenue net of subsidies is non-negative.*

It is evident that not all relative prices are self-financing. For example, if the government wishes to make the domestic relative price of exportable higher than that would prevail under free trade or if it wished to make the domestic relative price of the import competing good higher than that would prevail in autarky then this trade policy would necessarily require an import and/or export subsidy. The collection of tariff revenue would be negative. We exclude such cases by assuming that the government does not subsidize foreign trade. This means that the government will choose tariff/subsidy rates in such a way that the domestic price ratio will be within the bounds set by free trade and autarky price ratios. Formally, we state the following additional property of the pricing function, which is implicit in Findlay and Wellisz (1982):

(P5) (Self-financing). $P_i(\eta_i, \eta_{-i}) \in [P_i^*, P_i^a]$ for all η_i and η_{-i}, where P_i^a is the relative price of good i in autarky.

Property (P5) does not exclude the possibility of simultaneous existence of export subsidy and import tax in the announcement of government policies. This is perfectly consistent with property (P5). What it rules out are the combinations of those subsidy and tax rates that lead to higher subsidy payments than the tariff revenue collection. In other words, this assumption requires that the rationalized tariff rate be nonnegative.

Note that property (P5) by itself is not sufficient to preclude the possibility of free trade. Players may choose not to lobby at all or what they spend may counteract each other so that free trade prices are maintained. Now we will show that Findlay and Wellisz's (1982) conjecture is correct.

Corollary 5.1. *Suppose the conditions of Theorem 5.2 are satisfied with the pricing function satisfying (P1) - (P3) and (P5). If $(\widetilde{\eta}_i, \widetilde{\eta}_{-i})$ is a Nash equilibrium in the Tariff Game, then $P_i(\widetilde{\eta}_i, \widetilde{\eta}_{-i}) \neq P_i^*$.*

Proof: Suppose not, and assume that $P_i(\widetilde{\eta}_i, \widetilde{\eta}_{-i}) = P_i^*$. Let consider i as the owner of the specific-factor employed in the import-competing sector. Since P_i^* is the lower bound of P_i we must have $P_i(0, \eta_{-i}) \geq P_i^*$ for all $\eta_{-i} \in H_{-i}$. That is P_i will not fall below P_i^*, irrespective of the lobbying expenditure of the other player(s). So,

$$\Pi_i(0, \widetilde{\eta}_{-i}) \geq K_i \widetilde{R}_i(P_i^*)$$
$$> K_i \widetilde{R}_i(P_i^*) - \widetilde{\eta}_i$$
$$= K_i \widetilde{R}_i(P_i(\widetilde{\eta}_i, \widetilde{\eta}_{-i})) - \widetilde{\eta}_i.$$

Hence $\eta_i = 0$ yields a higher payoff than $\eta_i = \widetilde{\eta}_i$, given that $\eta_{-i} = \widetilde{\eta}_{-i}$. This implies that $\widetilde{\eta}_i$ is not a best response to $\widetilde{\eta}_{-i}$, which further implies that $(\widetilde{\eta}_i, \widetilde{\eta}_{-i}) \neq (0,0)$ is not a Nash equilibrium in the tariff game. A contradiction to the hypothesis.   Q. E. D.

Thus the corollary shows that if players spend non-zero amounts in lobbying the government at a Nash equilibrium in a Tariff Game then the domestic price ratio will diverge from its free trade value. The intuitive reason behind this result is pretty simple. If the domestic relative price does not diverge from the free trade relative price, which prevails even without lobbying the government, then why should the import competing sector spend resources in lobbying the government?

So far nothing has been said about the uniqueness of equilibrium in the game. The sufficient conditions for the uniqueness of equilibrium can be found in Friedman (1986). It suffices to note here that the conditions require, together with other conditions, that the payoff function of each player be concave in their respective strategy set. Lemma 5.2 has shown it to be quasiconcave. Unless further restrictions are imposed on the rental function it cannot be guaranteed that the sufficient condition will be satisfied generally and a unique Nash equilibrium will be attained in the tariff game.

5.6 Conclusion

This chapter has extended the existence result obtained by Coggins, et al., onto a productive political economy. It has shown that even if the government is responsive to the lobbying pressures of the interest groups, there exists at least one non-trivial Nash equilibrium of the political economy. Moreover, if the government is constrained to choose a tariff policy that is self-financing then each of the Nash equilibria will imply a positive tariff rate. In other words, this means that the domestic price ratio at every Nash equilibrium will be different from the free trade price ratio.

In order to show the existence of an equilibrium in a lobbying exchange economy Coggins, et al., had to impose one restriction on preferences, which they called '*own good bias*'. This restriction required that each player consume more of his own good than the one supplied by the other person. The proof of the existence theorem outlined in this chapter did not require that assumption for a productive economy. This result occurred partly because in the Coggins, et al.'s model the endowment of good for each player was fixed, but in our case sectoral output levels and, hence, the rental incomes are variable; and partly because Coggins, et al., measured player's payoffs in indirect utilities whereas this study used real net rental income as the payoffs to the players. It was thus possible to obtain much stronger results compared to previous studies with less severe assumptions. In fact, we obtained the existence results with the same set of assumptions on the pricing function as were in Findlay and Wellisz (1982).

One of the limitations of the noncooperative Nash solution is that if there are multiple equilibria (see Magee, Brock and Young, 1989 for such cases) it cannot specify a mechanism through which one of the equilibria will be selected. It is also frequently the case that the Nash process may lead to a suboptimal equilibrium in the game.[7] To resolve this problem some mechanism of refining the Nash equilibria, such as subgame perfectness, is required.

One of the fundamental assumptions of the noncooperative game is that the players make decisions in isolation. If there is a distinct possibility of increasing their payoff through communication, negotiation and adoption of a joint maximizing strategy then the assumption that rational players in a competitive environment always play a noncooperative game does not seem plausible. In the tariff game, for example, each player may spend resources in competitive lobbying just to protect himself against the predatory lobbying of the other. It is possible that they both might have been receiving lower payoffs than they would receive if they had agreed not to compete against each other.

In the next chapter we change the rules of the game, and allow the players to discuss, negotiate, and make binding agreements that are payoff (welfare) improving. This takes us to the study of the game in a cooperative form. However, as Kreps (1990: 505) has remarked 'this is not the cooperation borne of altruism or fondness of one's fellow player. This is cooperation arising from a self-interested calculation of the benefits and losses that may accrue from "polite" behaviour.'

Appendix-5A: Derivation of the properties of the pricing function of a support-maximizing government in a lobbying economy

The purpose of this Appendix is to demonstrate that the properties of the pricing function listed in Section 5.2 are consistent with a support maximizing behaviour of the government. In other words, we will show that the properties of the pricing function are sufficient for the maximum of the government's political support function. We follow Peltzman (1976) in deriving the political support function of the government.

We assume that in the political sphere the government exchanges policies for political support. In particular, this means that, besides policies that benefit everyone, if a policy change benefits one person or group and harms the other, and the beneficiary is able and prepared to offer increased support to the government that exceeds the loss in support from the losing person or group, then both the government and the winning player will be better off from this deal. Policy will thus be adjusted accordingly. This assumption does not presuppose any benevolence on the part of the government. It implies that policy changes are solely guided by the self-interest of the government driven by its desire to remain in power and are thus politically motivated.[8]

We further assume that with respect to each policy change involving a distributional issue the population can be divided into three groups according to their interest on the proposed policy change: the group that anticipates direct benefits and supports it; the group that anticipates a loss and therefore opposes it; and the third group that is uncertain about the effects of policy change on its welfare, and therefore is in a state of confusion as to whether or not to support the proposed policy change.

To be more specific, let us consider the case of an increase in the tariff rate on the imports of good 1. Clearly, the owners of the specific factor in sector 1 benefit from this change and therefore they form the first group - people who support the tariff increase. The owners of the specific factor in sector 2 lose from this change and therefore they form the second group - people who oppose the tariff change. The owners of the mobile factor, labour, may lose or gain from this change depending on their consumption pattern (tastes) known only to them, and the sizes of their income and commodity price change. If the workers are well informed, then they would, of course, either individually support or oppose the change, but there are costs involved in being well informed.

We further assume that people are distinguished by factor ownership and the ownership of specific factors is concentrated among a few and their gains or losses are relatively large compared with the information cost. Therefore they are fully aware of the likely consequences to them of the tariff changes. The owners of the mobile factor, workers in particular, are numerous. For anyone in this group the cost of information exceeds the benefit. Therefore, they remain rationally ignorant (Downs, 1957; Magee, Brock and Young, 1989). However, they make use of the 'free' information - voters' education - provided by the two 'interest groups' or the players. Each player can obtain more workers' support for the government by spending more resources on "voters' education". Hence the two interests will be contending in the political market in mobilizing workers' support to the government that will implement policies beneficial to them. The reason is as Peltzman (1976: 213) has aptly summarized -

> It is not enough for the successful group to recognize its interests; it must organize to translate this interest into support for the politician who will implement it. This means not only mobilizing its own vote, but contributing resources to the support of the appropriate political party or policy: to finance campaigns, to persuade the voters to support or at least not oppose the policy or candidate, perhaps occasionally to bribe those in office.

Given this stylization of the political process, the problem of the two players and the government being resolved simultaneously in the political market can be described as follows.

Recall from section 5.3 of the text that the problem of each player i is to choose its lobbying expenditure, η_i, to maximize

$$\Pi_i = K_i \tilde{R}_i (P_i(\eta)) - \eta_i; \qquad\qquad i = 1,2 \qquad\qquad (5A.1)$$

where, P_i is the relative price of good i. Note that once P_1 is determined, P_2 will be determined since it is the inverse of P_1. Therefore, we will focus on the government's choice of P_1 only and interpret the functions accordingly.

The government, on the other hand, is fully aware of the self-interested behaviour of the players. It understands that each player will spend resources in mobilizing political support for it only if the relative price it sets is going to yield them a higher payoff than otherwise. The government also understands that if a policy change hurts a player, then the player will divert his or her lobbying effort to oppose the policy changes and possibly finance the political campaign of the opposition. However, if the players somehow agree on a particular relative price (hence on a particular tariff rate), a political consensus will prevail. Implementation of this price will yield a maximum political support to the government, since there will be no organised group to oppose it. The lobbying contest takes place only if no agreement could be reached on the tariff rate. In this case the government will choose a relative price that maximizes political support for it.

Thus, the government chooses P_1 to maximize the following Peltzman-type political support function

$$S = \begin{cases} S^* & \text{if all players agree on a price } \hat{P_1} \\ S(\Pi_1(P_1(\eta)), \Pi_2(P_1(\eta))) & \text{if disagreement results} \end{cases} \quad (5A.2)$$

where, the support function $S(.)$ is strictly increasing and concave in each argument and $S^* \geq S(.)$.[9] The function (5A.2) clearly shows that the optimal choice of the government depends on the existing political environment - whether the players are cooperating with each other or not. We defer the study of this game in a cooperative environment until the next chapter. Here, we shall focus on the behaviour of the government in a noncooperative environment.

The act of maximizing support by the government and the act of maximizing payoffs by the private players interlocks the three in a political process. I this process each of the private players holds an opportunity to trade fruitfully with the government by mobilizing political support for a favourable price (or trade) policy and vice versa. For example, player 1 can mobilize increased support for the government by spending more on voters' education, if the government is prepared to provide enough protection to it by raising the tariff rate (or lowering the export subsidy). Similarly, player 2 can also mobilize additional political support for the government if it returns with lower protection to the import competing sector or with increased export subsidy. The government provides a favourable tariff rate to any of the players if he or she is prepared to spend resources sufficient to mobilize more political support than it would lose by implementing the policy.

The problems of the government and of the two players in a non-cooperative situation can be viewed as a Stackelberg game in which the government is the leader, and the two private players are Nash followers. The government, which is assumed to be fully informed of constraints and objectives of the Nash players, takes into account all possible reactions of the private players (subject to the equilibrium of the economic sphere) while maximizing its support function. It then obtains a solution function $P_1(\eta_1, \eta_2)$ to offer to the private players. This function will extract maximum support for it from the society whenever the players are in a Nash equilibrium. The purpose of this Appendix is to uncover the

109

properties of this pricing function. While doing so, we normalize capital stocks of both sectors to unity by the choice of units.

By differentiating equation (5A.1) we obtain the first order condition of the maximum to the Nash player i as:

$$\frac{d\Pi_i}{d\eta_i} = \frac{d\widetilde{R}_i}{dP_1}\frac{\partial P_1}{\partial \eta_i} - 1 = 0. \tag{5A.3}$$

The condition (5A.3) implies that each player will spend on lobbying as long as a unit of output spent on lobbying yields one extra unit of output in rental income. This condition can be rewritten as

$$d\widetilde{R}_i / dP_1 = 1/(\partial P_1 / \partial \eta_i) \tag{5A.4}$$

The necessary condition for the maximization of the government's support function can be written as

$$\frac{dS}{dP_1} = \sum_i \frac{\partial S}{\partial \Pi_i}\left[\frac{d\widetilde{R}_i}{dP_1} - \frac{\partial \eta_i}{\partial P_1}\right] = 0 \tag{5A.5}$$

This condition states that the government will choose the level of relative price so that at the margin the gain in support is exactly balanced by the loss in support that arises due to a small change in relative price. It can easily be seen that condition (5A.5) is satisfied whenever condition (5A.4) is satisfied provided the 'lobbying derivatives' (Baldwin, 1987) exist such that for each i

$$\partial \eta_i / \partial P_1 = 1/(\partial P_1 / \partial \eta_i). \tag{5A.6}$$

Since $d\widetilde{R}_1 / dP_1 > 0$ and $d\widetilde{R}_2 / dP_1 < 0$, it follows from condition (5A.4) that

$$\frac{\partial P_1}{\partial \eta_1} > 0 \text{ and } \frac{\partial P_1}{\partial \eta_2} < 0 \tag{5A.7}$$

at all nonzero values of η_1 and η_2. This means that the pricing function should be such that the relative price of commodity 1 increases with increased lobbying effort of player 1 and decreases with increased lobbying effort of player 2.

Conditions (5A.6) and (5A.7) follow automatically if the government offers a pricing function that has the properties (P1) and (P3) listed in Section 5.2.

Second Order Conditions: For each i, differentiating the first order condition (5A.3) with respect to η_i we get

$$\frac{d^2 \Pi_i}{d\eta_i^2} = \frac{d^2 \widetilde{R}_i}{dP_1^2}\left(\frac{\partial P_1}{\partial \eta_i}\right)^2 + \frac{d\widetilde{R}_i}{dP_1}\frac{\partial^2 P_1}{\partial \eta_i^2}. \tag{5A.8}$$

We know that $(\partial P_1 / \partial \eta_i)^2 > 0$, $d\widetilde{R}_1 / dP_1 > 0$, and $d\widetilde{R}_2 / dP_1 < 0$ we have the following conditions:

(i) If $d^2 \widetilde{R}_1 / dP_1^2 \leq 0$, then the sufficient (but not necessary) conditions for $d^2 \Pi_1 / d\eta_1^2 < 0$ is that $\partial^2 P_1 / \partial \eta_1^2 < 0$,

otherwise it is $\partial^2 P_1 / \partial \eta_1^2 < -(d^2 \widetilde{R}_1 / dP_1^2)(\partial P_1 / \partial \eta_1)$.

(ii) The sufficient condition for $d^2 \Pi_2 / d\eta_2^2 < 0$ is that $\partial^2 P_1 / \partial \eta_2^2 > 0$.

This means that if the government supplies a pricing function such that the conditions

$$\partial^2 P_1 / \partial \eta_1^2 < 0, \text{ and } \partial^2 P_1 / \partial \eta_2^2 > 0 \tag{5A.9}$$

are satisfied (with sufficiently large magnitude for $\partial^2 P_1 / \partial \eta_1^2$ if $d^2 \widetilde{R}_1 / dP_1^2 > 0$), then the second order conditions for the maximization of the payoff functions of the two Nash players are also satisfied whenever the first order conditions are met.[10]

A pricing function, however, will met requirements (5A.6), (5A.7) and (5A.9), if it is continuous in both arguments, productive and bounded - that is, if it satisfies properties (P1), (P3) and (P4) listed in Section 5.2.

We now check whether the second order condition for the government's support maximization also holds whenever it holds for the Nash players. Differentiating equation (5A.5) with respect to P_1 yields

$$\frac{d^2 S}{dP_1^2} = \sum_i \left[\left(\frac{d\widetilde{R}_i}{dP_1} - \frac{d\eta_i}{dp_1}\right)\frac{\partial^2 S}{\partial P_1 \partial \Pi_i} + \frac{\partial S}{\partial \Pi_i}\left(\frac{d^2 \widetilde{R}_i}{dP_1^2} - \frac{d^2 \eta_i}{dP_1^2}\right) \right]. \tag{5A.10}$$

When the first order conditions are satisfied for the Nash players we have $d\widetilde{R}_i / dP_1 = d\eta_i / dP_1$, therefore, it follows that

$$\frac{d^2 S}{dP_1^2} < 0 \text{ if and only if } \sum_i \left[\frac{\partial S}{\partial \Pi_i} \left(\frac{d^2 \widetilde{R}_i}{dP_1^2} - \frac{d^2 \eta_i}{dP_1^2} \right) \right] < 0 \qquad (5A.11)$$

Since $\partial S / \partial \Pi_i > 0$, a sufficient (but not necessary) condition for

$$\sum_i \left[\frac{\partial S}{\partial \Pi_i} \left(\frac{d^2 \widetilde{R}_i}{dP_1^2} - \frac{d^2 \eta_i}{dP_1^2} \right) \right] < 0 \qquad \text{is that}$$

$$\left(\frac{d^2 \widetilde{R}_i}{dP_1^2} - \frac{d^2 \eta_i}{dP_1^2} \right) < 0 \qquad \text{for each player } i. \qquad (5A.12)$$

Now it will be shown that the condition (5A.12) is satisfied whenever $d^2 \Pi_i / d\eta_i^2 < 0$, and the first order condition (5A.5) is satisfied. In other words, we will show that the second order condition for the maximization of the government's support function is satisfied whenever the payoff functions of the two Nash players are simultaneously maximized.

Since by differentiating equation (5A.6) we can see that

$$\frac{\partial^2 \eta_i}{\partial P_1^2} = -\left(\frac{\partial P_1}{\partial \eta_i} \right)^{-3} \frac{\partial^2 P_1}{\partial \eta_i^2}. \qquad (5A.13)$$

which is positive by condition (5A.9).

It follows from the first order and second order conditions (5A.4) and (5A.8) that

$$\frac{d^2 \widetilde{R}_i}{dP_1^2} < -\left(\frac{\partial P_1}{\partial \eta_i} \right)^{-3} \frac{\partial^2 P_1}{\partial \eta_i^2}. \qquad (5A.14)$$

Thus, equations (5A.13) and (5A.14) together imply that

$$\frac{d^2 \widetilde{R}_i}{dP_1^2} < \frac{\partial^2 \eta_i}{\partial P_1^2}$$

for each player i, and therefore, the condition (5A.12) holds.

Hence, if a government wants to maximize a Peltzman type political support function then it will offer a pricing function $P_1(\eta_1, \eta_2)$ such that (i) for all feasible $(\eta_1, \eta_2) \neq (0,0)$, it is continuous, and differentiable - i.e., (P1) is satisfied; (ii) it is strictly increasing and concave in the lobbying expenditure, η_1, of player 1 and decreasing and convex in the lobbying expenditure, η_2, of player 2 - i.e., (P3) is satisfied; and (iii) it is bounded - i.e., (P4) is satisfied. This pricing function guarantees that the political support of the government is maximized whenever the payoffs of the Nash players are maximized simultaneously. Since the pricing function is not yet defined at the origin, for the purpose of this chapter, we set $P_1(0,0) = P_1^*$. In other words, we assume that the government has no reason of its own to deviate from the free trade which is the property (P2) of the pricing function listed in Section 5.2.

It has been shown by Theorem 5.2 that at least one noncooperative Nash equilibrium exists in a political economy where the government offers a pricing function that satisfies properties (P1)-(P4). Now we have seen that if the government is a support maximizer, then it will offer a pricing function that precisely satisfies those properties. The implication of this result is that if there is a unique solution to the maximizing problem of the government and that of the Nash players then the relative price obtained at the Nash equilibrium of the lobbying game subject to a given pricing function, on the one hand, and the relative price obtained directly from the maximization of the political support function, on the other hand, are identical.

Since, the assumption of self-finance (P5) is a special case of the bounded pricing assumption (P4), the government will be maximizing its support within the self-finance constraint even if it offers a pricing function that satisfies (P1) - (P3), and (P5). Therefore, a government offering a pricing function that satisfies assumptions (P1)-(P4) or (P1) - (P3) and (P5) will henceforth be called a 'popular' or 'support maximizing' government. Conversely, a pricing function possessing properties (P1)-(P4) may be viewed as a function that did arise from the support-maximizing behaviour of the government.

Notes

1   Lobbying activities may take different forms - for example, mobilizing public support to the government or organization of a street demonstration against the government, or an outright bribe. This activity may also involve the use of factors. However, in this study the lobbying effort of each sector has been measured in equivalent units of output spent or lost in lobbying activities.

2   Note that $-i$ is the complementary set of i with respect to the player set, which is defined in section 5.4. However, in a 2-player game $i = 1$, if and only if $-i = 2$ and vice versa.

3   Here, we do not fix the numeraire, but assume that for each sector the commodity produced by the other sector is the numeraire. Therefore, the

relative prices of the two commodities satisfy $P_{-i} = P_i^{-1}$. In other words, the relative price of good 1 is the inverse of the relative price of good 2.

4   In the Appendix to the chapter we show that these properties are not arbitrary; they follow from the assumption that the government is a support maximizer.

5   For deadweight loss consideration see Becker (1983).

6   A correspondence φ from a subset S of a Euclidean space to a subset T of a Euclidean space is upper hemicontinuous (u. h. c.) at a point x^0 of S if there is a neighbourhood of x^0 in which φ is bounded, and for every sequence x^q in S converging to x^0 in S, and every sequence y^q in T converging to y^0 in T such that for every q, one has y^q in $\varphi(x^q)$, then y^0 is in $\varphi(x^0)$. Upper hemicontinuity of φ on S is defined as upper hemicontinuity at every point of S.

Similarly, A correspondence φ from a subset S of a Euclidean space to a subset T of a Euclidean space is lower hemicontinuous (l. h. c.) at a point x^0 of S if, for every sequence (x^q) in S converging to x^0 in S, and every y^0 converging to $\varphi(x^0)$, there is a sequence (y^q) in T converging to y^0 such that for every q, one has y^q in $\varphi(x^q)$. Lower hemicontinuity on S is defined as lower hemicontinuity at every point of S.

Continuity of a Correspondence at a point or on a set is defined as the conjunction of upper and lower hemicontinuity. (Debreu, 1982: 698-701).

7   We noted in Chapter 2 that Magee, Brock and Young (1989) have found several Prisoner's Dilemma equilibria in their simulations of the noncooperative game with Leontief production functions.

8   This assumption on the motivation of the government follows the tradition of the public choice literature. 'The central feature of that tradition is', as Brennan (1992: 13) describes, 'the searching out of invisible hand institutions, arrangements that achieve benign results without undue reliance on benevolent motivations. To test out whether such institutions are present or not, one must assume non-benevolent motivations: one does not test whether a plate is oven-proof by placing it in the cupboard.'

9   This is an indirect political support function that is based on the assumption that, besides players' own voting decisions, the political support/opposition of the 'ignorant' voter group depends on the lobbying efforts of the players which, in turn, are determined by the respective payoffs of the players (or the price function offered by the government) follows from the first-order condition (5A.3). See also Peltzman (1976).

10   This condition is noted in Wellisz and Wilson (1986: footnote 2) as a requirement for the existence of a Nash equilibrium.

6 Bargaining in the tariff game

Introduction

It was shown in the appendix to the previous chapter that if noncooperation prevails, then a support-maximizing government offers a pricing function that responds to the lobbying efforts of the private players. In this environment each player, who wants to maximize real rental-income net of lobbying expenditure, has an opportunity to obtain a favourable price by spending resources in lobbying the government. It was shown that at least one noncooperative Nash equilibrium exists in a political economy of this type. Furthermore, in all equilibria each player will spend a non-zero amount of resource in lobbying the government; and if the government is constrained by financing requirement then a positive tariff rate emerges at every equilibrium of the game.

However, the assumption of a noncooperation in the tariff game also implies that players do not communicate and cooperate with each other in adopting a joint strategy even if it may yield strictly higher payoffs to each of the players. Recognizing the restrictiveness of this approach we are changing the rules of the game in this chapter. Here, we will allow players to communicate, negotiate and enter into a binding agreement if it is individually rational to do so.

Each player is now free to choose between noncooperation and cooperation with the opponent. The inclusion of this possibility has expanded the strategy set of each player. Now, a player may choose to lobby the government, or may unilaterally decide not to lobby the government; or he may demand an agreement on a particular tariff rate and a binding commitment on not lobbying from the opponent before he stops lobbying the government for a more favourable tariff rate.

This change in the rules allows us to transform the tariff game into a standard bargaining problem, where players bargain over a tariff rate (or domestic relative price). We know that player 1, the import competing sector, will bargain for a higher tariff rate and player 2, the exporting sector, will bargain for a lower tariff rate (or for an increased export subsidy!). They may use all political means to communicate and negotiate the tariff rate that is mutually acceptable to them. The purpose of this chapter is to describe this process in the framework of the Nash bargaining theory and derive a solution to the bargaining problem in the tariff game. In so doing, we also put together several independent results produced by previous authors and provide an alternative way of characterising the generalized solution to any arbitrary Nash bargaining problem. We have accomplished this task in the following sequence of steps.

First, we establish that the bargaining problem in the tariff game is just a member of the class of standard bargaining problems. This correspondence has let us switch between an abstract bargaining problem and the bargaining problem in the tariff game freely whenever it is useful to do so. We then show that there is some reason to include bargaining power into the mathematical description of the game. We call it a *generalized bargaining game*, which is defined by the bargaining set, the disagreement payoffs, and the distribution of the bargaining power of the players. With this modification we show that the so-called asymmetric Nash solution to a bargaining problem is in fact symmetric. We provide this result as a corollary to Roth's Theorem that characterizes the Nash solution to an arbitrary bargaining game with asymmetric bargaining power. Since the solution is symmetric, we have called it the generalized Nash solution rather than the asymmetric Nash solution by which it is known in the literature.

In the second step, we ask why players reach an agreement in a bargaining game. Binmore, Rubinstein, and Wolinsky (1986) have argued that players reach in an agreement because (a) they have positive time-preference rates (so that they value the current above the future gain), and/or (b) they fear that a third party may intervene, in which case the opportunity of gain would be entirely lost. These factors increase each players' temptation to conclude the deal as early as possible. They have further shown that the very difference in players' fear of disagreement and the very difference in players' time-preference rates lead to the difference in a player's bargaining power, which is responsible for the asymmetric distribution of the gain from cooperation.

Aumann and Kurz (1977a) have also employed the concept of 'fear of ruin' - ruin meaning disagreement, another motivation for reaching in an agreement - and have shown that at the Nash equilibrium players hold identical fear of ruin. A natural question arises at this stage: whether the concept of fear of ruin used by Aumann and Kurz and the fear of disagreement used by Binmore, Rubinstein and Wolinsky is the same or not.

We have argued that the 'fear of disagreement' employed by Binmore, Rubinstein and Wolinsky and that employed by Aumann and Kurz are conceptually different; each provides a separate motivation for the players to reach in an agreement. We have further argued that unlike the 'fear of disagreement', Aumann and Kurz's concept of 'fear of ruin' can not be captured by differences in players' bargaining power. It is because the fear of ruin constantly changes during a single bargaining process as the players attain different levels of gains, while their relative bargaining power does not.

Since Aumann and Kurz's concept of 'fear of ruin' was defined for bargaining games with equal bargaining power; a generalization of the concept was, therefore, necessary to apply their result to games with unequal bargaining power. We have employed Svejnar (1986) to generalize this concept of fear of ruin so that both Aumann and Kurz's result and Binmore, Rubeinstein and Wolinsky's results could be used consistently.

We have shown that the equality of the generalized fear of ruin constitutes a separate characterization of the generalized Nash solution to an arbitrary Nash bargaining problem, including the tariff game. This result holds the key to the results that follow in subsequent chapters. We have also shown that if the fear functions are well-behaved, then the generalized Nash solution to the tariff game is not only unique but also is stable.

Our result is different from that obtained by Svejnar (1986), who showed that the generalized Nash solution also implies equality of generalized fear of ruin, and that equality of generalized fear of ruin together with usual axioms implies the generalized Nash solution. We have shown that equality of generalized fear of ruin, when each player holds a strictly positive fear of ruin, yields the generalized Nash solution without any reference to the other axioms. The advantage of this result is that we can now obtain the generalized Nash bargaining solution in a different way - using players' fear of ruin and the distribution of bargaining power only. This result seems to be very useful in simple and intuitive demonstration of the bargaining process and a deduction of the generalized Nash solution to a bargaining problem.

Finally, with a summary of the bargaining problem, we have stated the necessary and sufficient condition for the Nash solution to the bargaining problem of the tariff game. We have also attempted to identify the fear of ruin with the concept of endogenous bargaining power of the players.

This chapter is organised into five sections. The first section describes the setting of the game as a standard bargaining problem. The second section describes the Nash solution to the bargaining problem. It is argued that the generalized Nash solution to a bargaining problem that allows unequal bargaining power is not asymmetric as is commonly believed. In the third section, the bargaining process is described in terms the concept of fear of ruin. There we argue that the fear of disagreement referred to by Aumann and Kurz and the fear of disagreement referred to by Binmore, Rubinstein and Wolinsky are different. To cover both ideas a generalization of the concept of fear of ruin has been proposed. In the fourth section, the main result that the equality of generalized fear of ruin constitutes a separate characterization of the generalized Nash bargaining solution, is proved. Finally, in the fifth section the basic contention of the chapter has been summarized.

Thus this chapter examines the tariff game thoroughly in a bargain-theoretic framework. It obtains the necessary and sufficient condition for the generalized Nash solution to the bargaining problem in the tariff game, which charactrizes the equilibrium in the political sphere. The next chapter will take up this condition and embed it into the policy-exogenous equilibrium model of the economic sphere (described in Chapter 3) to obtain a (tariff-endogenous) general equilibrium model of the political economy.

6.1 Rules of the game and the bargaining problem

We continue to assume that the government is a support maximizer, but we allow for the possibility that the players may cooperate with each other.[1] In this environment, if the two players - owners of the specific factors in the two sectors - agree on a tariff rate, the best policy for the government is to implement the agreement. It will not only guarantee the maximum support to the government (see equation (5A.2), for example), but also save resources being wasted in competitive lobbying. If they disagree, then the game will be played as described in the previous chapter. The government behaves as a Stackelberg leader vis-à-vis the private players - it announces a pricing function that maximizes its political support subject to the reaction functions of the two coalitions (players). The two players behave as Nash players against each other taking the government's pricing function as given. The price (tariff rate) that arises at the Nash equilibrium of the lobbying game would be implemented.

Thus, if the two parties cooperate with each other - that is, they agree on a tariff rate and agree not to lobby the government for a different tariff rate - then, they receive the resulting rental income as their payoffs. If they could not reach in a cooperative agreement, then they would receive resulting rents at a noncooperative Nash equilibrium less their respective lobbying expenditures as their payoffs, as illustrated in Figure 6.1.

For simplicity, in Figure 6.1, identical Cobb-Douglas production technologies are assumed. The curve CD represents the rent transformation frontier (RTF) for given endowment of factors, and international prices (see Chapter 4). Suppose that the parties could not agree on any tariff rate, and chose to play a noncooperative game. Suppose further that a unique noncooperative Nash equilibrium is obtained with lobbying expenditures $\tilde{\eta}_1$ and $\tilde{\eta}_2$ yielding a domestic price ratio $\tilde{P}_1$. Then the rental payoffs, which are rental incomes net of lobbying expenditures, are given by $\tilde{\Pi}_1$ and $\tilde{\Pi}_2$ respectively to player 1 and player 2.

Recall that sectoral rental incomes are measured in units of own output. Let point E (in Figure 6.1) denote the payoff combination and the point R denote the combination of sectoral rental incomes at the noncooperative Nash equilibrium.

Then E shows the outcome in disagreement - the payoff to each player if they can not reach at an agreement.

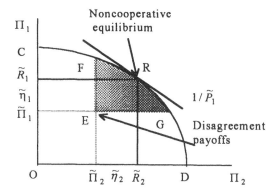

Figure 6.1   Payoffs in cooperation

However, if the two players cooperate, then they need not spend resources in competitive lobbying, and they can stay on the rent transformation frontier CD. For example, if the players had accepted the price $\tilde{P}_1$ and agreed not to participate in competitive lobbying, both would have received payoffs corresponding to the point R, which represents a combination of higher payoffs than those correspond to the point E.

Thus, given that E would be the outcome of noncooperation (disagreement), the shaded area EFG represents the set of payoff combinations that the two players can improve upon by choosing cooperation rather than noncooperation. The arc FG represents the set of feasible and Pareto efficient payoffs. Any point on it is strictly better than the point E, and any movement along it hurts either one player or the other.

As indicated in the previous chapter, a noncooperative Nash equilibrium may not be unique. In a case where multiple Nash equilibria exist it is not possible to identify *a priori* the disagreement payoffs with a particular noncooperative Nash equilibrium of the game. Since all the Nash equilibria are characterized by non-zero lobbying by all players (Lemma 5.4), the resulting payoffs at each of the noncooperative Nash equilibria are not on the curve CD, but lie inside it. Therefore, the above argument is equally applicable irrespective of which of the noncooperative Nash equilibria is attained.

In general, all payoffs represented by points in the area OCD are feasible outcomes and that the set of noncooperative Nash equilibria, which is a subset of feasible outcomes, can serve as a set of potential disagreement payoffs. The set of points that, in terms of payoffs, strictly dominate a Nash equilibrium point, such as E, is like the area EFG, and is always non-empty. Therefore, there is always an incentive to the players to become involved in a bargaining process and search for an agreeable tariff rate.

Further there are reasons to believe that all agreements reached in a tariff game will be enforceable. First, playing a noncooperative Nash equilibrium strategy is always a credible threat that can be issued by any player against the other player, and that works as a deterrent against possible deviant behaviour of either player. Second, as Shubik (1982) argued, constitutional arrangements and the presence of government as the enforcing agency makes players almost incapable of deviating from the agreement. Moreover, if the government is a support maximizer, as we have assumed, then it will have an incentive to implement such cooperative agreements. Third, the tariff game is a periodic game. It is played repeatedly. Cooperative outcomes of repeated games are, in general, self-enforcing (Fudenberg and Maskin, 1986; Friedman, 1986).

Therefore, the description of the political sphere in terms of a cooperative game is a natural representation of the rational behaviour on the part of the players.

Definition 6.1   (Bargaining Set).*Given disagreement payoffs* $\Pi^d \equiv (\Pi_1^d, \Pi_2^d)$ *let*

$$\mathfrak{R} = \Big\{ (\Pi_1, \Pi_2) \mid \Pi_1 \leq K_1 P_1^{-1} \beta_1^{-\sigma_1/(1-\sigma_1)}$$

$$\times \Big[P_1^{1-\sigma_1} - \alpha_1^{\sigma_1} \alpha_2^{-\sigma_2(1-\sigma_1)/(1-\sigma_2)}$$

$$\times (1 - \beta_2^{\sigma_2} (\Pi_2 / K_2)^{1-\sigma_2})^{(1-\sigma_1)/(1-\sigma_2)} \Big]^{1/(1-\sigma_1)}; \quad \Pi_i \geq \Pi_i^d \Big\} \qquad (6.1)$$

Then, $\mathfrak{R}$ *is a collection of all payoff combinations that are individually rational, and over which the players may bargain.* $\mathfrak{R}$ *is defined as the bargaining set.*

Note that the Pareto efficient boundary of the bargaining set is the segment of the rent transformation frontier (see equation 4.6) that has individually rational points. It has already been shown that if elasticities of factor substitution in both sectors are at least unity then the boundary of the bargaining set is concave to the origin (Proposition 4.2, Chapter 4). Therefore, points that are in area OCD form a convex set. Since the maximum output that a sector can produce in the event of specialization is finite (because of finite endowment of mobile factor(s) and concave production function), and since the rental income is always less than the level of output, the set $\mathfrak{R}$ is bounded. The set includes its boundary points, hence it is closed. The set $\mathfrak{R}$ is also compact and convex, because it is a subset of a 2-dimensional Euclidean space.

If the elasticities of factor substitution are sufficiently low to undermine the convexity of the bargaining set defined over certain outcomes, then as in the standard case (for example Nash, 1950) we can invoke the expected payoff approach that will guarantee the convexity of the corresponding bargaining set. Any concave function defined over $\Re$ will have its maximum in it.

If, the disagreement payoff, Π^d, is assumed to be predetermined and fixed, then the underlying bargaining problem in the tariff game satisfies conditions of the existence theorem proved by Nash (1953). If the disagreement payoff is not known a priori, then the bargaining problem in the tariff game still satisfies conditions of the existence theorem proved in Harsanyi (1963).

Thus, whether the disagreement payoffs are assumed to be predetermined or not (variable), the tariff game in cooperative form can be viewed as a standard bargaining problem.[2] However, in this chapter we will assume that the disagreement payoff is predetermined and therefore, the bargaining problem is defined by the pair $(\Re, \Pi^d)$.[3] Let **B** be the class of such 2-person bargaining games for which the underlying noncooperative game is given by Γ (see Chapter 5).

6.2   Nash solution to the bargaining problem in a tariff game

To solve a bargaining problem, several solution concepts have been proposed in the literature. The Nash solution is one of them. A short review of these solution concepts can be found in Datt (1989). He has also convincingly argued that Nash solution has a degree of generality not shared by other solution concepts. Several other studies that attempted to solve a standard bargaining problem by introducing various frictions into it have concluded that Nash solution is robust (see, Binmore, Rubinstein and Wolinsky, 1986; van Damme, 1986; Chun, 1988b; Chun and Thomson, 1990; Carlson, 1991).

Nash (1950, 1953), who studied 2-person bargaining games, defined a solution of a bargaining game in **B** as a function $\mu: \mathbf{B} \rightarrow \mathbf{R}^2$ such that for any $(\Re, \Pi^d) \in \mathbf{B}$ we have $\mu(\Re, \Pi^d) \in \Re$. In other words, a solution of the game is a rule for assigning a feasible payoff to each player. Roth (1979) has argued that this rule can also be interpreted as an arbitration procedure.

Nash (1953), in his seminal paper, used both strategic and axiomatic approaches to analyse the bargaining problem. In the strategic approach, he constructed a negotiation model, so-called 'demand game', in which each player (in a 2-person game) demands a particular utility payoff. If the demands of both the players are jointly compatible, then each one gets what is demanded; otherwise each receives the predetermined disagreement payoff.[4] Nash has shown that rational bargainers will agree on the payoff division that maximizes the Nash product over the feasible set.

In the axiomatic approach, Nash (1953) listed a set of eight general properties that any reasonable solution to the bargaining problem should possess. A deduction of logical solutions that satisfy the 'desirable' properties led Nash to the same solution that he obtained from the negotiation model - that the solution should maximize the Nash product! Nash, therefore, wrote,

> It is rather significant that this quite different approach yields the same solution. This indicates that the solution is appropriate for a wider variety of situations than those which satisfy the assumptions we made in the approach via the model (p. 136).

Subsequent authors have improved upon Nash's work and have neatly summarized his works. For example, Binmore (1987a) has listed 'somewhat freely adapted versions of Nash's axioms' as follows:

Axiom 1 (feasibility and strong individual rationality).
$$\Pi^d < \mu(\mathfrak{R}, \Pi^d) \in \mathfrak{R}.$$

That is, a solution to the bargaining problem should be feasible, and that it must be strongly individually rational. The second characteristic requires that each player should receive more in bargaining 'equilibrium' than that can be obtained in disagreement.

Axiom 2 (invariance).
For any increasing affine[5] transformation $\alpha: R^2 \to R^2$,
$$\mu(\alpha \mathfrak{R}, \alpha \Pi^d) = \alpha \mu(\mathfrak{R}, \Pi^d).$$

In other words, if the units of measurement and the origins of payoffs of the players were changed by any affine transformation, then the outcome of the new bargaining game will be equal to the conformable transformation of the original bargaining solution.[6] This requires that the 'real' solution should not depend on the chosen units of measurement. It should always be recoverable by inverse transformation on the solution. This axiom is also called Independence of Equivalent Utility (Payoffs) Representation.

Axiom 3 (independence of irrelevant alternatives).
$$\mu(\mathfrak{R}, \Pi^d) \in \wp \subseteq \mathfrak{R} \Rightarrow \mu(\wp, \Pi^d) = \mu(\mathfrak{R}, \Pi^d).$$

This axiom states that if $\wp$ is a subset of the original bargaining set $\mathfrak{R}$ and contains the original solution point $\mu(\mathfrak{R}, \Pi^d)$, then $\mu(\mathfrak{R}, \Pi^d)$ should also be the solution to the bargaining game $(\wp, \Pi^d)$. The intuition is that since the set $\wp$

was available when the bargaining set was $\Re$ and the players nevertheless chose $\mu(\Re, \Pi^d)$ should mean that they will choose $\mu(\Re, \Pi^d)$ when it is available in the game $(\wp, \Pi^d)$. This is a stipulation that the players be consistent.

Axiom 4 (efficiency).

$M > \mu(\Re, \Pi^d) \Rightarrow M \notin \Re$.

In other words, the axiom of efficiency requires that the solution picked by the μ rule should not be dominated by any other payoff combinations in the bargaining set. This axiom requires that the solution be Pareto optimal. There should be no possibility of increasing the payoff of one player without reducing the payoff of the other player.

Axiom 5 (symmetry).

If $\tau:(\Pi_1, \Pi_2) \to (\Pi_2, \Pi_1)$, then $\mu(\tau \Re, \tau \Pi^d) = \tau \mu(\Re, \Pi^d)$.

This axiom means that whoever is called the first player is immaterial. A player will get the same payoff whether she is called player 1 or player 2 - measured along the x-axis or measured along the y-axis. This axiom has strong implications and needs some scrutiny.

Definition 6.2 *A bargaining set $\Re$ is called symmetric if $(\Pi_1, \Pi_2) \in \Re \Leftrightarrow (\Pi_2, \Pi_1) \in \Re$. A bargaining game $(\Re, \Pi^d)$ is called a symmetric game if $\Re$ is symmetric and $\Pi_1^d = \Pi_2^d$.*

If $(\Re, \Pi^d)$ is a symmetric game, then Axiom 5 requires that $\mu_1(\Re, \Pi^d) = \mu_2(\Re, \Pi^d)$. The argument is as follows. Since the game is symmetric, nothing will be changed by a permutation of the players. In particular, $(\tau \Re, \tau \Pi^d) = (\Re, \Pi^d)$, therefore, $\mu(\tau \Re, \tau \Pi^d) = \mu(\Re, \Pi^d)$. That is, $\mu_i(\tau \Re, \tau \Pi^d) = \mu_i(\Re, \Pi^d)$. But $\mu_1(\tau \Re, \tau \Pi^d) = \tau \mu_1(\Re, \Pi^d) = \mu_2(\Re, \Pi^d)$ imply that $\mu_1(\Re, \Pi^d) = \mu_2(\Re, \Pi^d)$. Both players will gain equally over the disagreement payoffs. Therefore, in a symmetric game with $\Pi^d = 0$ if the bargaining solution rule μ satisfies the axiom of symmetry then the solution always lies on the ray of 45 degrees.

Theorem 6.1 (Nash's Theorem). *There is a unique solution possessing Axioms 1-5. It is the function* μ *defined by* $\mu(\mathfrak{R}, \Pi^d) = \overline{\Pi}$ *such that* $\overline{\Pi} \geq \Pi^d$ *and* $(\overline{\Pi}_1 - \Pi_1^d)(\overline{\Pi}_2 - \Pi_2^d) > (\Pi_1 - \Pi_1^d)(\Pi_2 - \Pi_2^d)$ *for all* $\Pi \in \mathfrak{R}$ *and* $\Pi \neq \overline{\Pi}$.

Proof: See Nash (1950, 1953), and Roth (1979).

Roth (1979) also showed, however, that a solution that satisfies Axioms 1-3 also satisfies the Axiom 4. Therefore, in the presence of Axioms 1-3 and Axiom 5, Axiom 4 - that the solution is required to be Pareto optimal - is redundant. The beauty of Nash's solution, nevertheless, lies in the result that the bargaining problem can be solved by maximizing the Nash product over the bargaining set.

Nash's bargaining solution is highly restrictive. It is based on the assumption that all 'significant differences between the players are those which are included in the mathematical description of the game' (Nash, 1953: p. 137). This implies that when the game is converted into the symmetric form, all differences between the players disappear. Nash (1953: p. 138) further argued that

> With people who are sufficiently intelligent and rational there should not be any question of 'bargaining ability', a term which suggests something like skill in duping the other fellow. The usual haggling process is based on imperfect information, the hagglers trying to propagandize each other into misconceptions of the utilities involved. Our assumption of complete information makes such an attempt meaningless.

Precisely because of this interpretation of the bargaining situation, a permutation of the players in a symmetric bargaining game brought no change in the bargaining set as well as the position of level curves of the Nash product. Therefore, identical payoffs were obtained by the players at the Nash equilibrium of a symmetric game. This argument clearly dismisses all possibilities but the bargaining set as that which differentiates the players. In view of recent developments in cooperative game theory, Nash's argument maintains, in particular, that the players have equal bargaining power or ability. [7]

Recent studies of bargaining problems have not only raised questions concerning the completeness of players' information on each other's utility function, but also have shown that there may exist factors influencing the outcome of bargaining that are not accounted for by the bargaining set and the disagreement point - the constituents of the mathematical description of a bargaining problem. In summary, they contend that players may very well have been endowed with uneven bargaining powers or weights, an issue which has not been adequately addressed by the theory of bargaining.

For example, Kalai (1977a) has shown that if an n-person bargaining game is played by two coalitions of size p and q (with p+q=n) such that within each coalition players have identical utility functions, then a non-symmetric Nash solution may arise even if the n-person game yields a symmetric Nash solution. In this case the source of apparent 'bargaining power' of the coalition is its membership. This was not envisaged by Nash. Similarly, the other sources of asymmetry are: players having different degrees of risk aversion (Roth, 1979), difference in the time preference rate (Rubinstein, 1982), different probability attached to the risk of breakdown of the negotiation (Binmore, Rubinstein, and Wolinsky, 1986), bargaining skill (Ohyama, 1989) and players possessing imperfect knowledge about each other (Harsanyi and Selton, 1972).[8]

In the case that players have unequal 'bargaining power', for whatever the reason, Nash's solution payoff to each player depends on the order in which the players are represented. In other words, this means that Nash's solution, as characterized by maximization of the 'Nash product', may not satisfy the axiom of symmetry.

To see this consider a symmetric bargaining game $(\Re, \Pi^d)$ with asymmetric solution. Let an ordered pair (Π_1, Π_2) such that $\Pi_1 \neq \Pi_2$ be the Nash product maximizing solution to a problem. Let τ be any player permutation. Since $(\Re, \Pi^d)$ is a symmetric game, we must have $(\Re, \Pi^d) = (\tau \Re, \tau \Pi^d)$. The Nash product maximizing solution vector of the permuted game $(\tau \Re, \tau \Pi^d)$ should also be equal to (Π_1, Π_2). But this means that player 2 will receive Π_1, and player 1 will receive Π_2. Hence, the solution depends on order in which the players are represented in the game.

Therefore, Nash's solution to the bargaining problem required an extension so that a solution satisfying the axiom of symmetry can be obtained even in the presence of unequal bargaining power.

In theories of bargaining the concept of 'bargaining power' is imprecisely defined (Binmore, Rubinstein, and Wolinsky, 1986: 186). To make the term more precise we state the following definition.

Consider a controlled bargaining situation $(A,0)$, where $A = \left\{ X \in R^2 \mid X_i \geq 0, \sum X_i \leq 1 \right\}$. In this game the players have identical *prospects* in agreement and in disagreement. If their payoffs at the solution of the game differ consistently every time they play the game $(A,0)$, then the result can be attributed to some unaccounted rule of the game that creates a difference between *otherwise identical players*.

Definition 6.3   (Bargaining Power). *Suppose that, in agreement, player 1 always gets δ times what player 2 gets in the controlled bargaining game $(A,0)$, where δ is some positive number. Then, the number δ measures some kind of power of player 1 over player 2; and therefore, the number δ is defined as the relative bargaining power of player 1.*

This definition of bargaining power accords well with that of Chamberlain and Kuhn (1965: p.170), who defined bargaining power as the ability to secure another's agreement on one's own terms.

Let Z be a vector of all variables, such as the time preference rate of the players, the players' belief that the opportunity of gain will evaporate or be snatched by a third party, the difference in players' skill of negotiation or coalitional strength of members, the difference between the degrees of free rider problem within each coalition and other unaccounted factors in the political environment etc., that influence the bargaining outcome but do not belong to the choice set of the bargainers. Then, we can infer, on the basis of previous studies referred above, that

$$\delta = \delta(Z) .$$

The functional dependence of relative bargaining power of player 1 on Z acknowledges that the relative bargaining power of a player is essentially a dynamic concept. It may change as the exogenous environment changes.

In a given environment Z, a value of δ equal to unity implies that the two players are equally powerful, neither is favoured against the other, and $\delta > 1$ implies that player 1 possesses more bargaining power than player 2, and vice versa.

We normalize the measure of bargaining power by defining

$$\Theta_1 = \frac{\delta}{1+\delta} \text{ , and } \Theta_2 = \frac{1}{1+\delta} . \tag{6.2}$$

Then, the parameter $\Theta_i(Z)$ satisfies $0 < \Theta_i(Z) < 1$, and $\sum_i \Theta_i(Z) = 1$; and therefore, it can be called the normalized bargaining power of player i.

With this definition of bargaining power, we can proceed on to the extension of Nash's bargaining solution in the presence of unequal bargaining power of the players. The following important theorem in this direction was proved by Roth (1979).[9]

Theorem 6.2 (Roth, 1979: Theorem 3). *For each strictly positive vector* Θ, *such that* $\sum_i \Theta_i = 1$, *there is a unique solution* μ *satisfying the axioms of feasibility, invariance and independence, such that* $\mu(A,0) = \Theta$ *where*

$$A = \left\{ X \in R^2 \,\middle|\, X_i \geq 0, \sum X_i \leq 1 \right\}.$$

For any bargaining game $(\Re, \Pi^d)$, $\mu(\Re, \Pi^d) = \overline{\Pi} \in \Re$, *such that* $\overline{\Pi} \geq \Pi^d$ *and*

126

$$\left(\overline{\Pi}_1 - \Pi_1^d\right)^{\Theta_1}\left(\overline{\Pi}_2 - \Pi_2^d\right)^{\Theta_2} > \left(\Pi_1 - \Pi_1^d\right)^{\Theta_1}\left(\Pi_2 - \Pi_2^d\right)^{\Theta_2}$$

for all $\Pi \in \Re$ *such that* $\Pi \geq \Pi^d$ *and* $\Pi \neq \Pi^d$.

Proof:　　See Roth (1979: 16-17), Binmore (1987a: 34-37), and Appendix-6B.

The first part of the theorem states that if the players possess different weights given by the vector Θ, and bargain over a 'pie' of size unity, represented by the symmetric bargaining set A with disagreement payoff equal to zero, then player i's share in the unit pie is just Θ_i. This explains why Θ_i has been defined as the bargaining power of player i (see also Binmore, 1987a and 1987b). This is the standard Nash solution to a symmetric bargaining game, which is also called the symmetric Nash bargaining solution. Thus, the Theorem 6.1 (Nash's Theorem) is a special case of Theorem 6.2 in which the players hold equal bargaining power.[10]

The second part of the theorem shows that in any bargaining game with predetermined disagreement payoffs, and a compact and convex bargaining set the solution to the bargaining problem that satisfies Axiom 1-3 is the one that maximizes the asymmetric Nash product over the bargaining set. The strict inequality implies that the solution is unique. That is, the payoff distribution that maximizes the asymmetric Nash product and the solution that satisfies the 'desirable' properties are one and the same. One implies the other.

A note of clarification is warranted here. It may appear that the solution to the bargaining game $(\Re, \Pi^d)$ that satisfies Axioms 1-3 does not necessarily satisfy Axiom 5 - the axiom of symmetry. Binmore (1987a), for example, has explicitly stated that the asymmetric Nash solution satisfies Axiom 5 if and only if the players have equal bargaining power. But this would mean that the solution depends on the way players are represented if players do not have equal bargaining power. If a player's payoffs are now measured along the x-axis, then she will receive a different payoff at the solution of the game than she would obtain had her payoffs were measured along the y-axis. This situation, certainly, is not satisfying.

However, once we isolate the axiom of symmetry from the hangover of identical bargaining power of the players and treat them independently it can be easily seen that the 'asymmetric' Nash solution is in fact symmetric. We will show this result as a corollary to Roth's Theorem. First, to highlight the role of bargaining power in the mathematical description of a bargaining game we state the following definition:

Definition 6.4　　(Generalized Bargaining Game). *A triplet* $(\Re, \Pi^d, \Theta)$ *is defined as a generalized bargaining game, where* $\Re$ *is a compact and convex bargaining* *set,* $\Pi^d \in \Re$ *is a predetermined disagreement payoff vector, and* Θ *is, as defined above, a given vector of (normalized) bargaining power of the players.*

Definition 6.4 recognizes the independent status of the information regarding the distribution of bargaining power between the players. Therefore, it is included in the mathematical description of the game. Curiously enough, previous writers, who recognized the role of the distribution of bargaining power in determining the solution of a bargaining game, did not include it in the description of the game. For example, in order to specify a solution to any bargaining game $(\Re, \Pi^d)$, Roth's Theorem (Theorem 6.2) requires a priori information on Θ. This is essentially equivalent to say that the game is defined by a triplet $(\Re, \Pi^d, \Theta)$. Clearly, Roth's Theorem holds for the bargaining problem $(\Re, \Pi^d, \Theta)$ as well as it holds for a bargaining problem $(\Re, \Pi^d)$ with given Θ.

With this definition of a generalized bargaining game, all of the axioms listed above can be restated accordingly by simply changing the description of the bargaining problem.[11] From now on the description $(\Re, \Pi^d)$ will be replaced by $(\Re, \Pi^d, \Theta)$ to mean a bargaining problem with bargaining set $\Re$, a predetermined disagreement point $\Pi^d \in \Re$ and an exogenously given allocation of bargaining power Θ.

Corollary 6.1 *For any bargaining game* $(\Re, \Pi^d, \Theta)$, *the solution* $\mu(\Re, \Pi^d, \Theta) = \overline{\Pi} \in \Re$ *such that*

$$\left(\overline{\Pi}_1 - \Pi_1^d\right)^{\Theta_1}\left(\overline{\Pi}_2 - \Pi_2^d\right)^{\Theta_2} > \left(\Pi_1 - \Pi_1^d\right)^{\Theta_1}\left(\Pi_2 - \Pi_2^d\right)^{\Theta_2}$$

for all $\Pi \in \Re$, $\Pi \geq \Pi^d$ *and* $\Pi \neq \Pi^d$ *satisfies Axiom 5, and therefore is symmetric.*

Proof: Let $H(\Pi_1, \Pi_2) = 0$ be the Pareto efficient boundary of the bargaining set $\Re$. Let $\overline{\Pi}$ maximize $\left(\Pi_1 - \Pi_1^d\right)^{\Theta_1}\left(\Pi_2 - \Pi_2^d\right)^{\Theta_2}$ subject to $H(\Pi_1, \Pi_2) = 0$. To visualize the effect of permutation, assume initially that player 1's payoffs are measured along the y-axis and player 2's payoffs are measured along the x-axis. Let $(\overline{\Pi}_2, \overline{\Pi}_1)$ represent the initial solution as shown in the panel (a) of the following Figure 6.2.

Now let us permute the players and measure player 1's payoffs along the x-axis and player 2's payoffs along the y-axis. The parameters Θ_1 and Θ_2 continue to measure the bargaining power of players 1 and 2 respectively (they have been permuted too). Compared to panel (a) the appearance of the bargaining set and the curvature of the level curve of the asymmetric Nash product have changed in panel (b). However, the problem is still to maximize $\left(\Pi_1 - \Pi_1^d\right)^{\Theta_1}\left(\Pi_2 - \Pi_2^d\right)^{\Theta_2}$ subject to $H(\Pi_1, \Pi_2) = 0$. Therefore, the solution vector is $(\overline{\Pi}_1, \overline{\Pi}_2)$ which is the permutation of the initial solution vector $(\overline{\Pi}_2, \overline{\Pi}_1)$.

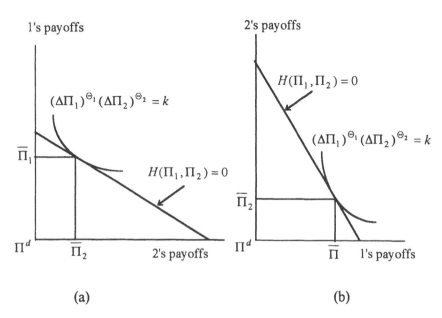

Figure 6.2   **Symmetry of Nash solution**

Thus, the unique solution vector that maximizes the 'asymmetric' Nash product over the bargaining set is simply permuted by a permutation of the players. The payoff received by each of the players is unaffected by the permutation.

Q. E. D.

Now, in the light of Definition 6.4, we restate Definition 6.2 as follows:

Definition 6.2a   *A bargaining set* $\Re$ *is called symmetric if* $(\Pi_1, \Pi_2) \in \Re$ $\Leftrightarrow$ $(\Pi_2, \Pi_1) \in \Re$. *A generalized bargaining game* $(\Re, \Pi^d, \Theta)$ *is a symmetric game if and only if* $\Re$ *is symmetric,* $\Pi_1^d = \Pi_2^d$ *and that* $\Theta_1 = \Theta_2$.

It is obvious that if a generalized bargaining game is symmetric, then the players will receive equal payoffs at the solution of the game. The argument is as follows: The game is symmetric implies that for any permutation τ on players we have $(\Re, \Pi^d, \Theta) = (\tau\Re, \tau\Pi^d, \tau\Theta)$. Therefore, $\mu(\Re, \Pi^d, \Theta) = \mu(\tau\Re, \tau\Pi^d, \tau\Theta)$. Since the solution function μ is symmetric, we must have $\mu(\tau\Re, \tau\Pi^d, \tau\Theta) = \tau\mu(\Re, \Pi^d, \Theta)$. That is, $(\mu_1, \mu_2) = \tau(\mu_1, \mu_2) = (\mu_2, \mu_1)$. Therefore, we have $\mu_1 = \mu_2$.

We know from Theorem 6.2 that a solution to the bargaining problem satisfies the Axioms 1-3 if and only if it maximizes the 'asymmetric' Nash product. Corollary 6.1 shows that the solution also satisfies the axiom of symmetry. This result holds as long as the bargaining power is assigned to the players, not to the axes. It, thus, follows from Roth's theorem and Corollary 6.1 that the solution to any arbitrary bargaining game, for a given distribution of bargaining power, satisfies all the five axioms as satisfied by the original Nash's solution if and only if it maximizes the corresponding asymmetric Nash product over the bargaining set. The only difference is that the original Nash solution applies in the case when all players have equal bargaining power. In the presence of uneven bargaining power it loses its symmetric property. The solution that follows from Theorem 6.2, however, applies to any arbitrary distribution of bargaining power provided that bargaining power of each player is strictly positive.[12]

For this reason, in what follows the so-called 'asymmetric' Nash solution to any bargaining game with arbitrary distribution of bargaining power will be called the *generalized Nash solution*. The product $\left(\Pi_1 - \Pi_1^d\right)^{\Theta_1}\left(\Pi_2 - \Pi_2^d\right)^{\Theta_2}$ will be called the *generalized Nash product*.

6.3   The bargaining process

Since the bargaining problem in the tariff game is essentially the same as any other abstract bargaining problem studied by game theorists, we can obtain insights into the underlying bargaining process from their studies as well. The explanation of the bargaining process most frequently referred to is that of Zuthen (1930). He assumed that in a bargaining process players offer proposals to each other, and postulated that each party will make concessions to his opponent once he finds that his opponent's determination is firmer than his own. Harsanyi (1956) has shown that this process of negotiation is mathematically equivalent to that of Nash's solution.[13]

In recent times, game theorists have started to study the bargaining process by specifying every move of the players (for example, Rubinstein, 1982). This is often called the sequential strategic approach. Rubinstein showed the existence of a unique perfect Nash equilibrium in any bargaining game, if players have sufficiently high time-preference rates and/or every player has to bear a fixed cost of bargaining for each period.

Binmore, Rubinstein and, Wolinsky (1986) not only studied bargaining problems using the sequential strategic approach but also studied the relationship between the solutions obtained from this approach and that of the axiomatic approach or static representation of a bargaining problem. Moreover, they examined the two motives behind the bargaining process that may induce the players to agree rather than to insist indefinitely on incompatible demands.

One of the motives studied by Binmore, Rubinstein and, Wolinsky (hereafter BRW) was the player's 'impatience to enjoy the fruits of an agreement,' which is concerned with the relative time preference of the players, and the other motive was the player's relative fear of disagreement.

If the players do not have a high enough time-preference rate, then they may keep on insisting on incompatible demands and no agreements may be reached. Making use of Rubinstein's seminal study (Rubinstein, 1982) Binmore (1987b) showed that the relative difference in the time preference rate of the players can be a source of unequal bargaining power of the players in the static representation of the game. Player with relatively higher time preference rate will have lower bargaining power. This result was also obtained by BRW.

In their comprehensive study of the strategic models of bargaining BRW also studied a game in which players faced an exogenous risk of breakdown of negotiations. They found a unique perfect equilibrium in this game as well. They have further shown that if the players differ in their beliefs concerning the likelihood of a breakdown of the negotiation, then the unique perfect equilibrium of the game approaches to the 'asymmetric' Nash bargaining solution to the static version of the game. The correspondence is that the bargaining power of a player will be lower if his estimate (or belief) of the probability of breakdown is relatively higher. Naturally, these results indicate that the generalized Nash solution is more appropriate in solving the bargaining problem in the tariff game than the original Nash solution since players may very well differ in their beliefs.

6.3.1   Fear of ruin: another fear of disagreement

To probe the fear of disagreement further, let us assume that the players hold identical beliefs about the external environments, have identical time preferences, etc., such that the players end with having equal bargaining power in BRW's sense. Now let us consider a situation as described in Figure 6.3.

Assume that RF is the rent transformation frontier (the Pareto efficient boundary of the bargaining set in an arbitrary bargaining game) and Π^o is a distribution of rents at any mutually acceptable relative price P_1^o.[14] Without loss of generality, let us take the case of player 1. Suppose further that for a small change of ΔP_1 in P_1 the resulting distribution of rent in market equilibrium is given by the point $\Pi^o + \Delta\Pi$. This means that player 1 gains by $\Delta\Pi_1$ and player 2 loses by $\Delta\Pi_2$ (for $\Delta\Pi_2 < 0$) if the price increase actually takes place. Therefore, player 1 may insist on such a price increase and player 2 is likely to oppose (or reject) it. Would player 1 insist on a price increase?

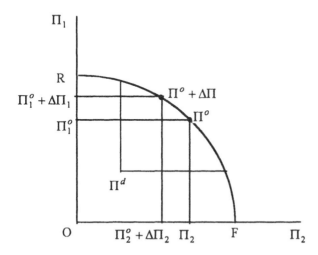

Figure 6.3   Fear of ruin

If player 1 insists on an increase in P_1, player 2 has two options: accept it, or quit the negotiation table and play a noncooperative game. Under this circumstance, insisting on such a price increase implies a gamble on the part of player 1. If it is accepted by player 2, player 1 will get a gain of $\Delta\Pi_1$; if player 2 rejects it and quits the table, player 1 is ruined. Player 1 will lose the entire gain of $\left(\Pi_1^o - \Pi_1^d\right)$, and end up with the disagreement payoff of Π_1^d.

Suppose that at Π^o, player 1 believes that if he insists on a small increase in price, then the probability that player 2 quits the negotiation and the disagreement results is $q_1(\Pi^o)$. Let $\bar{q}_1\left(\Pi_1^o, \Delta\Pi_1\right)$ be such that player 1 is indifferent between insisting on a price increase for a contingent gain of $\Delta\Pi_1$ with probability $(1 - \bar{q}_1)$ and accepting Π_1^o with certainty. That is, let

$$\Pi_1^o = (1 - \bar{q}_1)(\Pi_1^o + \Delta\Pi_1) + \bar{q}_1\Pi_1^d. \tag{6.3}$$

Then, $\bar{q}$ provides the threshold probability at Π^o such that $\bar{q}_1 > q_1$ implies that player 1 will insist on a price increase; $\bar{q}_1 \leq q_1$ implies that player 1 will prefer the certain outcome Π_1^o and will not insist on a higher price for his commodities. This means that $\bar{q}$ measures the 'boldness' of player 1 in an environment defined by (Π^o, Π^d).

Certainly, player 1, as can be seen from equation (6.3), will not risk the same amount of gain $\left(\Pi_1 - \Pi_1^d\right)$ for smaller amounts of contingent gains with identical probability distribution. To induce him to risk $\left(\Pi_1 - \Pi_1^d\right)$ for a gain that is smaller than $\Delta\Pi_1$ and remain indifferent ex ante, the probability of 'ruin' - that player 2 quits and disagreement results - has to be smaller than that corresponds to $\Delta\Pi_1$. Therefore, for given $\left(\Pi_1 - \Pi_1^d\right)$, the threshold probability $\bar{q}_1\left(\Pi_1^o, \Delta\Pi_1\right)$ declines as ΔP_1 gets smaller and smaller, and needs to be standardized to make a measure of player 1's boldness. Symmetric arguments can be made for player 2. Hence, the following definition due to Aumann and Kurz (1977a).

Definition 6.5   (fear of ruin). *Let*

$$q_i^*(P_1^o) = \lim_{\Delta P_1 \to 0} \frac{\bar{q}_i\left(\Pi_i^o, \Delta\Pi_i\right)}{|\Delta P_1|}, \tag{6.4}$$

then, $q_i^*(P_1^o)$ is a measure of boldness of player i at Π^o or at price P_1^o and, $f_i = (q_i^*(P_1^o))^{-1}$ is defined as a measure of player i's fear of ruin.[15]

The measure of boldness thus defined is 'the maximum probability of ruin per dollar of additional gains which player i is prepared to tolerate, for very small potential gains' (Roth, 1979: p. 50).

Moreover, it can be inferred directly from equation (6.3) that for a given contingent gain and his disagreement payoff, the maximum probability of ruin that player i is ready to accept declines as his payoff, Π_i, increases. Hence $\bar{q}_i(\Pi_i^o; \Delta\Pi_i)$ is a decreasing function and the fear of ruin is an increasing function of Π_i.

Solving equation (6.3) for $\bar{q}_i(\Pi_i^o; \Delta\Pi_i)$ we get

$$\bar{q}_i(\Pi_i^o, \Delta\Pi_i) = \frac{(\Pi_i^o + \Delta\Pi_i) - \Pi_i^o}{(\Pi_i^o + \Delta\Pi_i) - \Pi_i^d}. \tag{6.5}$$

Now, using equation (6.5) into the equation (6.4) we get

$$q_i^*(P_1^o) = \lim_{\Delta P_1 \to 0} \left[\frac{[(\Pi_i^o + \Delta\Pi_i) - \Pi_i^o] / |\Delta P_1|}{(\Pi_i^o + \Delta\Pi_i) - \Pi_i^d} \right]. \tag{6.6}$$

That is, player i's boldness at Π^o is given by

$$q_i^*(P_1^o) = \frac{\left| d\Pi_i / dP_1 \right\|_{P_1^o}}{\Pi_i^o - \Pi_i^d}. \tag{6.7}$$

Therefore, player i's fear of ruin, which is the inverse of the measure of player i's boldness, is given by[16]

$$f_i(P_1^o) = \frac{\Pi_i^o - \Pi_i^d}{\left| d\Pi_i / dP_1 \right\|_{P_1^o}}. \tag{6.8}$$

Thus, equation (6.8) defines the adapted version of Aumann and Kurz's concept of the fear of ruin. In general, at any relative price P_1 of commodity 1 such that $\Pi \in \Re$, we can write the fear functions, corrected for sign effects as follows.

$$f_1(P_1) = \frac{\Pi_1(P_1) - \Pi_1^d}{d\Pi_1(P_1) / dP_1} \tag{6.9a}$$

and,

$$f_2(P_1) = -\frac{\Pi_2(P_1) - \Pi_2^d}{d\Pi_2(P_1) / dP_1}. \tag{6.9b}$$

The derivative $d\Pi_i / dP_1$ measures the marginal ability of player i to obtain rents through price changes. It shows the change in the total rents obtained in sector i when the relative price of commodity 1 changes by one unit. The value of $d\Pi_i / dP_1$ is determined completely by the economic sphere.

Definition 6.6   *The fear functions $f_1(P_1)$ and $f_2(P_1)$ are said to be well behaved if for all P_1 that are relevant to bargaining (that is, such that $\Pi(P_1) \in \Re$) if $f_1'(P_1) > 0$ and $f_2'(P_1) < 0$, where prime denotes the derivative.*

The conditions which are sufficient in general for $f_1'(P_1) > 0$ and $f_2'(P_1) < 0$, are derived in Appendix-6A. It suffices here to note that the fear functions are well behaved under Assumption 4.1 - that the real rental functions are concave in the relative price of own-commodity.

The derivative properties of the fear functions indicate that player 1's fear of ruin increases as P_1 increases and player 2's fear of ruin increases as P_1 falls (or the relative price of commodity 2 increases).

Aumann and Kurz (1977a, 1977b) discovered that the Nash solution to a bargaining game 'calls for that compromise which makes the two players equally fearful of ruin, where ruin is here taken to mean disagreement' (P. 1149). This condition, the equality of fear of ruin, turns out to be identical to the first order condition of maximizing the Nash product over the bargaining set. The intuitive reason behind the equilibrating process is that the player who fears the most will concede. This explanation is similar to that of Zuthen's referred above.

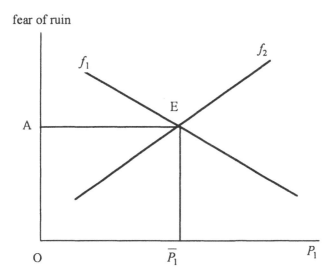

Figure 6.4   Bargained price: equality of fear of ruin

135

The Nash bargaining equilibrium is illustrated in Figure 6.4. $\overline{P}_1$ is the bargained price where both players are equally fearful of ruin. For all prices that are less than $\overline{P}_1$, player 2's fear of ruin exceeds player 1's fear of ruin. Hence player 2 concedes and prices are allowed to rise. For all prices greater than $\overline{P}_1$ player 1's fear of ruin exceeds the player 2's fear of ruin; therefore player 1 concedes. The price moves in favour of player 2.

6.3.2   Fear of ruin and fear of breakdown

It is important to distinguish between the fear of disagreement created by a positive probability of breakdown of the negotiation in BRW and the fear of ruin in Aumann and Kurz. In BRW the implied fear to each player is constant until the agreement is reached, whereas in Aumann and Kurz a player's fear increases as he receives an increasing gain from the bargain. Along the Pareto efficient frontier as the fear of one player increases the fear of the other player necessarily decreases. This is not the case with the concept of fear in BRW.

The types of fear of disagreement in these two studies are intrinsically different. This is because the sources of fear are different. In BRW players fear because they think that if an agreement can not be reached quickly, then the opportunity might be snatched by a third party, or may vanish by itself. For both players the source of fear, therefore, is the third party or a time factor. In the case of Aumann and Kurz, however, each player fears because the other player may refuse to agree. That is why the measure of the fear of ruin, as defined by Aumann and Kurz, increases with the gain of the player relative to the disagreement payoff. The source of the fear of ruin for each player is the other player (opponent). The fear of ruin exists even in the absence of a threat of a third party snatching the opportunity.

The implication of this discussion is that although the difference in players' perception of the risk of breakdown or the fear of disagreement as viewed by BRW is captured by the difference in bargaining power of the players, the fear of ruin as defined by Aumann and Kurz is not. Therefore, the fear of ruin constitutes a separate and an independent motive that not only affects the outcome of the game but also induces the players to reach an agreement through constant revisions of their incompatible demands.

6.3.3   Generalized Fear of Ruin

The property of the Nash bargaining solution, however, as discovered by Aumann and Kurz, that in equilibrium the players should be equally fearful of ruin holds, as in the case of the original Nash solution, only with equal bargaining power. It is because the above deduction is based on the assumption that the players hold equal bargaining power. An immediate problem is to explore whether or not a similar condition holds when there are reasons to believe that players hold unequal bargaining power.

For example, one of the reasons that players have unequal bargaining power is that they have unequal time preference rates. We know that $\varphi_1 < \varphi_2$ implies $\Theta_1 > \Theta_2$, where φ_i is the time preference rate of player i (Rubinstein 1982; Binmore 1987b: 71). Other things being equal, a player with higher time preference rate will be ready to reduce his demand by more than a player with lower time preference rate will be. This means that a player with higher time preference rate will have a greater fear of ruin than another player with a lower time preference rate. Similar arguments would follow, if we take the case of unequal fear of disagreement in BRW's sense - that is, the fear that the bargaining opportunity could be snatched by a third party.

It follows from the above that the fear of ruin held by each player comes from two sources: (1) the fear that a third party will intervene; and (2) the fear that the opponent will quit the bargaining table and disagreement will result. The measure of boldness as defined by the equation (6.4) and given by the equation (6.7) has to be understood in a broader context than it was defined for. In the case that there are many sources of fear, a measure of boldness (and a measure of fear of ruin) should represent the maximum tolerable probability of occurrence of either one or all of the events - for example, a third party intervenes and seizes the bargaining opportunity, or the gain simply evaporates over time or the opponent disagrees, and so on.

Therefore, it is now necessary to differentiate between a player's total boldness and a player's boldness vis-à-vis her bargaining opponent. We argue (on the basis of player's indifference) that, in any situation, a player has a fixed capacity to risk already attained gain. That measures her total boldness and is given by the equation (6.7). In order that a player insist on a favourable price (tariff) change and assume the risk of breakdown of negotiation the capacity to risk the gain should exceed the sum of risks that arise from all sources. A higher risk from a third party, therefore, reduces the capacity to risk the conflict with the bargaining opponent. That is, the higher a player's BRW type fear of disagreement (relative to the other player) the lower the player's boldness vis-à-vis his opponent and therefore the higher is the player's Aumann and Kurz type fear of ruin. Other things being equal, if the players have equal capacity to risk the conflict, the player who fears more than his opponent that a third party will snatch the opportunity will also display a greater fear of ruin vis-à-vis her opponent.

Let us consider again the situation described in Figure 6.3. If player 1 demands a price increase, then it will induce a bargaining process during which player 2 may disagree or a third party may intervene. If any of the events occur the disagreement payoff will result. The higher the demand the more it is likely that either of the events will occur.

As in BRW, let $a_i(\Delta P_1)$ be defined as follows:

$$a_1(\Delta P_1) = \begin{cases} 1 - e^{-a_1^* \Delta P_1} & \text{for} \quad \Delta P_1 > 0, \\ 0 & \text{for} \quad \Delta P_1 \leq 0. \end{cases} \qquad (6.10a)$$

$$a_2(\Delta P_1) = \begin{cases} 1 - e^{-a_2^*(-\Delta P_1)} & \text{for} \quad \Delta P_1 < 0, \\ 0 & \text{for} \quad \Delta P_1 \geq 0. \end{cases} \qquad (6.10b)$$

where, $a_i^* > 0$ and is independent of the current price. Then $a_i(\Delta P_1)$ denotes player i's subjective probability that a third party intervention occurs and that players have to receive the disagreement payoffs if she insists on a price change of ΔP_1.[17]

Similarly we can define Aumann and Kurz type fear of ruin as follows. Let,

$$b_1(\Delta P_1; P_1^o) = \begin{cases} 1 - e^{-b_1^*(\Delta P_1)} & \text{for} \quad \Delta P_1 > 0, \\ 0 & \text{for} \quad \Delta P_1 \leq 0. \end{cases} \qquad (6.11a)$$

and,

$$b_2(\Delta P_1; P_1^o) = \begin{cases} 1 - e^{-b_2^*(-\Delta P_1)} & \text{for} \quad \Delta P_1 < 0, \\ 0 & \text{for} \quad \Delta P_1 \geq 0. \end{cases} \qquad (6.11b)$$

where, $b_i^* > 0$ for each i such that b_1^* increases and b_2^* decreases with P_1.

Then, $b_1(\Delta P_1; P_1^o)$ denotes player 1's subjective probability that player 2 will declare disagreement if she demands a price increase of ΔP_1 and $b_2(\Delta P_1; P_1^o)$ denotes player 2's subjective probability that player 1 will declare disagreement if he demands a price fall of ΔP_1 given that P_1^o is a mutually acceptable price.

It is clear from these definitions that

$$a_i^* = \lim_{\Delta P_1 \to 0} (a_i / \Delta P_1) \text{ and, } b_i^* = \lim_{\Delta P_1 \to 0} (b_i / \Delta P_1), \qquad (6.12)$$

where, we take right-hand limit for player 1 and left-hand limit for player 2. It is clear from equation (6.12) that a_i^* and b_i^* yield player i's subjective valuation of the likelihood of the two types of risks per unit of price change when the proposed price changes are small.

Given this environment, we can search for the threshold probability of conflict with the opponent that player i can accept for small gains. At price P_i^o player i will demand a price change, at most, of size ΔP_1 such that the following equality holds:

$$\Pi_i^o = [a_i(\Delta P_1) + b_i(\Delta P_1) - a_i(\Delta P_1)b_i(\Delta P_1)]\Pi_i^d$$
$$+ [1 - a_i(\Delta P_1)][1 - b_i(\Delta P_1)](\Pi_i^o + \Delta\Pi_i) \tag{6.13}$$

Note that $[a_i(\Delta P_1) + b_i(\Delta P_1) - a_i(\Delta P_1)b_i(\Delta P_1)]$ measures the probability that either of the events occurs and disagreement results, and $[1 - a_i(\Delta P_1)][1 - b_i(\Delta P_1)]$ measures the probability that agreement results and player i will obtain the contingent gain of $\Delta\Pi_i$ when he demands a price change of ΔP_1.

From equation (6.13) we get

$$[a_i(\Delta P_1) + b_i(\Delta P_1) - a_i(\Delta P_1)b_i(\Delta P_1)] = \bar{q}_i(\Delta P_1), \tag{6.14}$$

where,

$$\bar{q}_i(\Delta P_1) = \frac{(\Pi_i^o + \Delta\Pi_i) - \Pi_i^o}{(\Pi_i^o + \Delta\Pi_i) - \Pi_i^d}. \tag{6.15}$$

For small price changes, taking limits to both sides of (6.14) and (6.15) yields

$$a_i^* + b_i^* = q_i^* \tag{6.16}$$

where q_i^* is as defined in equation (6.7). Thus, equation (6.16) shows that the maximum probability of conflict with the opponent that player i is prepared to tolerate is the difference between the measure of her total boldness, q_i^*, and her subjective probability, a_i^*, that a third party intervenes. That is, given a_i^*, while negotiating for gains, b_i^* measures player i's boldness at Π_i^o vis a vis her opponent.

Definition 6.7 (Total Boldness). *The maximum probability of conflict with the external world that a player is prepared to accept for a small current gain is a measure of the player's total boldness in a given environment. The inverse of this measure is the player's total fear of ruin.*

Definition 6.8 (Residual Boldness). *Given other exogenous risks, the maximum probability of conflict with the opponent that a player is prepared to accept for small gains is defined as a measure of the player's residual boldness. The inverse of this measure is the player's residual fear of ruin.*

In the absence of a third party risk, as can be seen from equation (6.16), total boldness, which is equal to the Aumann and Kurz's measure of boldness as defined above, of a player coincides with her residual boldness. The presence of a third party risk (or any other factor that affects players' relative bargaining power) makes the matter quite different. A player, whose total boldness is much higher than his opponent, would be ready to concede during a bargaining process simply because his perception of the third party risk is much higher than that held by his opponent. The difference in the third party risk can help to reduce the gap between the residual boldness of the players, which matters the most during the process of a negotiation.

A difference in players' perception of a third party risk has reinforcing effects from two directions. On the one hand it affects players' bargaining power as shown by BRW, and on the other hand, as shown above, it also affects player's boldness vis-à-vis her opponent. A player assigns a higher probability to a third party intervention than his opponent means that he will have lower bargaining power relative to his opponent. For given total boldness, a player assigns a higher probability to a third party intervention certainly implies that he will be less bolder vis-à-vis his opponent as well.

This argument leads us to the conclusion that either one should focus on the residual boldness (or residual fear of ruin) in characterizing the bargaining solution or one should appropriately allow for the difference in players' perception of a third party risk to play a role together with a measure of player's total boldness in determining the bargaining outcome or characterizing the bargaining solution.

The role played by the third party risk clearly suggests that if there are other sources of the difference in bargaining power between the players besides the third party risk, then they may also affect a player's fear of ruin vis-à-vis her opponent in the bargaining process. If a player has relatively more bargaining power than her opponent, then the reason behind the advantage in the bargaining power also works favourably to dampen the fear of the player vis a vis her opponent. Since there can be several sources of fear or the characteristics that differentiate the players, and Aumann and Kurz's measure of fear of ruin is a total measure, the following alternative measure of residual fear is proposed to generalize the Aumann and Kurz result.

Definition 6.9   (Generalized Fear of Ruin)   *Let f_i be as defined by (6.9) and Θ_i be as defined by (6.2). Let $f_i^* \equiv f_i / \Theta_i$, then f_i^* is defined as player i's generalized fear of ruin.*

Thus the generalized fear of ruin will be equal to Aumann and Kurz's concept of fear of ruin if and only if players have equal bargaining power, that is, if the players are identical except the bargaining set.

140

Now, we state the following axiom initially proposed by Svejnar (1986):[18]

Axiom 6 (Equality of Generalized Fear of Ruin).
A solution to a bargaining game satisfies $f_i^* = f_j^*$ for $i \neq j$.

6.4 Generalized Nash bargaining solution in a tariff game and the generalized fear of ruin

In an n-person bargaining problem in which the object of bargaining is a division of a fixed 'pie'; the players endowed with unequal bargaining power have concave utility functions, U_i for each player i, defined on the size of their share in the 'pie'; the zero normalized (disagreement payoff transformed into zero by change of origin) bargaining set, denoted by S, is compact and convex in utility space; Svejnar proved quite generally that:

Theorem 6.3 (Svejnar). *There is a unique solution which satisfies Axioms 1-3, and Axiom 6. It is the solution that maximizes* $\prod_{i=1}^{n} U_i^{\Theta_i}$ *for all* $U \in S$.

Proof: See Svejnar (1986).

The proof of Theorem 6.3 outlined in Svejnar (1986) is quite general. So long as the bargaining set is compact, convex and contains at least one point that strictly dominates the disagreement payoff, the proof of the equivalence between (a) the bargaining solution satisfying the four axioms, and (b) the solution that maximizes the generalized Nash product over the bargaining set, remains valid.

However, Theorem 6.2 (Roth's Theorem) shows that the solution to the bargaining problem can be characterized without referring to Axiom 6. This implies that Axiom 6 is redundant in the presence of Axioms 1-3. This axiom will be more useful if it could characterize the generalized Nash bargaining solution in the absence of at least one of the Axioms 1-3. The following theorem shows that this is in fact the case.

Recall that if the international price ratio P_1^*, and the domestic factor endowments K_1, K_2 and L are exogenously given, and the elasticities of factor substitution in both the sectors are at least unity, then the bargaining problem $(\Re, \Pi^d, \Theta)$ is well defined for exogenously given disagreement payoff Π^d, and bargaining power distribution Θ.

Theorem 6.4 *If fear functions are well defined - that is, the derivatives of the rental functions with respect to the relative price do not vanish at all prices - then* there exists a unique solution $\mu(\mathfrak{R},\Pi^d,\Theta) = \Pi(\overline{P_1}) \in \mathfrak{R}$ to any bargaining problem $(\mathfrak{R},\Pi^d,\Theta)$ in the tariff game. This solution can be characterized by any of the following equivalent statements:

(i) $\overline{P_1} = \underset{\Pi(P_1)\in\mathfrak{R}}{argmax}\left[\Pi_1(P_1) - \Pi_1^d\right]^{\Theta_1}\left[\Pi_2(P_1) - \Pi_2^d\right]^{\Theta_2}$. That is, $\Pi(\overline{P_1})$ maximizes the generalized Nash product over the bargaining set.

(ii) $\mu(\mathfrak{R},\Pi^d,\Theta)$ satisfies Axioms 1-3. That is, the solution to the bargaining problem $(\mathfrak{R},\Pi^d,\Theta)$ satisfying the Axioms 1-3 selects $\Pi(\overline{P_1})$ as the outcome of the bargaining.

(iii) $f_i^*(\overline{P_1}) > 0$ for each i, and $f_i^* = f_j^*$, $i \neq j$ such that $\Pi(\overline{P_1}) \in \mathfrak{R}$. That is, at $\overline{P_1}$ each player i has a positive fear of ruin, and that players' generalized fears of ruin are equalized.

Proof: (i) holds, if and only if (ii) holds follows from Theorem 6.2. Therefore, it suffices to show that (i) holds if and only if (iii) holds.[19]
(a)   First we will show that (i) implies (iii). Suppose (i) holds. This implies that at $P_1 = \overline{P_1}$ the level curve of generalized Nash product is tangent to the boundary of the bargaining set. Their slopes are equal.

The slope of any level curve of Nash product is given by

$$\left.\frac{d\Pi_1}{d\Pi_2}\right|_{NP} = -\frac{\Theta_2}{\Theta_1}\left(\frac{\Pi_1(P_1) - \Pi_1^d}{\Pi_2(P_1) - \Pi_2^d}\right) \tag{6.17}$$

and since RTF is the boundary of the bargaining set, its slope is given by

$$\left.\frac{d\Pi_1}{d\Pi_2}\right|_{RTF} = \frac{d\Pi_1(P_1)/dP_1}{d\Pi_2(P_1)/dP_1}. \tag{6.18}$$

Therefore, at the solution point we must have

$$\frac{d\Pi_1(\overline{P_1})/dP_1}{d\Pi_2(\overline{P_1})/dP_1} = -\frac{\Theta_2}{\Theta_1}\left(\frac{\Pi_1(\overline{P_1}) - \Pi_1^d}{\Pi_2(\overline{P_1}) - \Pi_2^d}\right) \tag{6.19}$$

which means that

$$\frac{1}{\Theta_1}\left(\frac{\Pi_1(\overline{P_1}) - \Pi_1^d}{d\Pi_1(\overline{P_1})/dP_1}\right) = \frac{1}{\Theta_2}\left(-\frac{\Pi_2(\overline{P_1}) - \Pi_2^d}{d\Pi_2(\overline{P_1})/dP_1}\right). \tag{6.20}$$

Therefore, it follows from equation (6.9) that $f_1^*(\overline{P_1}) = f_2^*(\overline{P_1})$. Moreover, $\Pi_i(\overline{P_1}) > \Pi_i^d$ implies that $f_i^*(\overline{P_1}) > 0$ for each i. Thus, at the solution point of the game each player holds strictly positive fear of ruin and the generalized fear of ruin is equalized across the players.

(b) Conversely, we will show that (i) follows from (iii). Suppose that (iii) holds. First note that $f_i^*(\overline{P_1}) > 0$ implies that $\Pi(\overline{P_1})$ lies on the boundary of the bargaining set. If $\Pi(\overline{P_1})$ does not lie on the boundary of the bargaining set, then players can increase their payoffs without affecting the relative price. They can do so simply by cutting down their lobbying expenditure. This means that $\left| d\Pi_i(\overline{P_1})/dP_1 \right| = \infty$ in the neighbourhood of $\overline{P_1}$. As a consequence, each player's fear of ruin of at $\overline{P_1}$ would be zero. This contradicts with the hypothesis that $f_i^*(\overline{P_1}) > 0$. Therefore, $f_i^*(\overline{P_1}) > 0$ for each i imply that $\Pi(\overline{P_1})$ lies on the boundary of the bargaining set.

It can be seen by reversing the above steps that $f_1^*(\overline{P_1}) = f_2^*(\overline{P_1})$ implies the satisfaction of the condition for tangency of a level curve of the generalized Nash product to the boundary of the bargaining set at $\Pi(\overline{P_1})$. Concavity of the generalised Nash product and convexity of the bargaining set guarantee that the point of tangency is unique, and that second order condition of maximization of the generalized Nash product is satisfied. Therefore, (iii) holds implies that (i) holds. Hence the theorem.   Q. E. D.

Corollary 6.2   (Bargained tariff rate). *A tariff rate $\overline{T}$ is a unique outcome of bargaining in a tariff game if $\overline{T}$ satisfies $\overline{P_1} = P_1^*(1 + \overline{T})$.*

Proof: Since $\overline{P_1}$ is unique by Theorem 6.4, the proof follows from the assumption that tariff is the only wedge between the world and the domestic relative prices.   Q. E. D.

Corollary 6.3   *If the fear functions are well behaved, then the bargaining solution obtained under conditions of Theorem 6.4 is stable.*

Proof: This corollary will be proved by way of a graphic illustration.
Fear functions are well behaved implies, by definition, that player 1's fear of ruin increases and player 2's fear of ruin decreases as P_1 increases.

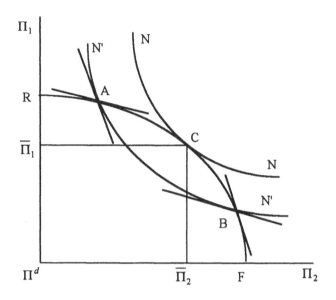

Figure 6.5   **Equality of players' generalized fear of ruin and the solution to a bargaining problem**

Let RF in Figure 6.5 represent the part of the RTF that forms the boundary of the bargaining set. Let a level curve of generalized Nash product labelled NN be tangent to the curve RF at the point C. Let P_1 be the domestic price ratio that corresponds to the point C, and $\Pi(\overline{P_1})$, be the payoff combination at price P_1. It follows from Theorem 6.4 that at point C the generalized fears of ruin are equalized across the players.

Now, suppose that, for some reason, the equilibrium is disturbed and the economy is at point B. Given unchanged values of the exogenous variables, the relative price should rise and the economy should move to the point C if the equilibrium at the point C is a stable one.

At the point B the generalized Nash product is not maximized. Obviously, B is not an equilibrium point. The two players will continue bargaining. Player 1 would like the relative price to *rise* and player 2 would like the relative price to *fall*. Since the absolute slope of the RTF is greater than the absolute slope of the Nash product curve at B, we can write

$$-\frac{d\Pi_1(\overline{P}_1)/dP_1}{d\Pi_2(\overline{P}_1)/dP_1} > \frac{\Theta_2}{\Theta_1}\left(\frac{\Pi_1(\overline{P}_1)-\Pi_1^d}{\Pi_2(\overline{P}_1)-\Pi_2^d}\right). \tag{6.21}$$

But this means that

$$\frac{-1}{\Theta_2}\left(\frac{\Pi_2(\overline{P}_1)-\Pi_2^d}{d\Pi_2(\overline{P}_1)/dP_1}\right) > \frac{1}{\Theta_1}\left(\frac{\Pi_1(\overline{P}_1)-\Pi_1^d}{d\Pi_1(\overline{P}_1)/dP}\right). \tag{6.22}$$

That is, at point B, by definition we have $f_2^* > f_1^*$. This means that player 2 will concede and the domestic relative price will rise. The process will continue until we reach the point C, where both players are equally fearful of each other quitting the negotiation.

Similarly, it can be seen that if the economy moves to points like A, then player 1's fear of ruin will exceed player 2's fear of ruin. Player 1 will concede and the price will fall.

6.5 Summary

It is clear from the above results that the Nash bargained solution in a tariff game can be obtained as a solution to the following maximizing problem:

$$\max\left[\Pi_1 - \Pi_1^d\right]^{\Theta_1}\left[\Pi_2 - \Pi_2^d\right]^{\Theta_2} \tag{6.23}$$

subject to the RTF,

$$\Pi_1 \leq K_1 P_1^{-1} \beta_1^{-\sigma_1/(1-\sigma_1)}\left[P_1^{1-\sigma_1} - \alpha_1^{\sigma_1}\alpha_2^{-\sigma_2(1-\sigma_1)/(1-\sigma_2)} \times \right.$$
$$\left.\left(1 - \beta_2^{\sigma_2}(\Pi_2/K_2)^{1-\sigma_2}\right)^{(1-\sigma_1)/(1-\sigma_2)}\right]^{1/(1-\sigma_1)} \tag{6.24}$$

and that $\Pi_i \geq \Pi_i^d$, for each player $i=1, 2$.

The inequality (6.24) is obtained from the equation (4.6) by appropriately replacing $K_i \widetilde{R}_i$ by Π_i. This substitution is allowed by the rule that in a cooperative game players need not spend resources in lobbying the government. The real-rent combinations along the RTF also are available to the players. Therefore, the boundary of the feasible set is the RTF. The inequality in (6.24) indicates that players may choose inefficient outcomes - either by inefficient allocation of resources or by playing noncooperation. The above bargaining problem is illustrated in Figure 6.6.

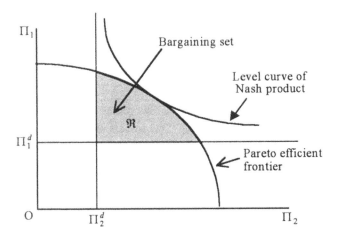

Figure 6.6   An illustration of a Nash bargaining solution

The level curves of the generalized Nash product defined by the function (6.23) are rectangular hyperbolas with asymptotes Π_1^d and Π_2^d. The presence of these asymptotes effectively restricts the solution payoffs to lie above the disagreement payoffs. The effective bargaining set is $\mathfrak{R}$, which lies to the north east of the disagreement point, (Π_1^d, Π_2^d). The tilt of the Nash product curve is determined by the magnitude of Θ_i. A higher value of Θ_i produces a tilt more towards the ith axis. The magnitude of Θ_i is an institutionally given datum and represents the 'bargaining power' of player i.

The maximand is concave and continuous; the constraint set is compact and convex; therefore there exists a unique maximum of the generalized Nash product in $\mathfrak{R}$. The first order condition of maximization problem, which is also sufficient, is that the Nash product (NP) curve be tangent to the Pareto efficient boundary of the feasible set - that is, the northeast boundary of the feasible set described by the equation (6.24). Replacing the sign of inequality by equality in (6.24) we can obtain the expression for the boundary of the feasible set, which is the rental transformation frontier (RTF).

The necessary and sufficient condition for the Nash solution to the bargaining problem is given by

$$\left(\frac{\Pi_1 - \Pi_1^d}{\Pi_2 - \Pi_2^d}\right) = -\frac{\Theta_1}{\Theta_2}\frac{d\Pi_1}{d\Pi_2}\Bigg|_{RTF}. \tag{6.25}$$

The payoff combination $\overline{\Pi} \equiv (\overline{\Pi}_1, \overline{\Pi}_2)$, that satisfies the condition given by the equation (6.25) is the solution to the bargaining problem. The relative price, and hence the tariff rate, that corresponds to this solution payoff is the outcome of the bargaining in a tariff game. More formally, a rationalized tariff rate $\overline{T}$ satisfying

$$\overline{T} = \arg\max\left\{\left[\Pi_1(P_1^*(1+T)) - \Pi_1^d\right]^{\Theta_1} \times \right.$$
$$\left.\left[\Pi_2(P_1^*(1+T)) - \Pi_2^d\right]^{\Theta_2}\Big|\Pi \in \Re\right\} \tag{6.26}$$

is the unique Nash bargained solution to the tariff game.

Theorem 6.2 (Roth's Theorem) has shown that the generalized Nash bargained solution is unique. It is also individually rational, independent of scale of measurement, and independent of irrelevant alternatives. Corollary 6.1 has shown that the solution is also symmetric. Roth's result also guarantees that the solution is efficient.

Aumann and Kurz have shown that at the Nash bargaining solution players' fear of ruin are equalized. Theorem 6.4 extends this result by showing that the equality of fear of ruin can constitute a separate characterization - i.e., it is a sufficient as well as a necessary condition of the Nash bargaining solution. Aumann and Kurz's result holds when players have equal bargaining power. But the characterization of the generalized Nash bargaining solution in terms of generalized fear of ruin provided by Theorem 6.4 holds for any arbitrary distribution of bargaining power among the players. It is shown that at the generalized Nash bargaining solution players' generalized fears of ruin are equalized. Clearly, Aumann and Kurz's result is a special case of this result.

Furthermore, it is shown in Corollary 6.3 that the generalized Nash bargaining solution is stable when the fear functions are well behaved. Appendix-6A provides a generally sufficient condition for fear functions to be well behaved.

This chapter has differentiated the concept of fear of disagreement as suggested by BRW and that suggested by Aumann and Kurz. It is argued here that they have addressed two different sources of fear. In BRW the source of fear is either the external world or time, whereas in Aumann and Kurz the source of fear is the opponent. The proposed generalization of fear of ruin not only embraces both of these fear concepts but also accommodates any other differences between the players that are capable of affecting the bargaining power of the players.

Now, it can be seen from the equation (6.25) that at the bargained outcome, the gain of player 1 relative to the gain of player 2 over the disagreement payoff depends on two terms: the ratio of the institutionally given bargaining power of the players, Θ_1 / Θ_2, and the slope of the rental transformation frontier. Begin and Karp (1991) have named the second term as the 'endogenous' bargaining power and the first term as 'exogenous' bargaining power of the players.

The role of these two terms in determining the outcome can best be viewed with the help of the following figure.

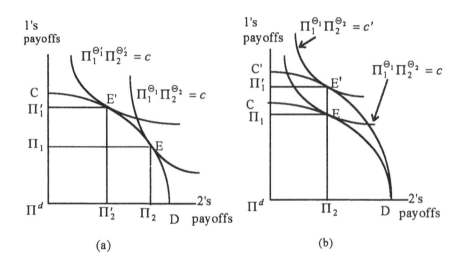

Figure 6.7 **Effects of changes in endogenous and exogenous bargaining power on the bargaining outcome**

The two panels in the above figure reflect the effect of the difference in the two types of bargaining power of the players. In panel (a) two generalized Nash product curves that correspond to different exogenous bargaining power distribution, holding the endogenous bargaining power constant, are drawn. The curves were drawn on the assumption that $\Theta_1 < \Theta'_1$. The result is that under unchanged economic circumstances, increased exogenous bargaining power of player 1 has the effect of increasing payoff to player 1.

In panel (b) two rental possibility frontiers are drawn to reflect an exogenous expansion in sector 1. The exogenous bargaining power distribution has been held fixed. The new rent possibility set defined by the transformation frontier C'D contains the rent possibility set defined by the rent transformation frontier CD. Hence in equilibrium, they are able to attain a higher Nash product with the rental possibility curve C'D than with CD. The figure has been so drawn that the gain goes to player 1 only. Thus the relative difference in the gain over the disagreement payoff can be attributed to change in the 'endogenous' bargaining power of the players.

Thus the 'endogenous' bargaining power can be viewed as being determined by the technologies of production, and the distribution of players' market power. This study assumes that all markets are competitive, therefore, possession of a meaningful market power by any one of the players has been ruled out. However, some advantages due to technological and installed capacity differences are still there.

If the slope of the RTF is defined to measure the distribution of endogenous bargaining power among players, then a movement along a rental transformation frontier implies a change in the slope of the frontier and therefore, in turn, implies a change in the endogenous bargaining power of the players. However, given a disagreement payoff, the RTF, and a distribution of exogenous bargaining power, one and only one point of the frontier will constitute a solution and other points of the frontier will be irrelevant. The endogenous bargaining power will be determined by the solution of the game, not the other way round. If endogenous bargaining power is to determine the solution of the game then such a movement along a given RTF should not be regarded as change in the endogenous bargaining power of the players. It follows that a frontier defines a particular configuration of 'endogenous' bargaining power of the players. A change in 'endogenous' bargaining power can arise only if the location of the RTF is changed.

In fact, the slopes of a given RTF show the economic limitation of the political system in transferring rents from one sector to the other sector. A shift in the frontier changes the constraint faced by the political system. For example, at each rental income of sector 1, the rent transformation frontier C'D has a greater absolute slope than the rental transformation frontier CD. This means that player 1 can obtain more rents per unit loss in the rental income of player 2 along the frontier C'D than along the frontier CD. Therefore, it can be argued[20] that the frontier C'D implies a greater 'endogenous' bargaining power of player 1 than implied by the frontier CD.

It can be seen from equation (6.9) that the slope of the RTF plays a crucial role in determining each player's total fear of ruin. For given disagreement payoffs, at each payoff level of player 1 the steeper the RTF the less fearful is player 1. Therefore, a biased outward shift of the RTF favouring player 1 has the effect of making player 1 bolder (that is, less fearful of ruin), and making player 2 less bolder (that is more fearful of ruin). Thus an increase in the 'endogenous' bargaining power of a player can also be viewed as an increase in the total boldness of the player and vice versa. The interpretation of the Nash bargaining solution in terms of generalized fear of ruin is, therefore, consistent with endogenous and exogenous dichotomy of bargaining power of the players.

Given the exogenous bargaining power coefficients, $\Theta' s$, equation (6.25) with appropriate definitional equations and the policy exogenous general equilibrium model of the economic sphere, as described in Chapter 3, are sufficient to solve for the bargained tariff rate. However, in the absence of reliable information on the exogenous bargaining power of the players we can study the comparative static properties of the equilibrium tariff rate under the assumption that the distribution of the exogenous bargaining power of the players are not affected by changes in the exogenous variables.

In the next chapter, we will combine the generalized Nash bargaining game with the policy exogenous general equilibrium model of an open economic sphere to obtain a tariff endogenous general equilibrium model of the political economy. A combination of the condition (6.25) that identifies the generalized Nash bargaining solution with the conditions of equilibrium in the economic sphere yields a set of conditions that characterize the general equilibrium of the political economy. A study of this model will be undertaken in the next chapter.

Appendix-6A: Derivative properties of the fear functions

Let us Recall Aumann and Kurz's fear of ruin at price P_1 :
Player 1's fear of ruin is defined by

$$f_1(P_1) = \frac{\Pi_1(P_1) - \Pi_1^d}{d\Pi_1 / dP_1}, \qquad (6A.1)$$

and player 2's fear of ruin is defined by

$$f_2(P_1) = -\frac{\Pi_2(P_1) - \Pi_2^d}{d\Pi_2 / dP_1}. \qquad (6A.2)$$

Differentiating equation (6A.1) with respect to the relative price yields

$$\frac{df_1(P_1)}{dP_1} = \frac{1}{(\Pi_1')^2}\left((\Pi_1')^2 - (\Pi_1 - \Pi_1^d)\frac{d^2\Pi_1}{dP_1^2}\right). \qquad (6A.3)$$

Therefore, the sufficient condition for $df_1(P_1) / dP_1 > 0$ is that $d^2\Pi_1 / dP_1^2 \leq 0$.

Satisfaction of the condition means that player 1's fear of ruin increases with P_1. Given the differentiability of the rental function, the necessary and sufficient condition for $df_1(P_1)/dP_1 > 0$ is that the term in the parentheses on the right be positive.

Similarly, differentiating (6A.2) with respect to P_1 yields

$$\frac{df_2(P_1)}{dP_1} = -\frac{1}{(\Pi_2')^2}\left((\Pi_2')^2 - (\Pi_2 - \Pi_2^d)\frac{d^2\Pi_2}{dP_1^2}\right) \tag{6A.4}$$

A sufficient condition for $df_2(P_1)/dP_1 < 0$ is that $d^2\Pi_2/dP_1^2 \leq 0$. If this condition is satisfied then an increase in P_1 implies a fall in player 2's fear of ruin. That is, at a higher relative price of commodity 1, player 1 becomes more fearful of ruin and player 2 becomes bolder. At a lower relative price of commodity 1, player 1 becomes bolder and player 2 becomes more fearful of ruin.

If second order derivatives of the payoff functions with respect to P_1 are nonpositive, then we are done. If this is not the case, that is if $d^2\Pi_i/dP_1^2 > 0$, then the information is not sufficient to determine the sign of the derivative of the fear functions as the relative price changes. The purpose of this Appendix is to obtain conditions under which $df_1(P_1)/dP_1 > 0$ and $df_2(P_1)/dP_1 < 0$ when the second order derivatives of the payoff functions are positive.

If the underlying production functions are continuously differentiable and the elasticities of factor substitution are finite then the sectoral payoff functions are continuously differentiable in P_1. Therefore, under these standard conditions, we can use Taylor series to approximate the sectoral rental functions. The series can, then, be used to evaluate the slope of fear of ruin functions of the players.

First, consider the case of player 1. Since Taylor series can be constructed around any arbitrary value of P_1 provided the derivatives exist, we can choose P_1^* such that $\Pi_1(P_1^*) = \Pi_1^d$. Then, for all P_1 such that $\Pi(P_1) \in \Re$ we have $P_1 \geq P_1^*$. The second order Taylor series expansion of the payoff function $\Pi_1(P_1)$ around P_1^* can be written as

$$\Pi_1(P_1) = \Pi_1^d + a(P_1 - P_1^*) + b(P_1 - P_1^*)^2. \tag{6A.5}$$

where, $a = \Pi_1'(P_1^*) > 0$; $b = (1/2)\Pi_1''(P_1^*) > 0$.

and the derivative of the payoff function is given by

$$d\Pi_1/dP_1 = a + 2b(P_1 - P_1^*) \tag{6A.6}$$

Therefore, the fear function can be written as

$$f_1(P_1) = \frac{a(P_1 - P_1^*) + b(P_1 - P_1^*)^2}{a + 2b(P_1 - P_1^*)}.$$

(6A.7)

Differentiating the fear function with respect to P_1 yields after simplification

$$\frac{df_1(P_1)}{dP_1} = \frac{a^2 + 2[b(P_1 - P_1^*)]^2 + 2ab(P_1 - P_1^*)}{\left[a + 2b(P_1 - P_1^*)\right]^2} > 0.$$

(6A.8)

Similarly, we can obtain a Taylor series approximation of the rental income function for player 2 by expanding around P_1^a where $\Pi_2(P_1^a) = \Pi_2^d$. Then for all P_1, such that $\Pi(P_1) \in \Re$, we must have $P_1 \le P_1^a$.

For player 2, we can write

$$\Pi_2(P_1) = \Pi_2^d + c(P_1 - P_1^a) + e(P_1 - P_1^a)^2$$

(6A.9)

where, $c = \Pi_2'(P_1^a) < 0$ and $e = \Pi_2''(P_1^a)/2$.

If $e \le 0$, then we are done. So suppose that e > 0. Following steps similar to what we did for player 1 we can obtain

$$\frac{df_2(P_1)}{dP_1} = -\frac{c^2 + 2[e(P_1 - P_1^a)]^2 + 2ce(P_1 - P_1^a)}{\left[c + 2e(P_1 - P_1^a)\right]^2}$$

$$= -\frac{\left[c + e(P_1 - P_1^a)\right]^2 + \left[e(P_1 - P_1^a)\right]^2}{\left[c + 2e(P_1 - P_1^a)\right]^2} > 0$$

(6A.10)

where,

$$f_2(P_1) = -\frac{c(P_1 - P_1^a) + e(P_1 - P_1^a)^2}{c + 2e(P_1 - P_1^a)}.$$

These results remain valid if we use Taylor series of third order, provided that the third order derivative of the rental function remain nonnegative for player 1 and nonpositive for player 2 at the point of expansion. As we increase the order of expansion, the signs of the derivatives of the fear functions become ambiguous.

Therefore, the sufficient conditions for fear functions to be well behaved are that

(i)   the elasticities of factor substitution be finite; and

(ii)   either of the following two conditions holds:

    (a)   the second order derivatives of the rental functions with respective to P_1 are nonpositive everywhere;

    (b)   all third and higher order derivatives of the rental functions with respect to the relative price vanish at the point of expansion.

The first condition assures that there are no corner solutions. This condition together with the continuous differentiability of the output supply functions with respect to price, then, guarantees the differentiability of the rental functions at each price.

The second condition is related to the higher order derivatives of the rental functions. This condition is satisfied if rental functions, in the relevant range for bargaining, are approximately quadratic (concave or convex as the case may be) in relative price of either commodity. The presence of nonlinearities makes it difficult to assess whether the condition (ii) is satisfied or not.

However, the rental functions are bounded and strictly increasing in relative price of own commodity, eventually at higher prices, the second order derivatives of the rental functions with respect to the relative price of own commodity have to be nonpositive.

Condition (i) is normally satisfied. We do not normally expect factors of production to be perfectly substitutable. Condition (ii) may be violated in some cases. Particularly this condition may be violated if the rental functions are wavy, though strictly increasing in relative price of own commodity. If this is so, then the bargaining solution that equalizes generalized fear may not be stable. Player 1's generalized fear or ruin may fall as the relative price of commodity 1 rises and player 2's generalized fear of ruin may fall as the relative price of commodity 2 rises. Thus, each player may like to put demands that are likely to be incompatible. Hence, we regard condition (ii) as a condition for stability of the bargaining solution. However, in this study, we assume that the conditions (i) and (ii) are satisfied.

Appendix-6B: Proof of Roth's Theorem

We will prove Roth's Theorem by way of the following lemma. The proof basically follows Binmore (1987a).

Lemma 6.1   *Consider a bargaining problem (A, 0) where,*

$$A = \left\{ (x_1, x_2) \mid x_1 + x_2 \leq 1; x_1 \geq 0, x_2 \geq 0 \right\}.$$

If $\mu(A,0) = (x_1^*, x_2^*)$ is a solution to the bargaining problem $(A,0)$ that satisfies axioms of feasibility, invariance and independence, then

(i) $\mu(A,0) = (x_1^*, x_2^*)$ is efficient;

(ii)   there exists a $\tau \in (0,1)$ such that $x_1^* = \tau$ and $x_2^* = 1 - \tau$; and

(iii) $(x_1^*, x_2^*) = \max\limits_{(x_1,x_2) \in A} x_1^{\tau} x_2^{(1-\tau)}$.

Conversely, for any given $\tau \in (0,1)$, if $(x_1^*, x_2^*) = \max\limits_{(x_1,x_2) \in A} x_1^{\tau} x_2^{(1-\tau)}$, then $x_1^* = \tau$ and $x_2^* = 1 - \tau$, and the solution x^* satisfies axioms of feasibility, invariance, and independence. Moreover, the solution x^* is unique.

Proof: (i) Let us consider the following figure:

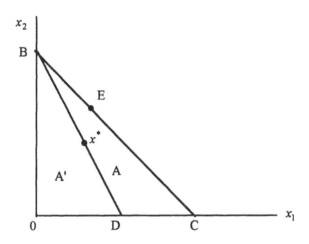

Let the area OBC represent the symmetric bargaining set A, of which the line BC represents the Pareto efficient boundary of the set A. Let $\mu(A,0) = (x_1^*, x_2^*)$ be a solution of the bargaining problem that satisfies the three axioms.

Since x^* satisfies the axiom of feasibility and it is individually rational, we must have $x^* > 0$. Suppose that the solution x^*, which satisfies the three axioms, does not lie on BC. Let BD be the line passing through the point B and x^*. Then the area OBD forms a subset of the area OBC. Let us call it the set A'. The set A' contains both points, the disagreement point 0 and the solution point x^*, and is a subset of the set A. Therefore, by the axiom of independence, $\mu(A',0) = x^*$.

154

Let α be an affine transformation which maps $0 \to 0$, $B \to B$ and $D \to C$. Then, by similarity αx^* lies on BC, it follows that $\alpha x^* \neq x^*$. By invariance, $\mu(\alpha A',0) = \alpha\mu(A',0) = \alpha x^*$. But, since $\alpha A' = A$, therefore, $\mu(\alpha A',0) = \mu(A,0) = x^*$. But this is a contradiction and therefore, x^* lies on BC, and so it is efficient.

(ii)   Let E be the point on BC which represents the solution vector x^*. Choose τ so that

$$\tau = \frac{BE}{BC}.$$

Since BC is a 45 degree line, it follows that $x_1^* = \tau$ and $x_2^* = 1 - \tau$.

(iii)   For τ given by (ii), a straightforward solution of the following maxmization problem

$$\max \quad x_1^\tau x_2^{(1-\tau)} \qquad \text{subject to} \qquad x_1 + x_2 = 1$$

is that $x_1^* = \tau$ and $x_2^* = 1 - \tau$.

To show the converse we will reverse the steps. For a given τ, x^* solves

$$\max \quad x_1^\tau x_2^{(1-\tau)} \qquad \text{subject to} \qquad x_1 + x_2 = 1$$

implies that $x_1^* = \tau$ and $x_2^* = 1 - \tau$.

Since the Pareto efficient boundary of the bargaining set A is a subset of the points satisfying $x_1 + x_2 = 1$, and x^* satisfies this equation, it is efficient. Obviously, $x^* > 0$ for $\tau \in (0,1)$, therefore it is individually rational and feasible.

Since the first order condition of the maximization problem remains unaltered by any positive affine transformation of the set A and the maximand, the solution x^*, therefore, satisfies the axiom of invariance.

Since, x^* is also the maximizer of $x_1^\tau x_2^{(1-\tau)}$ over any subset of the feasible set A that also contains x^* and 0, therefore, it satisfies the axiom of independence. Moreover, since the maximand is concave and the feasible set is compact and convex, the solution x^* is unique.   Q. E. D.

The major point of the lemma is that every solution to a bargaining game (A,0) that satisfies the three axioms induces a distribution parameter $\tau \in (0,1)$, and every distribution parameter induces a solution to the bargaining problem (A,0) that satisfies the three axioms. For a given $\tau \in (0,1)$, the induced solution to

155

the bargaining problem is unique, whereas there can be many solutions that satisfy the three axioms and induce many values of τ such that $\tau \in (0,1)$. In fact, all points on the boundary of the feasible set satisfy the three axioms and are potential solutions to the bargaining problem $(A,0)$.

The minimum information, in addition to $(A,0)$, required to obtain a unique solution is the ratio at which the players will receive their payoffs at the solution to the bargaining problem $(A,0)$. If this ratio, say $x_1 / x_2 = \delta$, is institutionally provided, then those points in the set A that lie on the ray of slope equal to δ become potential solution points. It is useful to note that if other axioms are not satisfied, then the condition that payoffs be divided according to δ alone is not sufficient to yield a unique outcome of the bargaining. For each $\delta > 0$, we can define a unique $\tau = \delta / (1+\delta) \in (0,1)$.

Since all solutions satisfying the three axioms lie on the efficient frontier, the intersection of the ray with the efficient boundary of the set A constitutes the unique solution to the bargaining problem $(A,0)$ for a given value of δ. Note that $\delta = 1$ yields the original Nash solution.

Appendix-6C: Proof of Theorem 6.4

Theorem 6.4   *For any bargaining problem* $(\mathfrak{R}, \Pi^d, \Theta)$ *in a tariff game, if the fear functions are well defined, the following statements are equivalent:*

(i) $\overline{P}_1 = \underset{\Pi(P_1) \in \mathfrak{R}}{\arg\max} \; \left[\Pi_1(P_1) - \Pi_1^d\right]^{\Theta_1} \left[\Pi_2(P_1) - \Pi_2^d\right]^{\Theta_2}$. *That is,* $\overline{P}_1$ *maximizes the generalized Nash product over the bargaining set.*

(ii) $\mu(\mathfrak{R}, \Pi^d, \Theta) = \Pi(\overline{P}_1)$, *that is* P_1 *is the price at the generalized Nash solution to the bargaining game* $(\mathfrak{R}, \Pi^d, \Theta)$ *with bargaining power distribution* Θ *that satisfies the Axioms 1-3.*

Proof: We have to show that (i) holds if and only if (ii) holds. Since the implication of (ii) by (i) is straightforward, we will show that (ii) implies (i).

Let us assume that $\overline{\Pi} = \Pi(\overline{P}_1)$ is the payoff combination that maximizes the generalized Nash product over the bargaining set $\mathfrak{R}$. Assume that $\mu(\mathfrak{R}, \Pi^d, \Theta)$ is the solution of the bargaining problem that satisfies Axioms 1-3. We have to show that $\mu(\mathfrak{R}, \Pi^d, \Theta) = \Pi(\overline{P}_1)$.

Let us define a set $\widetilde{\mathfrak{R}}$ such that

$$\widetilde{\mathfrak{R}} = \left\{ (\widetilde{\Pi}_1, \widetilde{\Pi}_2) \,\middle|\, \widetilde{\Pi}_i = \Theta_i \left(\frac{\Pi_i - \Pi_i^d}{\overline{\Pi}_i - \Pi_i^d} \right); \Pi \in \mathfrak{R} \right\}$$

It can be seen that $\widetilde{\mathfrak{R}}$ is obtained from $\mathfrak{R}$ by a positive affine transformation. The point $\overline{\Pi} \in \mathfrak{R}$ is transformed into $\Theta \in \widetilde{\mathfrak{R}}$, and $\Pi^d \in \mathfrak{R}$ is transformed into $0 \in \widetilde{\mathfrak{R}}$. We know that the payoff that maximizes the generalized Nash product is invariant under such transformations, therefore Θ solves the problem

$$\max_{\widetilde{\Pi} \in \widetilde{\mathfrak{R}}} \widetilde{\Pi}_1^{\Theta_1} \widetilde{\Pi}_2^{\Theta_2}.$$

We are done, if we can show that

$$\mu(\widetilde{\mathfrak{R}}, 0, \Theta) = \Theta.$$

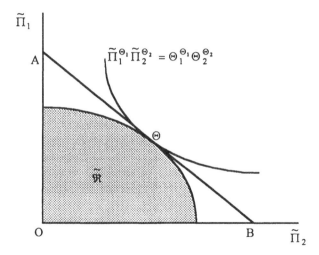

Since better -than -Θ set and the set $\widetilde{\mathfrak{R}}$ are both convex, Θ is in both the sets, hence by the separating hyper plane theorem, there is a unique hyper plane passing through Θ that is tangent to both the sets at Θ. AB is that line (hyper plane)

The slope of the generalized Nash product curve passing through Θ is given by

$$\frac{d\widetilde{\Pi}_1}{d\widetilde{\Pi}_2} = -\frac{\Theta_2}{\Theta_1} \cdot \frac{\widetilde{\Pi}_1}{\widetilde{\Pi}_2}.$$

Therefore, the slope of the tangent AB that passes through the point $(\widetilde{\Pi}_1, \widetilde{\Pi}_2) = (\Theta_1, \Theta_2)$ is -1.

Now, construct a set H of all points from the area OAB. Then the set H is symmetric. Therefore, by Lemma 6.1 $\mu(H,0,\Theta) = \Theta$.

But, since $\Theta \in \tilde{\Re} \subset H$, and the solution μ is independent of irrelevant alternatives, therefore, $\mu(\tilde{\Re},0,\Theta) = \Theta$. Now by applying inverse positive affine transformation, using the invariance property of μ, we can see that

$$\mu(\Re, \Pi^d, \Theta) = \Pi(\overline{P_1}).$$

Hence the condition (ii) implies the condition (i).   Q. E. D.

Notes

1   For analytical similarity between the choices of a support-maximizing government and a welfare maximizing government see Baldwin (1987).

2   It is very important to note that this study assumes that players are interested in maximization of the sectoral rents. How do the players use their rental income - whether they spend all in the consumption of the two goods or save and invest - is not analysed here. It is, in turn, assumed that the owners of the specific factors would behave nonstrategically as consumers.

This stylization implies that the two players bargain in terms of rental payoffs, or in terms of relative price or in terms of tariff rate but not in terms of utilities as the standard Nash bargaining process is formulated. In this sense the bargaining game that is studied here is an adapted version of the standard Nash bargaining game. Binmore (1987c) has studied such an adapted game for an exchange economy, and he preferred to call it a bartering game. In his bartering game players communicate not in terms of utilities but in terms of real quantities of commodities that are to be traded. We follow Binmore in this respect because it is more sensible to assume that players have perfect information on each other's rental prospects at different prices than to assume that they know each other's rental prospects and the utilities of the rental incomes at various prices as well. Furthermore, the assumption that production sectors strive for maximization of profit is fairly standard, and is quite common in studies of labour market that use bargain theoretic approach (for example, Datt, 1989).

3   The problem of identifying the disagreement payoffs will be dealt in the next chapter.

4   In fact, Harsanyi (1963) has shown quite generally that there exists an optimal threat strategy combination such that if the cooperation breaks down each of the player will find it best to play against the other player(s)

5   A map α is called an increasing affine transformation, if $\alpha(y) = ay + b$ where $a>0$ and b is any real number.

6   Note that the numerical value of rental income can be changed by changing the unit of output measurement, and a change in the origin can be brought by effecting a lump sum income transfer to and from a sector. We know that a lump sum tax, for example, does not affect the output decision of a production sector, whereas it affects the break even point. It is implicitly assumed that the lump sum taxes are never greater than the disagreement payoffs. This assumption is necessary to ensure that specialization will not be induced by the imposition of lump sum taxes or by the presence of some fixed costs. This requirement slightly restricts the nature of affine transformation that can be applied when we are dealing with rental income rather than 'utilities'. So long as the proofs of the theorems are concerned it is of no consequence.

7   Nash, in his 1950 paper, expressed this assumption explicitly, which he rejected in the 1953 paper.

8   Further references of the works that have independently obtained asymmetric Nash bargaining solutions can be found in Binmore (1987d: p.94).

9   In a 2-person case the theorem was first proved by Kalai (1977a).

10 Nash's solution to any arbitrary bargaining problem can be obtained easily using this property of the underlying symmetric bargaining problem.

11 Axiom 2 requires a different treatment. It should be read as follows: For any increasing affine transformation $\alpha: R^2 \to R^2$

$$\mu(\alpha \, \Re, \alpha \, \Pi^d, \Theta) = \alpha\mu(\Re, \Pi^d, \Theta) \, .$$

This is because bargaining power distribution is independent of unit of measurement of rental income. It has been normalized separately.

12 Otherwise the solution will not be unique. See Binmore (1987b).

13 Further details can be found in Harsanyi (1956), Roth (1979: 28-31).

14 To each player we can always take an offer of the other party as mutually acceptable price. Because, it will be agreed upon if the player in question accepts it.

15 See also Roth (1979) for similar arguments and definitions in terms of utilities.

16 In Aumann and Kurz (1977a) and Roth (1979) an equation similar to the equation (6.8) is directly used to define the fear of ruin that is later on shown to be related with the probabilistic measure of boldness. The order has been reversed in the present study because the concept of fear of ruin or boldness is best expressed in the belief system of the player. In any case the implication to the overall analysis is unchanged.

17 It is implicitly assumed that the length of a bargaining period depends on the size of price increase demanded. Insistence on a larger price increase raises the likelihood that the opponent will reject it and a disagreement results. If the opponent does not disagree, he will certainly take longer time in haggling

before he accepts it. But this increases the chance that a third party will intervene and the outcome will be the disagreement.

A slight abuse of notation may require some clarification. The relevant value of ΔP_1 is positive for player 1 and negative for player 2. That is, player 1 is interested in price increases and player 2 is interested in decreases of the relative price of commodity 1. By considering only the absolute value of ΔP_1 we can reduce unnecessary repetition of analogous equations. This is what is done here.

18 In Svejnar (1986) this axiom has been called "equality of fear of disagreement relative to bargaining power".

19 See Appendix-6C for (ii) implies (i).

20 This interpretation of endogenous bargaining power is consistent with Beghin and Karp's explanation endogenous bargaining power. See Beghin and Karp (1991), footnote 4.

7 A general equilibrium model of a political economy and comparative static results

Introduction

In Chapter 2, we reviewed a selection of the existing theories of tariff determination to examine the current state-of-the-art in modelling the tariff formation process. The review indicated that there exists a substantial body of literature, which subscribes to the view that tariffs may consistently be viewed as an outcome of simultaneous equilibrium in the political as well as economic spheres of the political economy. The tariff formation process in the political sphere, however, was generally portrayed as a noncooperative game in which the policy maker as well as the private interest groups behaved strategically to further their own self-interests. Following this literature we started with modelling the economic sphere of a small open political economy.

In Chapter 3, a stylized 2-sector, 3-factor policy exogenous model was constructed to describe an equilibrium in the economic sphere of a political economy. From this model a rent transformation frontier describing a locus of equilibrium combinations of rental incomes at different tariff rates was derived in Chapter 4. It showed that the owners of specific factors have conflicting interests on the government's choice of the tariff rate and therefore served as an interface between the economic and the political spheres of the political economy.

Following previous work, we studied the strategic interaction between the government and private interest groups in Chapter 5. We argued that the government, as a Stackelberg leader, can extract the maximum political support for itself if it offers a lobbying-sensitive pricing function to the interest groups. The owners of specific factors (the interest groups) would then play a noncooperative tariff game by choosing the amount of their predatory lobbying expenditure, to maximize their own rental income. It was shown that at least one noncooperative Nash equilibrium exists in such political economies; and at all Nash equilibria each player spends a non-zero amount of resource in lobbying the government. Moreover, if the government is constrained by financing requirements, then a positive tariff rate emerges at all Nash equilibria of the game. All of these results together imply that both players are better off in cooperation than in non-cooperation, because they both can save resources spent in lobbying the government.

We, therefore, viewed the tariff-setting game in a cooperative framework and analyzed the problem of tariff determination as a Nash bargaining problem in Chapter 6. There we viewed all political activities as integral parts of the bargaining process and derived the necessary and sufficient condition for a generalized Nash solution to the bargaining problem of the underlying tariff game.

In this chapter we shall combine the results obtained in previous chapters and derive a set of conditions that characterizes the equilibrium in a tariff (policy)-endogenous general equilibrium model (PEGEM) of a small open political economy. In particular, the condition describing the bargaining equilibrium in the tariff game, which is the condition for an equilibrium in the political sphere, is combined with the conditions of equilibrium in the economic sphere to describe the general equilibrium in the political economy. The political economy, which is in a state of general equilibrium, is then subjected to comparative static experiments to analyze the (comparative static) responses of the bargained tariff rate to various exogenous shocks.

This chapter is organised into seven sections. The first section describes the full model by collecting all the equilibrium conditions. The second section discusses the problems concerned with the identification of the disagreement payoffs. We argue that the concept of minimum expectation, suggested by Roth (1977), can be employed as a reference point in bargaining to operationalize the concept of disagreement.

In section three we obtain the players' minimum expectation in the tariff game under two different government types - coercive and support maximizing. First, we consider a coercive-type government, which rules by force, and derive players' minimum expectation under this regime. It is argued that minimum expectation of each player, in this case, is zero. We then consider the case with a support maximizing government, which offers a pricing function that satisfies assumptions (P1)-(P3), and (P5). We argue that, in this case, the minimum expectation of the exporting sector (player 2) is the payoff at the autarkic equilibrium, and the minimum expectation of the import-competing sector (player 1) is the payoff at the free trade equilibrium. This completes the groundwork to operationalize the PEGEM.

The comparative static responses of the bargained tariff rate are derived in section four. First, we derive and explain the comparative static results under the assumption that the government is coercive. The results are unambiguous. Intuitive explanations of these results are provided with geometric illustrations. With a support-maximizing government the response of the bargained tariff rate, however, becomes ambiguous.

Section five summarizes the chapter. The difficulties we faced in obtaining clear-cut analytical results highlight the necessity for numerical simulations of the model which is deferred until the next chapter.

7.1 The PEGEM: A policy-endogenous general equilibrium model

We recall from the previous chapter that the necessary and sufficient condition for the generalized Nash solution to the bargaining problem in the tariff game is given by

$$
\frac{\Pi_1 - \Pi_1^d}{\Pi_2 - \Pi_2^d} = -\frac{\Theta_1}{\Theta_2} \frac{d\Pi_1}{d\Pi_2}\bigg|_{RTF}.
\tag{6.25}
$$

where $\Pi_i = K_i \tilde{R}_i$, is the rental income of sector i in units of own-commodity. We normalize capital stocks by setting $K_1 = K_2 = 1$. With this normalization the rental rate at the initial equilibrium equals the rental income of each sector.

We can obtain from equation (4.8) that the slope of the RTF is given by

$$
\frac{d\Pi_1}{d\Pi_2}\bigg|_{RTF} = \frac{K_1}{K_2} \frac{d\tilde{R}_1}{dR_2} = -\frac{K_1 \tilde{R}_1}{K_2 R_2}\left(\frac{\lambda_2 \sigma_2 S_{L1}}{\lambda_1 \sigma_1 S_{L2}}\right) = -\frac{\Pi_1}{\Pi_2}\left(\frac{\lambda_2 \sigma_2 S_{L1}}{\lambda_1 \sigma_1 S_{L2}}\right).
\tag{7.1}
$$

The right hand side of equation (7.1) can be simplified by noting $\lambda_i = L_i / L$ is the share of sector i in the total employment of labour, and the distributive share of labour $S_{Li} = WL_i / P_i Y_i$, where $P_2 = 1$ by the choice of the numeraire. Using these definitions, equation (7.1) can be rewritten as

$$
\frac{d\Pi_1}{d\Pi_2}\bigg|_{RTF} = -\frac{\Pi_1}{\Pi_2}\left(\frac{\sigma_2 Y_2}{\sigma_1 Y_1 P_1}\right).
\tag{7.2}
$$

Alternately, we can also write

$$
\frac{d\Pi_1}{d\Pi_2}\bigg|_{RTF} = -\frac{\sigma_2 S_{K1}}{\sigma_1 S_{K2} P_1}
\tag{7.3}
$$

where, $S_{Ki} = \Pi_i / Y_i$ is the distributive share of capital in sectoral output in each sector i.

Now substituting the expression for the slope of the RTF from equation (7.2) into equation (6.25) we get

$$\frac{\Pi_1 - \Pi_1^d}{\Pi_2 - \Pi_2^d} = \frac{\Theta_1}{\Theta_2} \frac{\Pi_1}{\Pi_2} \left(\frac{\sigma_2 Y_2}{\sigma_1 Y_1 P_1} \right). \tag{7.4}$$

Alternately, the equation (7.4) can also be written as

$$\frac{\Pi_1 - \Pi_1^d}{\Pi_2 - \Pi_2^d} = \frac{\Theta_1}{\Theta_2} \left(\frac{\sigma_2 S_{K1}}{\sigma_1 S_{K2} P_1} \right). \tag{7.5}$$

This condition can be explained as follows. We know that Π_1 is a strictly increasing, and Π_2 is a strictly decreasing function of P_1, the left-hand side of equation (7.5) is a strictly increasing function of P_1 for a given value of Π^d. Given that $\sigma_1 \geq 1$ and $\sigma_2 \geq 1$, we also know that S_{K1} is a nonincreasing function of P_1, and S_{K2} is a nondecreasing (constant in the Cobb-Douglas case) function of P_1. Therefore, for a given distribution of bargaining power, the right-hand side of equation (7.5) is a strictly decreasing function of P_1. Thus, a unique domestic relative price satisfies, as discussed in the previous chapter, the necessary and sufficient condition for the solution to the bargaining problem. A non-unique situation may arise if σ_1 is close to zero and σ_2 is very large.

Now we combine equation (7.4) with the policy-exogenous general equilibrium model developed in Chapter 3. Recalling equations from Table 3.2, the system of equations that describes the general equilibrium of the political economy can be written as in the following Table 7.1.

Table 7.1 describes a system of 15 equations in 15 endogenous variables, including the rationalized tariff rate. For given values of exogenous variables and parameters the system, in principle, can be solved for the 15 endogenous variables. The solution vector of endogenous variables describes the full equilibrium of the politico-economic system of the stylized economy.

This system demands more information than a conventional policy-exogenous CGE model does. In addition to the information required by a conventional CGE model, it requires information on the distribution of the players' bargaining powers and information on disagreement payoffs, Π^d. With respect to the distribution of bargaining powers, we make the following assumption.

Assumption 7.1 *The distribution of bargaining power between the players is exogenously given and it is unaffected by small changes in the values of exogenous variables.*

Table 7.1
**PEGEM: A policy (tariff) endogenous general equilibrium model
of a small open political economy**

The political sphere

Condition for bargaining equilibrium:

$$\frac{\Pi_1 - \Pi_1^d}{\Pi_2 - \Pi_2^d} = \frac{\Theta_1}{\Theta_2} \frac{\Pi_1}{\Pi_2} \left(\frac{\sigma_2 Y_2}{\sigma_1 Y_1 P_1} \right). \tag{7.4}$$

Real rental income:

$$\Pi_i = K_i R_i / P_i, \qquad\qquad i=1,2. \tag{7.6}$$

The economic sphere

The supply functions of domestic production sectors:

$$Y_j = K_j \beta_j^{-1/\rho_j} \left[1 - \alpha_j^{1/(1+\rho_j)} \left(W / P_j \right)^{\rho_j/(1+\rho_j)} \right]^{1/\rho_j}; \qquad j=1,2. \tag{3.11}$$

Consumer demand functions:

$$C_j = (\delta_j / P_j) \sum_{i=1}^{2} (P_i Y_i + \Phi T_i P_i^* M_i); \qquad j=1,2. \tag{3.19}$$

Equilibrium in the market of good 1:

$$C_1 = Y_1 + M_1. \tag{3.21}$$

Domestic price determination:

$$P_1 = P_1^* (1 + T_1^R). \tag{3.26}$$

Trade balance constraint:

$$P_1^* M_1 + P_2^* M_2 = 0. \tag{3.23}$$

Sectoral labour demand:

$$L_j = K_j \alpha_j^{1/(1+\rho_j)} \beta_j^{-1/\rho_j} \left[\left(P_j / W \right)^{\rho_j/(1+\rho_j)} - \alpha_j^{1/(1+\rho_j)} \right]^{1/\rho_j}; \ j = 1,2. \tag{3.14}$$

Labour market equilibrium:

$$L = \sum_{j=1}^{2} L_j. \tag{3.15}$$

Virtual rental rates:

$$R_j = \beta_j^{-1/\rho_j} \left(P_j^{\rho_j/(1+\rho_j)} - \alpha_j^{1/(1+\rho_j)} W^{\rho_j/(1+\rho_j)} \right)^{(1+\rho_j)/\rho_j}; \ j = 1,2. \tag{3.12}$$

Total number of equations 15.

Table 7.1 (continued)

List of endogenous variables:

Π_j $j = 1,2.$: 2 Sectoral rental incomes

Y_j $j = 1,2.$: 2 Sectoral outputs

C_j $j = 1,2.$: 2 Domestic demands

M_i $i = 1,2.$: 2 Net import quantities

L_j $j = 1,2.$: 2 Sectoral employment of labour

R_j $j = 1,2.$: 2 Sectoral rental rates in units of commodity 2

W : 1 Wage rate in units of commodity 2

P_1 : 1 Price of commodity 1 in units of commodity 2

T_1^R : 1 Rationalized tariff rate

Total number of endogenous variables: 15.

List of exogenous variables:

Π_j^d $j = 1,2.$: 2 Disagreement payoffs

K_j $j = 1,2.$: 2 Endowments of sector specific capital stocks

L : 1 Endowment of Labour in the economy

P_1^* : 1 International relative price of commodity 1

P_2 : Price of the numeraire commodity (always unity).

Total number of exogenous variables: 7.

Parameters:

σ_j $j = 1,2.$: 2 Elasticities of factor substitution

δ_j $j = 1,2.$: 2 Budget share parameter of C-D utility function

α_j, β_j $j = 1,2.$: 4 Distributive parameters of CES production functions

Θ_1, Θ_2 : 2 Parameters reflecting the bargaining power of players

In Chapter 6, it was argued that bargaining power is affected by factors such as the time-preference rates of the players, their subjective probability that a third party will snatch the bargaining opportunity and so on. In this light, Assumption 7.1 does not seem to be too restrictive. More importantly, it paves a clear way towards the comparative static analysis of the PEGEM. We will now move to identify disagreement payoffs to the players which is the only additional information required by the PEGEM compared to the PXGEM.

7.2 Identification of disagreement payoffs

A disagreement payoff is the payoff that a player will receive if players fail to reach an agreement. A natural candidate for this is the payoff at a noncooperative Nash equilibrium of the tariff game. But, there are two problems which make the use of payoffs at a noncooperative Nash equilibrium less attractive. First, the possibility of multiple Nash equilibria can not be dismissed a priori, and there seems no clear way of identifying which one of them will be attained if there is a disagreement. Second, even if there are reasons to believe that a unique Nash equilibrium will be attained, the government's pricing function has to be specified before any Nash equilibrium can be computed. This would further require a good knowledge of the government's political support function, which is not yet fully understood.

The solution to the bargaining problem discussed in Chapter 6, however, is based on given disagreement payoffs. So long as these are known before the bargaining game is played, any arbitrary pair of payoffs can be a candidate for the disagreement payoffs. All results obtained in Chapter 6 remain valid, since none of them is based on the assumption that the disagreement payoff is a noncooperative Nash solution.

A particularly interesting alternative candidate for the disagreement payoff is the minimum expectation payoff proposed by Roth (1977). Roth's concept of minimum expectation can be defined in the following way.

Let $\overline{\mathfrak{R}}$ be the set of all feasible payoff combinations. For each player i, define

$$\Pi_i^{\max} = \max\left\{ \Pi_i \,\middle|\, (\Pi_i, \Pi_{-i}) \in \overline{\mathfrak{R}} \right\}; \text{ and}$$

$$\Pi_i^{\min} = \max\left\{ \Pi_i \,\middle|\, (\Pi_i, \Pi_{-i}^{\max}) \in \overline{\mathfrak{R}} \right\}.$$

Definition 7.1 **(*minimum expectation*).** *The payoff combination* $\Pi^{\min} \equiv (\Pi_1^{\min}, \Pi_2^{\min})$ *represents the minimum expectation of the players in cooperation. The payoff combination* $\Pi^{\max} \equiv (\Pi_1^{\max}, \Pi_2^{\max})$, *which is also called* *the ideal point, represents the aspiration levels of the players in cooperation* (see Figure 7.1).[1]

One attractive feature of the point of minimum expectation is that it represents the payoff to each player when the bargaining opponent has been able to secure the best feasible outcome for herself, say by forming a coalition with the government or by pre-emptive lobbying. In other words, for each player, the payoff combination Π^{min} corresponds to the opponent's dictatorial solution. The payoff combination Π^{min} therefore represents the worst outcome to each player.

Roth (1977) has shown that the Nash solution to the class of bargaining problems in which the disagreement payoff is given by Π^{min} satisfies all the axioms as satisfied by the original Nash solution. The only difference between the two is that Nash's solution is independent of irrelevant alternatives (axiom of independence) other than the disagreement point, whereas the new solution will be independent of irrelevant alternatives other than the point of minimum expectation.

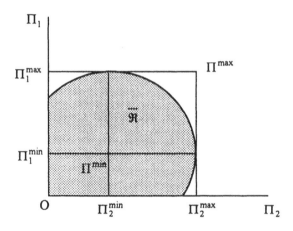

Figure 7.1   The point of minimum expectation

Thomson (1981) has argued that the disagreement point in a bargaining problem simply serves as a reference point to which players find it natural to compare any proposed compromise. He has suggested several possible candidates for such a reference point. However, requiring that the point satisfy some desirable properties can considerably shorten the list of reference points. One such property, as suggested by Thomson, is that the point of reference be sensitive to changes in the set of feasible outcomes. In this respect the point of minimum expectation, suggested by Roth, displays another attractive feature that is not possessed by other points like the status quo - the point of minimum expectation could be changed by changes in the boundary of the feasible set.

Furthermore, Thomson also proposed the following two essential properties of a reference point:[2]

1. That it be invariant with respect to positive affine transformations; and

2. That it be invariant with respect to symmetrization of almost symmetric bargaining problems.

Thomson has found (in his Lemma 2) that the point of minimum expectation satisfies the two desirable properties of a reference point.[3]

It is important to keep in mind that the solution to a bargaining problem based on the minimum expectation payoffs is not necessarily equal to the Nash solution if the true disagreement payoffs are already known (for example, the status quo or zero) and are different from the minimum expectation payoffs. Therefore, a solution based on player's minimum expectations yields, at best, a Nash-like solution to a bargaining problem, which satisfies axioms similar to those as satisfied by the Nash solution.

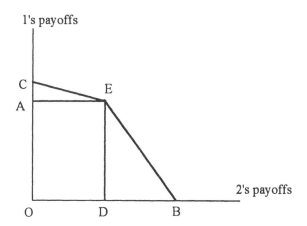

Figure 7.2   Discontinuity of the point of minimum expectation

In general, the operational definition of the disagreement payoffs in the theory of bargaining has remained unclear. Identification of the disagreement payoffs has, therefore, been suggested as a matter of modelling judgement (Binmore, Rubinstein, and Wolinsky, 1986). The payoff at the minimum expectation appears to be a natural candidate for the disagreement payoffs because it possesses desirable properties of a reference point and the concept of minimum expectation itself is well defined and operational.

However, the point of minimum expectation, as pointed out by Thomson, has a serious limitation that it is *not always* continuous in the feasible region. A small change in the feasible region, in some cases, may lead to radical changes in the point of minimum expectation. Consider Figure 7.2, for example.

Suppose that the initial set of feasible outcomes is OAEB. Then player 1's minimum expectation is 0, and player 2's minimum expectation is OD. Now if the set of feasible outcomes is expanded to OCEB, (point C very close to point A) then the minimum expectation of each player will be zero. Therefore, with a small increase in the feasible set the point of minimum expectation moved from D to the origin. If the payoff at the point of minimum expectation is used as the disagreement payoff, the bargaining solution may also change abruptly for small changes in the set of feasible outcomes. This situation is also not very satisfactory, particularly for the validity of comparative static results. The continuity of the point of minimum expectation with respect to the feasible set in the tariff game is, therefore, worth examining.

7.3 Minimum expectation in the tariff game

In this section we derive expressions for the minimum expectation payoffs of the players under two different political environments. First, we consider a special case in which the government rules by force and then we consider the case in which the government is based on political supports.

In the first case we allow for the possibility that any of the players may form a coalition with the government and chose a policy that best suits the winning player. The government balances its budget, if necessary, by taxing the losing player and other nonstrategic agents in the economy. We shall call this type of government a coercive government and obtain players' minimum expectations under it.[4]

In the case of a support maximizing government we recall from Chapter 5 that it offers a pricing function satisfying properties (P1)-(P3) and (P5) if cooperation breaks down in the political sphere. We shall call this type of government a popular government, and obtain players' minimum expectation under it.

7.3.1   Minimum expectation under a coercive government: a special case

If a player fails to form a coalition with the 'coercive' government, for whatever the reason, then the result could be that his rental income is taxed to sustain the price that benefits the winning player most. This means that the worst outcome in disagreement would require a player to surrender all of his rental income to finance the government's budget deficit created by the price which is most favourable to his opponent. This in turn implies that, given that they both do not know (before the game is played) who will be the loser, the payoff at the minimum expectation of each player under a coercive government is zero. Therefore, we write

$$\Pi^{min} = (0,0) \, . \tag{7.7}$$

It is interesting to note that the point of minimum expectation, in this case, has been located without first locating the aspiration level of the players.

Continuity of the point of minimum expectation in this case is, therefore, not a problem at all since the point of minimum expectation, under coercive behaviour of the government, does not change as the RTF shifts due to changes in the factor endowments. It, nevertheless, loses its sensitivity with respect to changes in the boundary of the feasible (or the bargaining) set.

The case with $\Pi^d = \Pi^{min} = (0,0)$ is interesting for three reasons. First, it greatly simplifies the model and analytical results are possible. It can illustrate the mechanism of endogenous determination of the tariff rate. Second, it corresponds to a *potentially* dictatorial type of government. The results, therefore, will show the behaviour of bargained tariff rates under a particular political environment where the government can be captured by one of the bargaining parties, if no agreement is reached during the bargaining process. Third, more interestingly, $\Pi^d = 0$ corresponds to Brock, Magee, and Young's *economic black hole* and could be considered as the worst possible noncooperative Nash equilibrium outcome in the tariff game.[5]

7.3.2   Minimum expectation under a support-maximizing government

It follows from Definition 7.1 that location of the point of minimum expectation requires a knowledge of the aspiration level (ideal point) of the players. In the tariff game, where players are attempting to maximize the rental incomes, it is natural to think that the best outcome for each player is attained when the employment of labour (the mobile factor) is completely specialized in his favour. In other words, player 1 would aspire to a tariff rate that eliminates employment of labour in the exporting sector and player 2 would aspire for a tariff rate that eliminates the employment of labour in the import competing sector.[6]

A tariff rate, however, will require a complementary financing policy if it is not self-financing. Rational players will take into account the effects of such policies on their own payoffs while determining their aspiration levels. For example, player 1 may not like to push for a domestic relative price that is higher than that it would be at the autarky even though it implies a higher rental income, if she has to bear all the subsidy cost. This is equivalent to subsidizing her production out of her own rental income. The payoffs at such prices will be correspondingly less than the rental incomes by the amount of subsidy cost. Nevertheless, player 1 would certainly prefer to have such a higher-than-autarky price if taxing someone else in the economy finances it. Symmetric arguments can be made for player 2 - the exporting sector.

In the model studied here, the tariff revenue is transferred to the national consumer (see equation (3.19) in Table 7.1), which encompasses the government, owners of the sector-specific factors, and the labourers. This means that even though the government's budget constraint is always satisfied (with the aggregate budget constraint) the extent of the gain from the tariff revenue or the cost of the subsidy to each individual player remains unknown. Thus the model can not yield payoffs to each player including his share in the tariff revenue or in the subsidy costs. As a result, the problem of identifying each player's aspiration level and, hence, the point of minimum expectation remains unresolved. We have considered this limitation as the price to be paid for the simplicity of the present model.[7]

Even in a model that attempts to address the distributional issues explicitly, numerous ways of financing a tariff induced budget or trade deficit can, nevertheless, be conceived. At least a somewhat arbitrary rule of distributing the tariff revenue needs to be spelled out clearly. Therefore, the point of minimum expectation or the aspiration level of the players can be identified only after the mode of balancing the government's budget is specified.

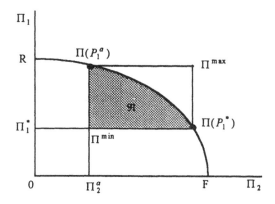

Figure 7.3   **Minimum expectation under a support-maximizing government**

In our case, however, the government is revenue constrained. It has been argued in Chapter 5 that such a government offers, in disagreement, a pricing function that satisfies property (P5). This means that the domestic relative price is bounded by the free-trade and the autarky relative prices.

This further means that the aspiration level of player 1 corresponds to the upper bound (at autarky) and the aspiration level of player 2 corresponds to the lower bound (at free trade) of P_1. This implies that player 1's (the import competing sector) minimum expectation is the payoff at the free trade price and player 2's (the exporting sector) minimum expectation is the payoff at the autarkic price (see Figure 7.3). Therefore, we write

$$\Pi^{min} = (\Pi_1^*, \Pi_2^a),\qquad\qquad\qquad (7.8)$$

where, Π_1^* is the rental income of the import-competing sector at the free-trade price, and Π_2^a is the rental income of the exporting sector at the autarky price.

The minimum expectation given by $\Pi^{min} = (\Pi_1^*, \Pi_2^a)$ has the following interesting properties:

1. It is well defined, because both free trade and autarky equilibria are well defined concepts and exist for all non-zero factor endowment configurations;

2. For a given factor endowment, payoffs at the free trade price and at the autarky price are unique;

3. It is a continuous function of the feasible set. The argument is as follows. Since production functions are continuously differentiable in factors, and commodity demand functions are differentiable in commodity prices, all rental functions and the autarky equilibrium price are continuous functions of factor endowments. This implies that the RTF is continuous in factor endowments, and therefore, the payoffs at the free trade price and at the autarky price are continuous in factor endowments. Therefore, $\Pi^{min} = (\Pi_1^*, \Pi_2^a)$ is continuous in the feasible set, since factor endowment changes are the only sources that bring change in the feasible set ;

4. It is sensitive to changes in the boundary of the feasible set; because as the RTF shifts with a change in factor endowment, so do the points of free-trade and autarkic equilibria.
5. Finally, it also satisfies Thomson's two desirable properties of a reference point, as referred above in Section 7.2.

Because of these properties we have decided to measure the disagreement payoffs by the payoffs at the minimum expectation of the players. However, depending upon the nature of the government payoffs at the minimum expectation of the players may be (0,0) or (Π_1^*, Π_2^a). Both cases will be considered in the comparative statics of the model. It is, however, useful to note that $\Pi^{min} = (\Pi_1^*, \Pi_2^a)$ is consistent with the support-maximizing behaviour of the government.

7.4 Comparative static results

7.4.1 Comparative static results I: coercive government

If the government does not care about its support because it is coercive or dictatorial, then the pricing function offered by the government may not satisfy some of the properties - especially, the bounded pricing and self-financing - listed in Chapter 5. The minimum expectation of a player in this political environment is straight forward and model solution quite simple compared to those in a political environment where the government is based on popular politics. For this reason we have considered the case of a coercive government first.

7.4.1.1 The PEGEM under a coercive government In this section, we derive a version of the PEGEM that is applicable under a coercive government. We know that under a coercive government the minimum expectation of players is at the origin. Therefore, substituting $\Pi^d = 0$ into equation (7.4) and solving for P_1 we obtain

$$P_1 = \left(\frac{\Theta_1 \sigma_2}{\Theta_2 \sigma_1}\right) \frac{Y_2}{Y_1}. \tag{7.9}$$

Linearizing equation (7.9) around the 'observed' full equilibrium we obtain

$$p_1^o = (\theta_1 - \theta_2) + (y_2^o - y_1^o). \tag{7.10}$$

At unchanged bargaining powers, whatever they may be, equation (7.10) reduces to

$$p_1^o = y_2^o - y_1^o. \tag{7.11}$$

This equation is exactly the same as the autarky rule of price that was obtained in Appendix-3B. It shows that if some exogenous shock leads the outputs of the two sectors, in the new equilibrium, to grow at different rates, then the relative price of the commodity growing at the faster rate will fall.[8]

In order to get a more precise meaning out of the equation (7.11) we combine it with the linearized version of the PXGEM described in Table 3.3. This yields the linearized version of the PEGEM that is listed in Table 7.2. Once again as in Chapter 3, we have ignored the four equations of the demand side. This has no consequence to our analysis, since in this political economy the supply side is still independent of the demand side of the economic sphere.

7.4.1.2 Responses of the tariff rate. The system described in Table 7.2 contains 9 equations in 9 endogenous variables, including the tariff rate. It can be solved for each of the endogenous variables in terms of changes in the exogenous variables to obtain the elasticity formulae.

In fact, part of the job has already been done in Chapter 3. Using equations (3.50), and (3.51) that yield the responses of sectoral output levels we can obtain the expression for the differential of the sectorial output growth as

$$
\begin{aligned}
y_2^o - y_1^o = \frac{1}{A^o} & \left[\left(\frac{\lambda_1^o \sigma_1}{S_{K1}^o} + \frac{\lambda_2^o \sigma_1 S_{L1}^o}{S_{K1}^o} + \lambda_2^o \sigma_2 \right) k_2 \right. \\
& - \left(\frac{\lambda_2^o \sigma_2}{S_{K2}^o} + \frac{\lambda_1^o \sigma_2 S_{L2}^o}{S_{K2}^o} + \lambda_1^o \sigma_1 \right) k_1 \\
& \left. - \left(\frac{\sigma_2 S_{L2}^o}{S_{K2}^o} \frac{\lambda_1^o \sigma_1}{S_{K1}^o} + \frac{\sigma_1 S_{L1}^o}{S_{K1}^o} \frac{\lambda_2^o \sigma_2}{S_{K2}^o} \right) p_1 + \left(\frac{\sigma_2 S_{L2}^o}{S_{K2}^o} - \frac{\sigma_1 S_{L1}^o}{S_{K1}^o} \right) l \right]
\end{aligned}
\tag{7.12}
$$

where, $A^o = \lambda_1^o \sigma_1 / S_{K1}^o + \lambda_2^o \sigma_2 / S_{K2}^o > 0$.

Solving equation (7.11) for p_1^o using equation (7.12) we get

$$
\begin{aligned}
p_1^o = B^{-1} & \left[\left(\frac{\lambda_1^o \sigma_1}{S_{K1}^o} + \frac{\lambda_2^o \sigma_1 S_{L1}^o}{S_{K1}^o} + \lambda_2^o \sigma_2 \right) k_2 \right. \\
& \left. - \left(\frac{\lambda_2^o \sigma_2}{S_{K2}^o} + \frac{\lambda_1^o \sigma_2 S_{L2}^o}{S_{K2}^o} + \lambda_1^o \sigma_1 \right) k_1 + \left(\frac{\sigma_2 S_{L2}^o}{S_{K2}^o} - \frac{\sigma_1 S_{L1}^o}{S_{K1}^o} \right) l \right];
\end{aligned}
\tag{7.13}
$$

Table 7.2
Linearized version of PEGEM: coercive government behaviour

The political sphere:

$$p_1^o = y_2^o - y_1^o.$$ (7.11)

The economic sphere:

The output supply functions:

$$y_j^o = k_j + \sigma_j \left(\frac{S_{Lj}^o}{S_{Kj}^o} \right)(p_j^o - w^o); \qquad\qquad j = 1, 2.$$ (3.36)

Labour demand functions:

$$l_j^o = k_j + \frac{\sigma_j}{S_{Kj}^o}(p_j^o - w^o); \qquad\qquad j = 1, 2.$$ (3.37)

The labour market equilibrium condition:

$$l = \sum_{j=1}^{2} \lambda_j^o l_j^o.$$ (3.38)

Sectoral rental rates:

$$r_j^o = \frac{1}{S_{Kj}^o}(p_j^o - S_{Lj}^o w^o); . \qquad\qquad j = 1, 2.$$ (3.39)

Price equations:

$$p_1^o = p_1^* + \tau^o t, \quad \text{and}$$ (3.40)

$$p_2^o = 0.$$ (3.41)

where, $B = A^o + \left(\dfrac{\sigma_2 S_{L2}^o}{S_{K2}^o} \dfrac{\lambda_1^o \sigma_1}{S_{K1}^o} + \dfrac{\sigma_1 S_{L1}^o}{S_{K1}^o} \dfrac{\lambda_2^o \sigma_2}{S_{K2}^o} \right) > 0$.

Recalling that the factor creating a wedge between the domestic relative price and the world relative price is the tariff rate (see equation (3.40) in Table 7.2) it follows from equation (7.13) that

$$\tau t = -p_1^* + B^{-1} \left[\left(\frac{\lambda_1^o \sigma_1}{S_{K1}^o} + \frac{\lambda_2^o \sigma_1 S_{L1}^o}{S_{K1}^o} + \lambda_2^o \sigma_2 \right) k_2 \right.$$

$$\left. - \left(\frac{\lambda_2^o \sigma_2}{S_{K2}^o} + \frac{\lambda_1^o \sigma_2 S_{L2}^o}{S_{K2}^o} + \lambda_1^o \sigma_1 \right) k_1 + \left(\frac{\sigma_2 S_{L2}^o}{S_{K2}^o} - \frac{\sigma_1 S_{L1}^o}{S_{K1}^o} \right) l \right]. \qquad (7.14)$$

Before we derive comparative static results from equation (7.14), we recall the definitions of some variables and parameters which it involves.

First, from equation (3.24) and (3.32) we know that $\tau = 1/(1 + T_1^R)$, where, $T_1^R = (T_1 - T_2)/(1 + T_2)$ is the rationalized tariff rate - a single tariff rate that is equivalent to the joint imposition of an import tax at rate T_1, and an export subsidy (tax if negative) at rate T_2; and $t = 100 \times dT_1^R$ is the change in the percentage point (not the percentage change) of the rationalized tariff rate.

The term $(1 + T_1^R)$ can be viewed as the rate of protection offered to the import competing sector, and therefore, the term τt, which represents the percentage change in $(1 + T_1^R)$, can also be viewed as the percentage change in the rate of protection awarded to the import competing sector. If, in the initial full equilibrium, $T_1^R > 0$ - that is, the economy was taxing trade - then we obtain $0 < \tau < 1$. Similarly, $\tau = 1$ for $T_1^R = 0$, and $\tau > 1$ for $-1 < T_1^R < 0$. If we exclude the possibility of subsidizing imports or taxing exports at rates greater than 100% as practically implausible, then the parameter τ is always positive.

Furthermore, the share parameters $\lambda_1, \lambda_2, S_{K1}, S_{K2}, S_{L1}$ and S_{L2} are always positive. Elasticities of factor substitution, σ_1 and σ_2, are also positive.

Now by setting any three of the four exogenous variables - p_1^*, k_1, k_2 and l, in turn equal to zero we can obtain the comparative static results as follows:

$$\frac{\tau t}{p_1^*} = -1 < 0; \qquad (7.15)$$

177

$$\frac{\tau t}{k_1} = -B^{-1}\left(\frac{\lambda_2^o \sigma_2}{S_{K2}^o} + \frac{\lambda_1^o \sigma_2 S_{L2}^o}{S_{K2}^o} + \lambda_1^o \sigma_1\right) < 0; \tag{7.16}$$

$$\frac{\tau t}{k_2} = B^{-1}\left(\frac{\lambda_1^o \sigma_1}{S_{K1}^o} + \frac{\lambda_2^o \sigma_1 S_{L1}^o}{S_{K1}^o} + \lambda_2^o \sigma_2\right) > 0; \text{ and} \tag{7.17}$$

$$\frac{\tau t}{l} = B^{-1}\left(\frac{\sigma_2 S_{L2}^o}{S_{K2}^o} - \frac{\sigma_1 S_{L1}^o}{S_{K1}^o}\right) \gtrless 0 \quad as \quad \frac{\sigma_2 S_{L2}^o}{S_{K2}^o} \gtrless \frac{\sigma_1 S_{L1}^o}{S_{K1}^o}. \tag{7.18}$$

These results can be summarized as follows. For small changes, other things remaining the same -

Result 7.1   Any change in the relative price of the import competing good in the world market is exactly offset by domestic tariff changes leaving the domestic relative price unchanged.

Result 7.2   If a sector experiences an exogenous increase in the stock of its specific factor, then the rate of protection awarded to this (growing) sector will decline and the rate of protection awarded to the other sector will rise.

Result 7.3   An exogenous increase in the supply of the mobile factor (labour) in the economy may lead to a fall or a rise in the rate of protection awarded to a sector depending on the relative ease of factor substitution and factor intensity between the two sectors.

7.4.1.3   Discussion of the result 7.1.   This result implies that if, say, the price of the domestic exportable rises in the world market then, *ceteris paribus*, either the export subsidy will fall or the import tax will increase to such an extent that the increase in the rationalized tariff rate will exactly offset the effect of the world price change on the domestic relative price. The domestic economy will be fully insulated against the terms of trade shocks. No reallocation of resources will take place. Why do we get this result?

Suppose that $\Pi(P_1^*)$ represent the distribution of rents at free trade, and $\Pi(P_1^o)$ represent the payoffs at the generalized Nash bargaining equilibrium. Then, at the domestic relative price P_1^o players' generalized fear of ruin are equal. Suppose further that, other things remaining the same, the price of the home exportable good rises in the world market to $\overline{P_1}^*$ such that $\overline{P_1}^* < P_1^*$.

At an unchanged tariff rate (policy) the relative price of the import competing good in the domestic market will fall at the same proportional rate as it did in the world market. Let the new domestic relative price be $\overline{P}_1$. Consequently, PXGEM predicts that the rental income of the import competing sector will fall and that of the exporting sector will rise compared to the initial equilibrium. Thus, the players will slide from the point $\Pi(P_1^o)$ to the point $\Pi(\overline{P}_1)$ along the RTF (see Figure 7.4). As a result, the gain of player 1 relative to the reference point (origin) declines, and that of player 2 increases.

We know that each player's fear of ruin (disagreement) depends directly on the size of the gain relative to the minimum expectation it follows that at $\overline{P}_1$ player 2 will be more fearful of player 1 declaring disagreement than player 1 fears of player 2 declaring disagreement.[9] To restore equality in players' generalized fear of ruin player 2's payoffs has to be reduced and that of player 1 has to raised by tariff changes. Therefore, in the new sequence of bargaining process prompted by the world price change, player 2 will ultimately concede, leading to a higher tariff rate in the new equilibrium.

The new tariff rate will be such that the induced domestic relative price remains unaffected, since the RTF and the level curves of the generalized Nash product are unaffected by changes in the international terms of trade, and therefore, the equilibrium point will also remain unaffected.

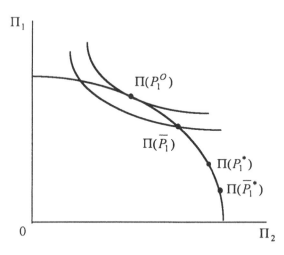

Figure 7.4   Bargained tariff rate and world price changes

179

7.4.1.4   Discussion of the result 7.2.   The following explanation can be given for the result that an exogenous increase in the stock of the specific factor in the import-competing sector would lead to a fall in the rationalized tariff rate and/or a rise in the export subsidy. The remaining results (the effect of an increase in the stock of the specific factor in the exporting sector, and the Result 7.3, that is the effect of an increase in the supply of the mobile factor) can be explained in a similar way.

In order to simplify the diagrammatic exposition we have assumed, in drawing Figure 7.5, that production functions are Cobb-Douglas in both sectors.

Suppose that E_o, the point of tangency of Nash product N_o to the rent transformation frontier CD, is the initial equilibrium of the tariff game. Suppose further that the capital stock in sector 1 increases exogenously. Then, the RTF will shift upwards to C'D. PXGEM predicts that, at an unchanged tariff rate and therefore at an unchanged domestic relative price, the output and rental income of sector 1 will increase and the output and rental income of sector 2 will fall. The point E_1 describes the combination of the rental incomes (in economic equilibrium) of the two sectors.

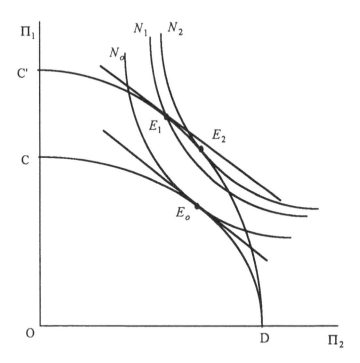

Figure 7.5   Effects on the bargained tariff rate of an increase in K_1

From equation (7.3) it can be seen that the slope of the RTF depends only on the relative price, since the distributive shares are constant under Cobb-Douglas production functions. This means that if point E_1 on C'D and point E_o on CD correspond to the same relative price, then the slopes of the respective frontiers at points E_o and E_1 should be equal. However, the absolute slope of the Nash product curve at E_1 will exceed the slope of the Nash product curve at E_o (by homotheticity,[10] see the curve labelled N_1). Therefore, the curve N_1 will not be tangent to the frontier C'D at E_1. However, their slopes indicate that at E_1 player 1's fear of ruin will exceed player 2's fear of ruin. Therefore, in the new bargaining process, induced by the shock, player 1 will concede and the tariff rate on imports of commodity 1 will fall, leading to a fall in the relative price of commodity 1 in the domestic market. The new bargained equilibrium will be attained at E_2 on C'D where both players will again be equally fearful of ruin.

The results, though consistent with general intuition in terms of the direction of responses, are very strong. In particular, the result that the domestic economy will be fully insulated against any terms of trade change in the world market can be debated. However, it should be noted that the results are subject to the assumption that the government is expected to be unconstrained with respect to tariff rates, and as a result the point of minimum expectation was the origin. The reference point, thus assumed, was insensitive to changes in the economic environment.

7.4.2   Comparative static results II: support-maximizing government

In this section we will study comparative-static properties of the bargained tariff rate under the assumption that the government is a support maximizer. It has been shown in the appendix to Chapter 5 that if the government is a support maximizer and satisfies self-financing constraint, then it will offer a pricing function satisfying properties (P1) - (P3), and (P5). In particular, property (P5) implies that the relative price offered by the government always falls between the autarkic and the free trade relative prices.

In the following subsections we first modify the model to incorporate the consequence on players' minimum expectation of this change in the assumption on the nature of the government. The model is then used to derive the comparative static response of the bargained tariff rate when the world price changes. Details of the other comparative static results are provided in the Appendix-7A.

7.4.2.1   The PEGEM under a support-maximizing government
As discussed in Section 7.3.2, with a support-maximizing government the payoff at the minimum expectation of the import competing sector will be equal to the payoff at the free-

trade price and the minimum expectation payoff of the exporting sector will be equal to the payoff at the autarkic price. That is, we have

$$\Pi^d = \Pi^{\min} = (\Pi_1^*, \Pi_2^a)$$

To keep the comparative-static analysis tractable and obtain analytical results, we assume that the production functions in both sectors are Cobb-Douglas (not necessarily identical). This assumption implies that $\sigma_1 = \sigma_2 = 1$, and all distributive shares will be constant at all equilibria. In particular, it can be seen from equations (3.28) and (3.29) that $S_{Ki} = \beta_i$, and $S_{Li} = \alpha_i$ for each sector i.

With these modifications the first-order condition of bargaining equilibrium (7.4) can be written as

$$\frac{\Pi_1 - \Pi_1^*}{\Pi_2 - \Pi_2^a} = \frac{\Pi_1}{\Pi_2} \frac{\Theta_1 Y_2}{\Theta_2 P_1 Y_1}. \tag{7.19}$$

Holding bargaining powers constant, equation (7.19) can be linearized and written in terms of percentage changes of the variables as

$$D_1(\pi_1^o - \pi_1^*) - D_2(\pi_2^o - \pi_2^a) = y_2^o - y_1^o - p_1^o \tag{7.20}$$

where,

$$D_1 = \frac{\Pi_1^*}{\Pi_1^o - \Pi_1^*} > 0, \text{ and} \tag{7.21}$$

$$D_2 = \frac{\Pi_2^a}{\Pi_2^o - \Pi_2^a} > 0. \tag{7.22}$$

Linearizing the equation (7.6), percentage changes in real rental incomes can be expressed as:

$$\pi_i^o = k_i + r_i^o - p_i^o \tag{7.23}$$

where it is understood that commodity 2 is the numeraire, and therefore, $p_2^o = 0$.

Table 7.3
Linearized version of the PEGEM under Cobb-Douglas
production functions and the self-financing assumption

The political sphere:

$$D_1(\pi_1^o - \pi_1^*) - D_2(\pi_2^o - \pi_2^a) = y_2^o - y_1^o - p_1^o. \tag{7.20}$$

$$\pi_i^o = k_i + r_i^o - p_i^o. \tag{7.23}$$

The economic sphere:

The output supply functions:

$$y_j^o = k_j + \sigma_j \left(\frac{S_{Lj}^o}{S_{Kj}^o}\right)(p_j^o - w^o); \qquad\qquad j = 1, 2. \tag{3.36}$$

Labour demand functions:

$$l_j^o = k_j + \frac{\sigma_j}{S_{Kj}^o}(p_j^o - w^o); \qquad\qquad j = 1, 2. \tag{3.37}$$

The labour market equilibrium condition:

$$l = \sum_{j=1}^{2} \lambda_j^o l_j^o. \tag{3.38}$$

Sectoral rental rates:

$$r_j^o = \frac{1}{S_{Kj}^o}(p_j^o - S_{Lj}^o w^o); \qquad\qquad j = 1, 2. \tag{3.39}$$

Price equations:

$$p_1^o = p_1^* + \tau^o t, \quad \text{and} \tag{3.40}$$

$$p_2^o = 0 \tag{3.41}$$

Now the linearized version of the PEGEM can be written as in Table 7.3. Note that the systems of equations in Table 7.3 and 7.2 differ in two respects. First, the elasticities of factor substitution are set to unity in Table 7.3 because we are assuming Cobb-Douglas production functions. Second, the point of minimum expectation in Table 7.3 is not the origin. The system presented in Table 7.3 allows the payoff at the reference point (disagreement payoff) to respond to changes in exogenous variables.

7.4.2.2   World price changes and the response of the tariff rate   Now we shock the model with a small change in the relative price of the import competing good in the international market assuming that the factor endowment remains unchanged.

Since $k_i = 0$ for each sector i, it follows from equation (7.23) that

$$\pi_i^o = r_i^o - p_i^o \text{, and } \pi_i^* = r_i^* - p_i^* .$$

Hence using equations (3.46) and (3A.6) that describe the response of rental functions in PXGEM (Chapter 3) we can write

$$\pi_1^o = \frac{p_1^o \lambda_2^o S_{L1}}{A^o S_{K1} S_{K2}} \text{, and } \pi_1^* = \frac{p_1^* \lambda_2^* S_{L1}}{A^* S_{K1} S_{K2}} . \tag{7.24}$$

It has also been shown in Chapter 4 that the RTF does not shift with respect to any change in the international terms of trade; it simply induces a movement along the RTF. In other words, the shape of the product transformation frontier is unaffected by the terms of trade change in the international market. Therefore, for a given taste and endowment, the autarkic equilibrium is unaffected by changes in the international terms of trade. This implies that

$$\pi_2^a = 0 .$$

From equation (3.47) and equation (7.23) we get

$$\pi_2^o = r_2^o = -\frac{\lambda_1^o S_{L2} p_1^o}{A^o S_{K1} S_{K2}} . \tag{7.25}$$

Similarly, by setting elasticities of factor substitution equal to unity, and holding endowment of factors constant, we obtain from equation (7.12) that

$$y_2^o - y_1^o = -\frac{1}{A^o S_{K1} S_{K2}} (\lambda_1^o S_{L2} + \lambda_2^o S_{L1}) p_1^o . \qquad (7.26)$$

Substituting these results (that follow from PXGEM) into equation (7.20) of linearized PEGEM (Table 7.3) we get

$$D_1 \left(\frac{\lambda_2^o S_{L1}}{A^o S_{K1} S_{K2}} p_1^o - \frac{\lambda_2^* S_{L1}}{A^* S_{K1} S_{K2}} p_1^* \right) + D_2 \frac{\lambda_1^o S_{L2}}{A^o S_{K1} S_{K2}} p_1^o$$

$$= -\frac{1}{A^o S_{K1} S_{K2}} (\lambda_1^o S_{L2} + \lambda_2^o S_{L1}) p_1^o - p_1^o . \qquad (7.27)$$

Solving this equation for p_1^o we obtain

$$\frac{1}{A^o S_{K1} S_{K2}} \left(D_1 \lambda_2^o S_{L1} + D_2 \lambda_1^o S_{L2} + 1 \right) p_1^o = D_1 \frac{\lambda_2^* S_{L1}}{A^* S_{K1} S_{K2}} p_1^* . \qquad (7.28)$$

Since the coefficients on both sides of equation (7.28) are positive, it follows that

$$\frac{p_1^o}{p_1^*} > 0 . \qquad (7.29)$$

Inequality (7.29) shows that the relative price of commodity 1 in the domestic market moves with the relative price of commodity 1 in the world market. In particular, it states that if the relative price of the domestic exportable increases in the world market, then the relative price of the exportable in the domestic market will also increase. Equation (7.28) can be solved, for the percentage change in the protection rate, as

$$\tau t = \frac{1}{1 + D_1 \lambda_2^o S_{L1} + D_2 \lambda_1^o S_{L2}} \times$$

$$\left[D_1 A^o S_{L1} \left(\frac{\lambda_2^*}{A^*} - \frac{\lambda_2^o}{A^o} \right) - D_2 \lambda_2^o S_{L2} - 1 \right] p_1^* \qquad (7.30)$$

It can be shown that $\lambda_2^* / A^* > \lambda_2^o / A^o$ since $\lambda_2^* > \lambda_2^o$ by Proposition 3.1, but this is not sufficient to sign the terms enclosed in the brackets. Therefore, it can not be said a priori that the tariff rate will fall or rise as the relative price of the import-competing good rises in the world market. Thus all the unambiguous results regarding the behaviour of the bargained tariff rate obtained in the previous case disappear as we allow the point of minimum expectation to respond to changes in the exogenous variables.

The situation becomes still worse as we perform comparative-static experiments by changing factor endowments. In these cases even the direction of changes of the domestic relative price appeared ambiguous let alone the response of the bargained tariff rate (see Appendix-7A).

7.5 Summary

In this chapter, we obtained a policy endogenous general equilibrium model (PEGEM) by combining conditions that characterize the Nash bargaining equilibrium in the political sphere with conditions that characterize an equilibrium in the economic sphere of a political economy. By arguing that the payoffs at the point of minimum expectation can reasonably be a good reference point for bargaining in the tariff game, the concept of disagreement was made operational.

The comparative static responses of the bargained tariff rate were studied under two different assumptions on the nature of the government.

First, we considered the case of a coercive government, which had no restraint in choosing the domestic relative price. Consequently, the minimum expectations of both players were zero. The comparative static results, in this case, were conclusive and it was found, in particular, that the bargained tariff rate moved in the opposite direction to exactly offset the effect of a change in the world relative price on the domestic relative price.

When it was assumed that the government is a support maximizer, which maintains some restraint in choosing the domestic relative price, the minimum expectations of player 1 and 2 were given by the free trade and the autarkic equilibrium payoffs respectively. In this case, the minimum expectation payoffs became not only nonzero but also sensitive to changes in the exogenous variables. It was not possible to sign the comparative static responses of the tariff rate as the exogenous variables change. However, as in previous studies, it was found that ceteris paribus the domestic relative price always moves in the same direction as the international relative price moves. A clear-cut answer can be obtained by simulating the model numerically which is done in the following chapter.

Appendix-7A: Derivation of comparative static results under a popular government and Cobb-Douglas production functions

From equation (7.23) we have,

$$
\begin{aligned}
\pi_1^o - \pi_1^* &= (k_1 + r_1^o - p_1^o) - (k_1 + r_1^* - p_1^*) \\
&= (r_1^o - p_1^o) - (r_1^* - p_1^*).
\end{aligned}
\tag{7A.1}
$$

For a given tariff rate, equation (3.46) can be used to obtain

$$
r_1^o - p_1^o = \frac{\lambda_2^o S_{L1}}{A^o S_{K1} S_{K2}} p_1^o - \frac{S_{L1}}{A^o S_{K1}} (\lambda_1^o k_1 + \lambda_2^o k_2 - l)
\tag{7A.2}
$$

Symmetrically, we can obtain from equation (3A.6) that

$$
r_1^* - p_1^* = \frac{\lambda_2^* S_{L1}}{A^* S_{K1} S_{K2}} p_1^* - \frac{S_{L1}}{A^* S_{K1}} (\lambda_1^* k_1 + \lambda_2^* k_2 - l).
\tag{7A.3}
$$

Using equations (7A.2) and (7A.3) into equation (7A.1) we can express $(\pi_1^o - \pi_1^*)$ in terms of percentage change in the relative price, and percentage change in factor quantities.

Similarly, from equation (7.23), noting that commodity 2 is the numeraire in PXGEM, we can also write

$$
\begin{aligned}
(\pi_2^o - \pi_2^a) &= (k_2 + r_2^o) - (k_2 + r_2^a) \\
&= r_2^o - r_2^a.
\end{aligned}
\tag{7A.4}
$$

Substituting $\sigma_1 = \sigma_2 = 1$ in defining equations (3B.11) - (3B.15) and then simplifying the terms in equation (3B.18) yields

$$
r_2^a = S_{L2}(k_2 - l).
\tag{7A.5}
$$

This equation shows that under a Cobb-Douglas production function, changes the rental income in sector 2 is independent of changes in the capital stock in sector 1.[11]

Therefore, making use of the result obtained in equation (3.47) together with equation (7A.5) we can write

$$r_2^o - r_2^a = -\frac{\lambda_1^o S_{L2}}{A^o S_{K1} S_{K2}} p_1^o$$

$$-\left(\frac{\lambda_1^o S_{L2}}{A^o S_{K2}} + S_{L2}\right) k_2 + \left(\frac{S_{L2}}{A^o S_{K2}} + S_{L2}\right) l. \tag{7A.6}$$

Substituting equation (7A.6) in equation (7A.4) we can express $(\pi_2^o - \pi_2^a)$ in terms of percentage change in the relative price and percentage change in factor quantities.

Finally, using equation (7.12) we can obtain

$$y_2^o - y_1^0 - p_1^o = \frac{1}{A^o S_{K1}} k_2 - \frac{1}{A^o S_{K2}} k_1$$

$$+ \frac{(S_{K1} - S_{K2})}{A^o S_{K1} S_{K2}} l - \frac{1}{A^o S_{K1} S_{K2}} p_1^o. \tag{7A.7}$$

Substituting equations (7A.1), (7A.4), and (7A.7) in equation (7.20) of the text we obtain

$$\left(D_1 \frac{\lambda_2^o S_{L1}}{A^o S_{K1} S_{K2}} + D_2 \frac{\lambda_1^o S_{L2}}{A^o S_{K1} S_{K2}} + \frac{1}{A^o S_{K1} S_{K2}}\right) p_1^o$$

$$= D_1 \frac{\lambda_2^* S_{L1}}{A^* S_{K1} S_{K2}} p_1^* + \left[D_1 \frac{S_{L1}}{S_{K1}} \left(\frac{\lambda_1^o}{A^o} - \frac{\lambda_1^*}{A^*}\right) - \frac{1}{A^o S_{K2}}\right] k_1$$

$$+ \left[D_1 \frac{S_{L1}}{S_{K1}} \left(\frac{\lambda_2^o}{A^o} - \frac{\lambda_2^*}{A^*}\right) - D_2 S_{L2} \left(\frac{\lambda_1^o}{A^o S_{K2}} + 1\right) + \frac{1}{A^o S_{K1}}\right] k_2$$

$$+ \left[D_1 \frac{S_{L1}}{S_{K1}} \left(\frac{1}{A^*} - \frac{1}{A^o}\right) + D_2 S_{L2} \left(\frac{1}{A^o S_{K2}} + 1\right) + \frac{S_{K1} - S_{K2}}{A^o S_{K1} S_{K2}}\right] l. \tag{7A.8}$$

It is obvious that the coefficients of the variables p_1^o and p_1^* are positive, whereas the coefficients of the endowment variables k_1, k_2 and l, are ambiguous (we need specific values of the parameters to determine) in their signs. Thus, algebraically, we have the following comparative static results:

(i) $\quad \dfrac{p_1^o}{p_1^*} > 0$;

(ii) $\dfrac{p_1^o}{k_1} \gtrless 0$;

(iii) $\dfrac{p_1^o}{k_2} \gtrless 0$ and

(iv) $\dfrac{p_1^o}{l} \gtrless 0$.

Moreover, as we evaluate further, even the effect of changes in the world relative price on the bargained tariff rate becomes ambiguous in sign. The nice and clear result obtained in the previous case disappears here suggesting a need for a numerical simulation of the model.

Appendix-7B: Minimum expectation and the comparative static results when specialization in labour employment is feasible

If specialization in the employment of labour is feasible, then the aspiration level of player 1 is the rental income that can be obtained when all labour in the economy is employed in sector 1. Sector 2 will produce its output employing capital only. Therefore the payoff to the specific factors in sector 2, in this case, will be equal to its output. This represents the minimum expectation of player 2. Similarly, the aspiration level of player 1 is the rental income that it can obtain when all labour in the economy is employed in sector 2. Sector 1 will produce its output employing its capital stock only. Therefore, if this happens, the payoff to the specific factor in sector 1 will be equal to the quantity of output produced in sector 1.

We know that if $L_i = 0$, then $Y_i = \beta_i^{-1/\rho_i} K_i$ since the production functions are assumed to be CES in both sectors. Therefore, the minimum expectation of each player i is given by

$$\Pi_i^{min} = \beta_i^{-1/\rho_i} K_i .\qquad(7B.1)$$

Now, replacing Π_i^d by Π_i^{min} defined by equation (7B.1) and linearizing the PEGEM given in Table 7.1 we can obtain the linearized version of the model as

Table 7B.1
Linearized version of the PEGEM: specialized labour employment in disagreement

The political sphere:

$$D_1'(\pi_1^o - \pi_1^{\min}) - D_2'(\pi_2^o - \pi_2^{\min}) = y_2^o - y_1^o - p_1^o .$$ (7B.3)

$$\pi_i^o = k_i + r_i^o - p_i^o$$ (7B.4)

$$\pi_i^{\min} = k_i \qquad\qquad i = 1, 2.$$ (7B.5)

The economic sphere:

The output supply functions:

$$y_j^o = k_j + \sigma_j\left(\frac{S_{Lj}^o}{S_{Kj}^o}\right)(p_j^o - w^o); \qquad\qquad j = 1, 2.$$ (3.36)

Labour demand functions:

$$l_j^o = k_j + \frac{\sigma_j}{S_{Kj}^o}(p_j^o - w^o); \qquad\qquad j = 1, 2.$$ (3.37)

The labour market equilibrium condition:

$$l = \sum_{j=1}^{2} \lambda_j^o l_j^o .$$ (3.38)

Sectoral rental rates:

$$r_j^o = \frac{1}{S_{Kj}^o}(p_j^o - S_{Lj}^o w^o); . \qquad\qquad j = 1, 2.$$ (3.39)

Price equations:

$$p_1^o = p_1^* + \tau^o t, \quad \text{and}$$ (3.40)

$$p_2^o = 0$$ (3.41)

listed in Table 7B.1. Where, as in equation (7.11), for each player i, D_i' is defined as

$$D_i' = \frac{\Pi_i^{\min}}{\Pi_i^o - \Pi_i^{\min}} = \frac{\beta_i^{-1/\rho_i}}{(R_i^o / P_i^o) - \beta_i^{-1/\rho_i}} > 0 . \tag{7B.2}$$

Comparative static results : Making use of equations (7B.4) and (7B.5) equation (7B.3) can be written as

$$D_1'(r_1^o - p_1^o) - D_2'(r_2^o) = y_2^o - y_1^o - p_1^o . \tag{7B.6}$$

We can obtain from equation (3.46) that

$$r_1^o - p_1^o = \frac{\lambda_2^o \sigma_2 S_{L1}^o}{A^o S_{K1}^o S_{K2}^o} p_1^o - \frac{S_{L1}^o}{A^o S_{K1}^o}\left(\lambda_1^o k_1 + \lambda_2^o k_2 - l\right), \tag{7B.7}$$

and from equation (3.47) we obtain

$$r_2^o = -\frac{\lambda_1^o \sigma_1 S_{L2}^o}{A^o S_{K1}^o S_{K2}^o} p_1^o - \frac{S_{L2}^o}{A^o S_{K2}^o}\left(\lambda_1^o k_1 + \lambda_2^o k_2 - l\right). \tag{7B.8}$$

Substituting the expressions for $(r_1^o - p_1^o)$ from equation (7B.7) and for r_2^o from equation (7B.8) into equation (7B.6) we obtain

$$y_2^o - y_1^o - p_1^o = \left(\frac{D_1' \lambda_2^o \sigma_2 S_{L1}^o}{A^o S_{K1}^o S_{K2}^o} + \frac{D_2' \lambda_1^o \sigma_1 S_{L2}^o}{A^o S_{K1}^o S_{K2}^o}\right) p_1^o$$
$$-\left(\frac{D_1' S_{L1}^o}{A^o S_{K1}^o} - \frac{D_2' S_{L2}^o}{A^o S_{K2}^o}\right)\left(\lambda_1^o k_1 + \lambda_2^o k_2 - l\right). \tag{7B.9}$$

Substituting the expression for $(y_2^o - y_1^o)$ from equation (7.12) into equation (7B.9) and solving for p_1^o we obtain

$$\Omega p_1^o = \left[\left(\frac{D_1' S_{L1}^o}{A^o S_{K1}^o} - \frac{D_2' S_{L2}^o}{A^o S_{K2}^o}\right)\lambda_1^o\right.$$
$$\left. -\frac{1}{A^o S_{K2}^o}\left(\lambda_2^o \sigma_2 + S_{L2}^o \lambda_1^o \sigma_2 + \lambda_1^o \sigma_1 S_{K2}^o\right)\right]k_1$$

$$+ \left[\left(\frac{D_1' S_{L1}^o}{A^o S_{K1}^o} - \frac{D_2' S_{L2}^o}{A^o S_{K2}^o} \right) \lambda_2^o + \frac{1}{A^o S_{K1}^o} \left(\lambda_1^o \sigma_1 + S_{L1}^o \lambda_2^o \sigma_1 + \lambda_2^o \sigma_2 S_{K1}^o \right) \right] k_2$$

$$+ \left[\frac{1}{A^o} \left(\frac{\sigma_2 S_{L2}^o}{S_{K2}^o} - \frac{\sigma_1 S_{L1}^o}{S_{K1}^o} \right) - \left(\frac{D_1' S_{L1}^o}{A^o S_{K1}^o} - \frac{D_2' S_{L2}^o}{A^o S_{K2}^o} \right) \right] l. \qquad (7B.10)$$

where,

$$\Omega = \left[\left(\frac{D_1' \lambda_2^o \sigma_2 S_{L1}^o}{A^o S_{K1}^o S_{K2}^o} + \frac{D_2' \lambda_1^o \sigma_1 S_{L2}^o}{A^o S_{K1}^o S_{K2}^o} \right) \right.$$

$$\left. + \frac{\sigma_1 \sigma_2}{A^o S_{K1}^o S_{K2}^o} \left(\lambda_1^o S_{L2}^o + \lambda_2^o S_{L1}^o \right) + 1. \right] > 0 \qquad (7B.11)$$

As in the case of coercive government, it follows from equation (7B.10) that changes in tariff rate will exactly offset any change in terms of trade in the international market. Thus the domestic economy will be insulated from terms of trade shock. This result follows because the variable p_1^o responds only to domestic endowment changes, but not to changes in the international relative price.

The effects of changes in the endowment variables in the domestic relative price are unclear. The size and direction of effects can only be obtained after the numerical simulation of the model.

Notes

1 See also Friedman (1986) pp. 160-62.
2 These properties are required in establishing the correspondence between a solution that maximizes the Nash product and a solution that satisfies all the axioms that characterize a bargaining solution.
3 See Thomson (1981) for details and for other candidates for reference points.
4 Posner (1974) distinguished three forms of political system: (i) entrepreneurial - which sells favourable legislation to industries that value it most; (ii) coercive - which awards legislation to groups that are able to make credible threats to retaliate with violence if society does not give them favourable treatment; (iii) democratic - legislation is awarded by the vote of elected representatives of the people.
5 Magee, Brock and Young have defined an economic black hole, in the context of a long-run model in which both capital and labour are involved in predatory lobbying, as a situation in which all of the economy's factor endowment is exhausted in predatory lobbying. See Magee, Brock and Young (1989: 223). A

short-run analogue of their economic black hole can be defined as a situation in which the owners of the specific factors exhaust all of their rental incomes in predatory lobbying. So, if in a noncooperative Nash equilibrium each player exhausts his rents in predatory lobbying and obtains zero payoffs, then the equilibrium tariff thus determined may be defined as the black hole tariff.

6   In such a case one sector will employ all labour and the other sector will be producing outputs employing its sector-specific capital stock only. Production of outputs with a single factor is possible under CES production function. The worst outcome for each sector is not to be able to employ the mobile factor. Therefore, the rental income and the payoff at the point of minimum expectation of each sector will be equal to the level of output thus produced. Comparative static results with minimum expectation thus defined are reported in Appendix-7B.

7   For a clear approach to the problem of distributing the recycled tariff revenue and its impact on the endogenous tariff rate see Long and Vousden (1991). They have shown that if the players do not differ in their risk preferences significantly, then a failure to account for the tariff revenue changes in the players' payoffs will have no qualitative consequence on the final result. It simply makes the modelling aspect more complicated. However, if there are reasons to believe that the players differ in their risk preferences significantly, then it follows from their result that the omission may affect the result qualitatively. We ignore the tariff revenue changes in accounting players' payoffs by assuming that players have almost identical risk preferences.

8   Note that equation (7.11) remains independent of the way tariff is distributed. Therefore, as far as the results of this section are concerned, the distribution of the tariff revenue does not matter.

9   For details see the discussion of point B in the proof of Corollary 6.3.

10   When the payoffs at the point of minimum expectation are zero for both players, then the generalized Nash product reduces to a Cobb-Douglas type function. So, the generalized Nash product is clearly homothetic for the same reason as the Cobb-Douglas production function is - that the slopes of level curves at any point depend only on the ratio of the payoffs at that point.

11   See also the discussion following equation (3B.18) in Appendix-3B. One implication of this result is that the payoff of player 2 in the autarkic equilibrium, which is the minimum expectation of player 2, remains unaffected by changes in the capital stock in sector 1, since the price of commodity 2 has been held fixed by the choice of the numeraire.

8 Some illustrative simulations of the PEGEM

Introduction

Comparative static results derived in the previous chapter clearly indicate that, even in this simple model of a political economy, an unambiguous prediction of the direction of responses of the bargained tariff rate to exogenous shocks may not be possible if the point of minimum expectation also responds to the shocks. The algebraic expressions become quite complex and involve various shares corresponding to different equilibrium points and the payoffs at the point of minimum expectation all of which are themselves affected by the shocks. An alternative approach is to solve the PEGEM numerically and draw conclusions inductively, which is the main purpose of this chapter. By doing so we will accomplish two tasks: we will show that the PEGEM is in fact operational, and we will examine the endogenous response of the tariff rate to various exogenous shocks.

Though numerical simulation is a useful technique in resolving ambiguities, it has its own limitations. Results obtained from a numerical simulation are not valid generally. They reflect the behaviour of endogenous variables under a particular environment conditioned by the chosen, estimated or the observed values of parameters and exogenous variables of the model. To overcome this limitation and retain the flavour of generality we have, therefore, opted to calibrate the model to several stylized data sets and parameter values covering some extreme cases and perform comparative static experiments with each of them separately. These experiments gave us an opportunity to see whether or not there is some pattern in the response of the bargained tariff rate.

Interestingly, the bargained tariff rate displayed a general pattern in its comparative static response to exogenous shocks over a range of trade regimes and parametric configurations of the economic sphere. In particular, the direction of the response of the bargained-tariff rate under a popular government appeared to follow the same pattern as it did under a coercive government (see Chapter 7). The precise magnitudes of responses are, of course, different.

This chapter is divided into seven sections. The first section sets up the analytics of the simulation model, which is simply the linearized version of the PEGEM, as set out in Table 7.1. The second section describes the technique used to calibrate the model; the possibility of errors due to linearization, and the types of data sets required to maintain a flavour of generality in the results.

The third section discusses simulation results in two parts. In the first part, we focus on the behaviour of the bargained tariff rate in three different political economies that differ regarding the parameter of the political sphere, but have the same economic sphere. The difference in the political sphere has been constructed indirectly by imposing different tariff regimes on otherwise identical economies. The underlying differences in the bargaining power of individual players have been inferred from the equilibrium data sets representing the three different political economies. In the second part, we focus on the behaviour of the bargained tariff rate in political economies that differ in their economic spheres but have had the same (an intermediate) tariff regime.

The testable propositions that follow from these simulations are listed in section four. The credibility of these hypotheses is evaluated against the results reported in previous studies. In section six we have applied the PEGEM to explain commonly raised issues such as why comparative advantage of a nation may shift with factor accumulation and so on. Finally, this chapter is concluded in section seven.

8.1   PEGEM: The simulation model

The linearized version of the PEGEM in its full form is listed in Table 8.1. This model describes the linearized conditions for equilibrium in the political as well as in the economic sphere of the political economy. The condition for equilibrium in the political sphere is the condition for a generalized Nash solution to the bargaining problem in the tariff game described in Chapter 6. The conditions for equilibrium in the economic sphere are the ones that constitute the PXGEM described in Chapter 3. Recall from the previous chapter that in the PEGEM the tariff rate is determined at the equilibrium of the political sphere, while the rest of endogenous variables are determined at the equilibrium of the economic sphere. The general equilibrium of the political economy is attained when both spheres are simultaneously in equilibrium. This occurs when the values of endogenous variables determined at the equilibrium of the economic sphere at a given tariff rate also satisfy the condition for equilibrium in the political sphere, which produces the same tariff rate.

The economic sphere of the PEGEM contains three sub-models of which one is factual and two are counterfactual (see Table 8.1). The first component, which is the factual one, is the basic sub-model that lists the conditions of equilibrium in the observed state of the economic sphere. It is simply the linearized version of the PXGEM component of the PEGEM listed in Table 7.1. The set of equations in the basic sub-model differs from the set of equations listed in Table 7.3 or in Table 7.4 (see Appendix-7B) in that it includes the demand side of the economy, namely equations (8.1), (8.3), (8.4), and (8.6), which have been ignored so far.[1] Equations pertaining to the demand side which are being added to the set of equations listed in Table 7.3 can be obtained in the following way.

Linearizing the consumer demand equation (3.19) we can obtain

$$c_j^o = -p_j^o + \sum_{i=1}^{2} H_i^o (p_i^o + y_i^o) + H_3^o z^o, \qquad j = 1\,2. \qquad (8.1)$$

where,

$$H_i^o = \frac{P_i^o Y_i^o}{\sum\limits_{i=1}^{2} P_i^o Y_i^o + Z^o}, \qquad i = 1, 2; \qquad (8.2a)$$

$$H_3^o = \frac{Z^o}{\sum\limits_{i=1}^{2} P_i^o Y_i^o + Z^o} \qquad (8.2b)$$

and Z^o represents the tariff revenue at the observed equilibrium of the economy. In percentage change form it can be expressed as

$$z^o = p_1^* + m_1^o + t / T_1^o \qquad (8.3)$$

where, t is the change in percentage points of the rationalized tariff rate, T_1^o, on imports of good 1.

The defining equations (8.2a) and (8.2b) show that the H_i^o terms are the shares of sectoral value-added and tariff revenue respectively in total income, which is the sum of the sectoral value-added and the tariff revenue, of the national (representative) consumer.

To clear the market of good 1 we must have $C_1^o = Y_1^o + M_1^o$. Expressing this condition in percentage change form we get

$$c_1^o = J_1^o y_1^o + J_2^o m_1^o \qquad (8.4)$$

where,

$$J_1^o = \frac{P_1^o Y_1^o}{P_1^o C_1^o},$$ (8.5a)

and $$J_2^o = \frac{P_1^o M_1^o}{P_1^o C_1^o}$$ (8.5b)

are respectively shares of the domestic output and imports in the domestic consumption of good 1.

We have already noted that the trade balance constraint represents the market clearing condition for the foreign exchange. Expressing the trade balance constraint in percentage change form and noting that good 2 is the numeraire we get

$$m_2^o = p_1^* + m_1^o.$$ (8.6)

Note that equations (8.4) and (8.6) require that the markets for good 1 and the foreign exchange continue to clear after each disturbance to the economy, and the labour market will continue to clear by equation (3.38). Nothing has, however, been said about the market of good 2, which will continue to clear by Walras' Law.

The second component of the full model has been called the free trade sub-model. It describes the equilibrium of the economy under free trade. This set of equations has been obtained from Table 3A.1 by adding, as in the main model, equations (8.7) - (8.9) that represent the demand side of the economy. The way these demand side equations have been derived is similar to that in the basic sub-model. Note that in this sub-model neither there is a variable for the tariff revenue nor the tariff rate since they do not mean anything under the free trade regime. This free-trade sub-model will yield changes in the minimum expectation of player 1 as exogenous variables change.

The third component of the PEGEM has been called the autarky sub-model. Equations listed in this group have been copied from Table 3B.2. Note that under autarky the market of each commodity clears domestically. There are no net imports and, therefore, whatever be the underlying tariff rate tariff revenue collection is always zero. Since there is no trade, the trade balance constraint is meaningless. We have stated the market clearing condition for good 1 and the market of good 2 will clear by Walras' Law. This component of the model yields the behaviour of the endogenous variables if the economy maintains an autarkic regime before and after a given shock. In particular, this sub-model yields an expression for the behaviour of the minimum expectation of player 2 - the exporting sector.

Table 8.1
Simulation model of a political economy: PEGEM
(The Full Model)

The Political Sphere:

$$D_1(\pi_1^o - \pi_1^*) - D_2(\pi_2^o - \pi_2^a) = y_2^o - y_1^o - p_1^o. \tag{7.20}$$

$$\pi_i^o = k_i + r_i^o - p_i^o. \tag{7.23}$$

Economic Sphere: the PXGEM

(a) The basic sub-model:

Output supply functions:

$$y_j^o = k_j + \sigma_j \left(\frac{S_{Lj}^o}{S_{Kj}^o} \right)(p_j^o - w^o); \qquad j = 1, 2. \tag{3.36}$$

Consumer demand, and tariff revenue:

$$c_j^o = -p_j^o + \sum_{i=1}^{2} H_i^o(p_i^o + y_i^o) + H_3^o z^o, \qquad j = 1\,2. \tag{8.1}$$

$$z^o = p_1^* + m_1^o + t / T_1^o. \tag{8.3}$$

Market clearing equations:

$$c_1^o = J_1^o y_1^o + J_2^o m_1^o, \tag{8.4}$$

(Trade balance constraint):

$$m_2^o = p_1^* + m_1^o. \tag{8.6}$$

Labour demand functions:

$$l_j^o = k_j + \frac{\sigma_j}{S_{Kj}^o}(p_j^o - w^o); \qquad j = 1, 2. \tag{3.37}$$

The Labour market equilibrium condition:

$$l = \sum_{j=1}^{2} \lambda_j^o l_j^o. \tag{3.38}$$

Sectoral rental rates:

$$r_j^o = \frac{1}{S_{Kj}^o}(p_j^o - S_{Lj}^o w^o); \qquad j = 1, 2. \tag{3.39}$$

Table 8.1 (contd.)

Price equations:

$$p_1^o = p_1^* + \tau^o t, \tag{3.40}$$

and, $p_2^o = 0$. $\tag{3.41}$

(b) The free trade sub-model:

Output supply functions:

$$y_j^* = k_j + \sigma_j \left(\frac{S_{Lj}^*}{S_{Kj}^*} \right)(p_j^* - w^*); \qquad j = 1, 2. \tag{3A.1}$$

Consumer demand:

$$c_j^* = -p_j^* + \sum_{i=1}^{2} H_i^* (p_i^* + y_i^*) ; \qquad j = 1, 2. \tag{8.7}$$

Market clearing conditions:

$$c_1^* = J_1^* y_1^* + J_2^* m_1^*, \tag{8.8}$$

(Trade balance constraint):

$$m_2^* = p_1^* + m_1^*. \tag{8.9}$$

Labour demand functions:

$$l_j^* = k_j + \frac{\sigma_j}{S_{Kj}^*}(p_j^* - w^*); \qquad j = 1, 2. \tag{3A.2}$$

The labour market equilibrium condition:

$$l = \sum_{j=1}^{2} \lambda_j^* l_j^*. \tag{3A.3}$$

The rental rates:

$$r_j^* = \frac{1}{S_{Kj}^*}(p_j^* - S_{Lj}^* w^*); \qquad j = 1, 2. \tag{3A.4}$$

Price normalisation rule:

$$p_2^* = 0. \tag{3A.5}$$

Table 8.1 (contd.)

(c) Autarkic sub-model:

Output supply functions:

$$y_j^a = k_j + \sigma_j \left(\frac{S_{Lj}^a}{S_{Kj}^a} \right) (p_j^a - w^a); \qquad\qquad j = 1, 2. \qquad (3B.2)$$

Consumer demand:

$$c_j^a = -p_j^a + \sum_{i=1}^{2} H_i^a (p_i^a + y_i^a); \qquad\qquad j = 1, 2. \qquad (3B.3)$$

Market clearing condition:

$$c_1 = y_1. \qquad (3B.7)$$

Labour demand functions:

$$l_j^a = k_j + \frac{\sigma_j}{S_{Kj}^a} (p_j^a - w^a); \qquad\qquad j = 1, 2. \qquad (3B.4)$$

The labour market equilibrium condition:

$$l = \sum_{j=1}^{2} \lambda_j^a l_j^a. \qquad (3B.5)$$

The rental rates:

$$r_j^a = \frac{1}{S_{Kj}^a} (p_j^a - S_{Lj}^a w^a); \qquad\qquad j = 1, 2. \qquad (3B.6)$$

Price normalization rule:

$$p_2^a = 0. \qquad (3B.8)$$

8.2 Some strategic considerations

This section contains three subsections. The first subsection outlines the simulation strategy that will be employed in obtaining the counterfactual data sets. The second subsection outlines the solution method used to eliminate the linearization error in deriving the counterfactual data sets. In the third subsection we isolate main parameters whose values can potentially affect the generality of the results.

8.2.1 Simulation strategy and calibration of the PEGEM

It can be seen from Table 8.1 that the implementation of the model requires both factual and counterfactual information. Factual information, which includes the elasticities of factor substitution in the two sectors and various quantities and value shares at the observed state of equilibrium (or 'base year'), is required to calibrate the basic sub-model. Counterfactual information, which includes the quantity and value shares both at the free trade equilibrium and at the autarkic equilibrium, is required to calibrate the free trade sub-model and the autarkic sub-model of the PEGEM. In particular, values at these counterfactual equilibria are required to calibrate the coefficients D_1 and D_2 which describe the response of the minimum expectation of the players that are contained in equation (7.20). Since the free trade and the autarkic equilibria are not observable, the following 3-step strategy has been adopted to generate the required information (see Figure 8.1).

In the first step we calibrate the basic sub-model using the base year data set. The general nature of the data set required to obtain sufficient information to calibrate the basic sub-model and generic rules to calculate the relevant shares are outlined in the Appendix-8A. We assume that the elasticities of factor substitution are known from extraneous sources and remain constant throughout experiments.

The basic sub-model has 13 equations in 18 variables. It can be closed by treating five variables as exogenous and the rest endogenous. The five exogenous variables are: the two sector-specific capital stocks, the economy wide supply of labour, the world relative price and the rationalized tariff rate.

The above division of the variables into endogenous and exogenous categories is sufficient to close the model, and in what follows it is referred to as the *natural closure* of the basic sub-model. Once the model has been parameterized (either by calibration or estimation) it can be simulated for any given change in the exogenous variables.

In step 2, we perform two different simulations and update the state of the economy to two different new equilibria. In the first simulation, we shock the model by reducing the observed tariff rate to zero under the natural model closure and update the state of the economy to the new equilibrium. This will provide us with necessary data to mimic the economy had it followed the free trade policy.

For example, if, in the observed equilibrium, the rationalized tariff rate is 25 per cent ad valorem, then we set the change in percentage points of the rationalized tariff rate, $t = -25$, holding other exogenous variables constant. Simulation of the basic sub-model yields the effects of this tariff cut on the endogenous variables of the model. The result is then used to update the observed (or base year) data set, which then describes the state of the economy at the free trade equilibrium. In other words, this will depict the state of the economy had it followed the free trade policy instead of following what has been the observed policy. The updated data set is then used to calibrate the free trade sub-model of the PEGEM.

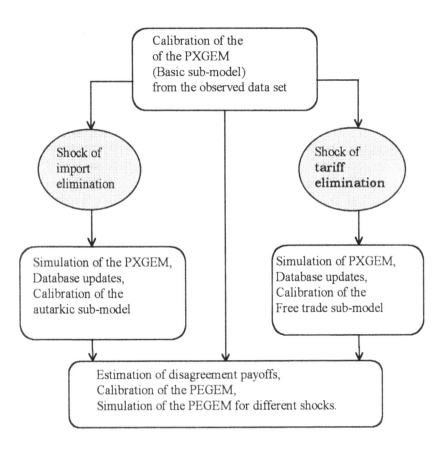

Figure 8.1   Simulation strategy

In the second simulation we change the closure of the model. This time we treat the tariff rate as an endogenous variable, and the net import of good 1 as the policy variable. This swapping of the endogenous and exogenous variable does not affect the total number of the endogenous variables in the model. Holding other exogenous variables constant, we apply an exogenous policy shock of 100 per cent reduction in the net import of good 1 and simulate the model to obtain its effect on the set of endogenous variables. The result of the simulation yields, among others, a percentage point increase in the rationalized tariff rate that would be consistent with zero imports of good 1. This will also imply a 100 per cent reduction in the export of good 2 since the model maintains a binding trade balance constraint. Thus, we obtain the tariff rate that induces zero trade in both commodities. Updating the base year data set using these results yields the level of endogenous variables that would describe the economy under the autarkic equilibrium. The updated data set is then used to calibrate the autarky sub-model of the PEGEM listed in Table 8.1.

In step 3 we make use of these two counterfactual descriptions of the economy with the observed one to calibrate the full model, which is then used to evaluate the behaviour of the bargained tariff rate as the exogenous variables change.

In the updated (counterfactual) data sets, nominal magnitudes are measured in units of commodity 2, since commodity 2 is the numeraire. The rental payment in sector 2 is the payoff of player 2 under autarky. Therefore, the rental payments of sector 2 under autarky represents the minimum expectation of player 2. To obtain the payoff of player 1 under free trade, which is measured in units of commodity 1, we have to divide the rental payments of sector 1 by the relative price of commodity 1 that would prevail at the free trade equilibrium. The relative price of commodity 1 can be obtained from the updated data set. For example, if, after the elimination of the tariff, the relative price of commodity 1 falls by 10 per cent, then the relative price of commodity 1 at the free trade equilibrium will be 0.90, since we have set it equal to unity at the observed equilibrium. To complete the calibration of the PEGEM, the coefficients D_1 and D_2 are estimated by combining the payoffs at the point of minimum expectation with the observed payoffs according to the defining equations (7.21) and (7.22).

8.2.2 *Simulation of the basic sub-model and linearization errors*

The system of equations in the basic sub-model is the linearized version of the system of nonlinear equations describing the PXGEM (the economic markets of PEGEM listed in Table 7.1). In other words, equations listed here (Table 8.1) are the linear approximations to the actual relationships among the model variables. Each curve, describing the actual functional relation, is replaced by its tangent at the point of observed equilibrium. Therefore the solutions obtained from the simulation of the linearized system will show movements along the tangents not along the actual curves thus producing linearization errors.

Linearization errors can be ignored for small changes or shocks. However, if the shocks are large in magnitude producing large changes in the endogenous variables, then the errors due to linearization may be significant.

In both of our simulations, which are required to calibrate the free-trade and the autarkic equilibria, the shocks can be quite large. Therefore, the linear solutions could produce large errors, and the description of the economy under the free trade regime or under the autarkic regime, obtained by following the above procedure, may be inaccurate. Clearly, the nature of the problem warrants the use of a solution procedure that can approximate the exact nonlinear solutions as accurately as desired.

We have used GEMPACK to simulate the models.[2] This software can obtain multi-step solutions by updating the data base after each step of simulation. For example if we select a 2-step solution of the model, then it will first divide the shock into two equal parts and performs linear simulation of the model for the first part of the shock. It then updates the base data, recalculates the shares, etc., and re-calibrates the model at the new point defined by the updated data set. Then, it simulates the model again for the second part of the shock. The basic principle can be understood as a polynomial approximation to a curve. By increasing the number of linear segments (of a given shock) the final solution can be made very close to the actual solution. Moreover, GEMPACK also provides an extrapolated solution using the Richardson extrapolation based on the results of 2 or 3 multi-step solutions.[3] The errors due to linear approximations can, therefore, be reduced to a negligible number by increasing the number of steps in the multi-step simulation.

While simulating the basic sub-model, we have used tariff revenue as a criterion to judge the accuracy of the results, since tariff revenue has to be zero at both the free trade equilibrium and the autarkic equilibrium. In each simulation we initially required the extrapolated solution based on three multi-step (2-step, 4-step, and 8-step) solutions. If the updated data after the simulation did not yield a zero tariff revenue collection, then the numbers of steps were increased to 5-steps, 10-steps, and 20-steps. If the tariff revenue still did not vanish in the updated data set, then the numbers of steps were increased further and so on until the tariff revenue vanished or became approximately zero. The updated data set is, then, checked to ensure that markets clear domestically at the autarkic equilibrium and the trade account balances at the free trade equilibrium. This final check ascertains that the update commands have been correctly specified and executed.

Though our simulation is intended to be illustrative only, we have insisted, in all cases, on extrapolated results.

8.2.3   Preliminary considerations on basic data sets

Now, we ask what sort of data sets should we construct to capture the possible extreme responses of the bargained tariff rate? On the basis of the analytical results obtained from the comparative static exercise of the previous chapter (see equation (7.30) in particular), one may suspect that the *direction* of response of the bargained tariff rate with respect to the world price change can possibly be *altered* if different data sets imply extremely different values for D_1 and D_2. Particularly, if D_1 is much larger than D_2 in one set and the opposite is true in the other then the tariff rate may rise in the first case and fall in the second as the price of good 1 rises in the world market. If this is true, then the direction of the tariff change for a given shock depends on where the economy initially is on the product (or rent) transformation frontier. It is because D_1 takes its near-maximum value if the observed equilibrium is very close to the free trade equilibrium and its near-minimum value if the observed equilibrium is close to the autarkic equilibrium. Similarly, D_2 takes its near-maximum value if the observed equilibrium is very close to the autarkic equilibrium and takes its near-minimum value if the observed equilibrium is very close to the free trade equilibrium (see equation (7.29) in particular). Therefore, one may argue that the direction of response of the bargained tariff rate will be different if the observed equilibrium is close to the free trade equilibrium instead of being close to the autarkic equilibrium.

Such an argument may not be valid because it fails to consider the general equilibrium effects of a movement of the observed equilibrium point on share-parameters. For example, consider the case with Cobb-Douglas production functions. It can be seen from equation (7A.8) or (7.30) that the effect of a terms of trade loss on the tariff rate can be positive if D_1 is sufficiently greater than D_2. This condition will be met by an observed equilibrium sufficiently close to the free trade equilibrium, but at the same time we will also find that the term $(\lambda_2^* / A^* - \lambda_2^o / A^o)$ in equation (7.30) will decline and tend to zero as the observed equilibrium moves closer towards the free trade equilibrium. Thus, in effect, the decline in the value of the term $(\lambda_2^* / A^* - \lambda_2^o / A^o)$ may more than offset the increase in the value of D_1 preventing the reversal of the direction of the response of the domestic tariff rate across different data sets as the international terms of trade change. Moreover, if the production functions are not characterized by unitary elasticities of factor substitution, then the distributive shares will also change and the exact behaviour of the tariff rate as exogenous variables change remains, nevertheless, an empirical issue.

Table 8.2
Basic data sets: observed and simulated equilibria in three different political economy with Cobb-Douglas production functions
(values in $)

	Wage	Rent	Value-added	Con. Exp.	Net Imp.	Price Level
(a) Almost free trade						
The observed data						
Sector 1	70	30	100	151	51	1.00
Sector 2	40	60	100	50	-50	1.00
Simulated autarky						
Sector 1	143	61	204	204	0	1.69
Sector 2	27	40	67	67	0	1.00
Simulated free trade						
Sector 1	68	29	97	149	52	0.98
Sector 2	40	61	101	49	-52	1.00
(b) Almost autarky						
The observed data						
Sector 1	70	30	100	102	2	1.00
Sector 2	40	60	100	99	-1	1.00
Simulated autarky						
Sector 1	71	31	102	102	0	1.01
Sector 2	40	59	99	99	0	1.00
Simulated free trade						
Sector 1	19	8	27	81	54	0.50
Sector 2	53	80	133	79	-54	1.00
(c) Intermediate tariff regime						
The observed data						
Sector 1	70	30	100	125	25	1.00
Sector 2	40	60	100	80	-20	1.00
Simulated autarky						
Sector 1	96	41	137	137	0	1.24
Sector 2	35	53	88	88	0	1.00
Simulated free trade						
Sector 1	49	21	70	111	41	0.80
Sector 2	45	67	112	71	-41	1.00

Thus, it follows that the parameters of concern are the distribution of bargaining power between the players and the two elasticities of factor substitution. The first one positions the observed equilibrium somewhere between free trade and the autarkic equilibrium, and the second one affects the shape of the RTF and hence the degree of ease with which rents can be transferred from one player to the other (it affects the behaviour of the distributive share parameters). To illustrate the role played both types of parameters and also maintain a flavour of generality we perform numerical simulations in two parts.

In part I we take an economic sphere with Cobb-Douglas production functions and let the political sphere differ. With identical economic spheres, political economies can differ in their political spheres only if they have different distribution of players' bargaining power. We know that differences in the distribution of bargaining power results into different tariff regimes we have chosen, for this exercise, three different states of general equilibrium: (a) *almost free trade*, which is characterized by a very low tariff rate, and a large volume of trade; (b) *almost autarky*, which is is characterized by a very high tariff rate, and almost no trade with rest of the world and (c) *an intermediate case* in which the tariff rate and the volume of trade with rest of the world is moderate. The hypothetical data sets used in the simulations are presented in Table 8.2. The underlying differences in the distribution of players' bargaining power are inferred from these figures and reported in Table 8.3.

In part II, we allow the economic sphere to differ by varying the elasticity of factor substitution while holding the observed equilibrium of the political economies at the intermediate tariff regime (case c).

8.3   Simulations of the PEGEM

8.3.1   Calibration, simulation, and discussion of the results: part I

Table 8.2 provides us with numerical description of observed equilibria of three different political economies, which have three different tariff regimes. These figures are values at domestic prices, where the units were chosen so as to make the domestic base-prices of both goods equal to unity. Therefore, the figures can also be regarded as expressions in units of either good, whatever is convenient. From the values of net imports it is apparent that the tariff revenue in cases (a) and (b) are 1 unit of the numeraire, whereas in case (c) it is 5 units of the numeraire. The rationalized tariff rate is 2 per cent in case (a), 100 per cent in case (b) and 25 per cent in case (c), whatever had been the actual rates of tariffs and subsidies.[4]

In each of the three cases, we followed the three-step simulation strategy, described above, to calibrate the PEGEM. The counterfactual data, the simulated autarky and the simulated free trade, were generated from the basic sub-model in the first two steps and are also reported in Table 8.2.

Given an 'observed' equilibrium of the political economy, the figures under corresponding simulated autarky indicate the state of the economy in equilibrium if the country adopts autarkic trade policy and yields the worst outcome to the exporting sector. Similarly, the figures under corresponding simulated free trade indicate the state of the economy if the country adopts a free trade policy and yields the worst outcome to the import competing sector. Clearly, these two simulated equilibria yield the required payoffs at the minimum expectations of the players. To repeat again, these figures were obtained by multi-step simulations of the PXGEM for shocks that eliminate all imports and the tariff rate respectively.

8.3.1.1 Estimates of the bargaining power of the players Since each of the observed data sets corresponds to the general equilibrium of a political economy, and the minimum expectation of player 1 is obtained at the free trade equilibrium and the minimum expectation of player 2 is obtained at the autarkic equilibrium, the data presented in Table 8.2 should satisfy the necessary and sufficient condition of the generalized Nash solution to the bargaining problem in the tariff game underlying the three political economies. We know that the bargaining equilibrium is given by condition (7.4), which is

$$
\frac{\Theta_1}{\Theta_2} = \frac{\Pi_2^o}{\Pi_1^o} \left(\frac{\Pi_1^o - \Pi_1^*}{\Pi_2^o - \Pi_2^a} \right) \left(\frac{\sigma_1 P_1^o Y_1^o}{\sigma_2 Y_2^o} \right).
$$

Now we use this condition to recover the underlying relative bargaining power of the players in the three political economies using figures from Table 8.2.

Table 8.3
The implied bargaining power of the players in the three political economies

	case(a)	case(b)	case(c)
Relative power of player 1, (Θ_1 / Θ_2)	0.0408	28.00	1.070
Bargaining power of player 1, (Θ_1)	0.0392	0.9655	0.517
Bargaining power of player 2, (Θ_2)	0.9608	0.0345	0.483

Table 8.4
Simulation results - part I, case (a): endogenous response of the tariff rate in a political economy with almost free trade situation

Endogenous variables	Effects of 1% increase in			
	P_1^*	K_1	K_2	L

Predictions of policy-endogenous general equilibrium model (PEGEM)

	P_1^*	K_1	K_2	L
y_1^o	0.48	0.44	-0.29	0.85
y_2^o	-0.49	-0.14	0.89	0.25
r_1^o	1.43	-0.57	-0.26	0.84
r_2^o	-0.49	-0.14	-0.10	0.25
w	0.73	0.22	0.16	-0.37
p_1^o	0.94	-0.02	0.03	-0.01
t	**-0.06**	**-0.02**	**0.03**	**-0.01**
π_1^o	0.48	0.44	-0.29	0.85
π_2^o	-0.49	-0.14	0.89	0.25
π_1^*	0.52	0.46	-0.32	0.86
π_2^a	0.00	0.00	0.60	0.40

Predictions of policy-exogenous general equilibrium model (PXGEM)

	P_1^*	K_1	K_2	L
y_1^o	0.51	0.45	-0.31	0.85
y_2^o	-0.52	-0.15	0.91	0.24
r_1^o	1.52	-0.54	-0.31	0.85
r_2^o	-0.52	-0.15	-0.09	0.24
w	0.78	0.23	0.13	-0.36
p_1^o	1.00	0.00	0.00	0.00

Table 8.5
Simulation results - part I, case (b): endogenous response of the tariff rate in a political economy with almost autarkic situation

Endogenous variables	Effects of 1% increase in			
	P_1^*	K_1	K_2	L

Predictions of policy-endogenous general equilibrium model (PEGEM)

Endogenous variables	P_1^*	K_1	K_2	L
y_1^o	0.02	0.31	-0.01	0.70
y_2^o	-0.02	-0.01	0.61	0.39
r_1^o	0.07	-0.97	0.57	0.41
r_2^o	-0.02	-0.01	-0.39	0.39
w	0.04	0.01	0.58	-0.59
p_1^o	0.05	-0.28	0.58	-0.29
t	**-1.89**	**-0.57**	**1.16**	**-0.58**
π_1^o	0.02	0.31	-0.01	0.70
π_2^o	-0.02	-0.01	0.61	0.39
π_1^*	1.37	0.70	-0.82	1.12
π_2^a	0.00	0.00	0.59	0.40

Predictions of policy-exogenous general equilibrium model (PXGEM)

Endogenous variables	P_1^*	K_1	K_2	L
y_1^o	0.51	0.45	-0.31	0.85
y_2^o	-0.52	-0.15	0.91	0.24
r_1^o	1.52	-0.54	-0.31	0.85
r_2^o	-0.52	-0.15	-0.09	0.24
w	0.78	0.23	0.13	-0.36
p_1^o	1.00	0.00	0.00	0.00

Table 8.6
Simulation results - part I, case (c):
endogenous response of the tariff rate
in a political economy with intermediate tariff regime

Endogenous variables	Effects of 1% increase in			
	P_1^*	K_1	K_2	L

Predictions of policy-endogenous general equilibrium model (PEGEM)

	P_1^*	K_1	K_2	L
y_1^o	0.28	0.38	-0.17	0.78
y_2^o	-0.28	-0.08	0.77	0.31
r_1^o	0.81	-0.75	0.11	0.64
r_2^o	-0.28	-0.08	-0.23	0.31
w	0.42	0.12	0.35	-0.47
p_1^o	0.54	-0.14	0.28	-0.14
t	**-0.57**	**-0.17**	**0.35**	**-0.17**
π_1^o	0.28	0.38	-0.17	0.78
π_2^o	-0.28	-0.08	0.77	0.31
π_1^*	0.73	0.52	-0.44	0.92
π_2^a	0.00	0.00	0.60	0.40

Predictions of policy-exogenous general equilibrium model (PXGEM)

	P_1^*	K_1	K_2	L
y_1^o	0.51	0.45	-0.31	0.85
y_2^o	-0.52	-0.15	0.91	0.24
r_1^o	1.52	-0.54	-0.31	0.85
r_2^o	-0.52	-0.15	-0.09	0.24
w	0.78	0.23	0.13	-0.36
p_1^o	1.00	0.00	0.00	0.00

Table 8.7
Simulation results - part I, case (d):
endogenous response of the tariff rate in a political economy similar to case (c) but factor intensity of the two sectors reversed

	Wage	Rent	Value-added	Con. Exp.	Net Imp.	Price Level
The observed data						
Sector 1	30	70	100	125	25	1.00
Sector 2	60	40	100	80	-20	1.00
Simulated autarky						
Sector 1	42	98	140	140	0	1.30
Sector 2	54	36	90	90	0	1.00
Simulated free trade						
Sector 1	22	52	74	110	36	0.80
Sector 2	64	43	107	71	-36	1.00

Predictions of policy-endogenous general equilibrium model (PEGEM)

Endogenous variables	Effects of 1% increase in			
	P_1^*	K_1	K_2	L
y_1^o	0.17	0.82	-0.07	0.25
y_2^o	-0.17	-0.12	0.47	0.65
r_1^o	0.68	-0.51	0.13	0.39
r_2^o	-0.17	-0.12	-0.53	0.65
w	0.11	0.08	0.35	-0.43
p_1^o	0.51	-0.33	0.19	0.14
t	**-0.61**	**-0.42**	**0.24**	**0.18**
π_1^o	0.17	0.82	-0.07	0.25
π_2^o	-0.17	-0.12	0.47	0.65
π_1^*	0.35	0.95	-0.14	0.19
π_2^a	0.00	0.00	0.40	0.60

212

It can be seen from Table 8.3 that the exporting sector had more bargaining power (approximately 24 times) than the import competing sector in case (a), whereas the import competing sector had more bargaining power (approximately 28 times) than the exporting sector in case (b). Both players had almost equal bargaining power in case (c).

8.3.1.2 Discussion of the simulation results The four columns in Tables 8.4 - 8.6 list percentage changes (with two exceptions) of endogenous variables over their observed values, as predicted by PEGEM and PXGEM, in response to a one percent increase in the exogenous variables.[5] The exogenous variables in the PEGEM are: the relative price of the import competing good in the international market, stock of specific-factor in sector 1, stock of specific-factor in sector 2, and the endowment of labour in the economy. Note also that PXGEM and PEGEM differ in their treatment of the tariff rate. PEGEM determines the tariff rate endogenously, whereas PXGEM treats tariffs as exogenously determined. Therefore, the results obtained from simulating the PXGEM represent the responses of the endogenous variables with respect to the exogenous variables had the tariff rates been held constant at the observed level. The PEGEM allows players to bargain and adopt a new tariff rate, if that is agreeable, as exogenous variables change. Hence, the results obtained by simulating the PEGEM take into account the endogenous responses of the tariff rate also while predicting the responses of other economic variables. Naturally, the predictions of the PXGEM and PEGEM are different.

For example, if the international terms of trade falls by a one percent, then PXGEM predicts, by definition, that the domestic relative price will also fall by a one percent. With PEGEM, however, the tariff rate may also change and therefore the change in the domestic relative price will not be the same as predicted by the PXGEM. The domestic relative price may fall by more or less than a one per cent. As a consequence, the other endogenous variables pertaining to the economic market, will also show a different response under PEGEM compared to the prediction of the PXGEM.

The simulation results are discussed in the following three sections. First, we explain only those aspects of the results that are due to the particular structures assumed in the model. These results will not necessarily hold when those particular structures, for example Cobb-Douglas production functions, are replaced by different ones. Then, we compare the responses of the endogenous variables under PXGEM with those of the PEGEM, and explain why the responses of the endogenous variables differ when the policy variable is also endogenous. Finally, we explain, both intuitively and mechanically, why the policy variable, the bargained tariff rate, changes in the direction as shown by the simulation results.

8.3.1.3 The consequences of assumed structures Following patterns appeared in the simulation results reported under PEGEM in Tables 8.4 - 8.6 are either simply due to the assumption of Cobb-Douglas production functions or because of the choice of the initial data sets or because of the small country assumption.

First, in each case and for each shock, we have obtained that the response of sectoral output, y_i^o, and the response of the payoff to player i, π_i^o, are identical. This is due to the assumption of Cobb-Douglas production functions, which implies that the factor shares in each sector remain globally constant.

Second, the rental income of player 2 at the autarkic equilibrium has remained constant (that is, its percentage changes are zeroes) on two occasions: when world price changes, and when the stock of capital in sector 1 changes. The first relationship follows from the independence of the autarkic equilibrium in the domestic market from world price changes. The second relationship is due to the property of Cobb-Douglas production functions in both sectors (See Appendix-3B).

Finally, the responses of the endogenous variables with respect to changes in each of the exogenous variables under PXGEM are exactly the same in all cases. This should be of no surprise because of two reasons: the small country assumption, and that the economic sphere is identical in all three cases. Given that the tariff rate is fixed, the small country assumption links the domestic relative price only to the world relative price. The domestic relative price is, therefore, independent of any change in domestic demand and supply conditions. Because economic spheres are identical, the each sector in the three cases employs the same amount of factors, applies the same production technology, produces the same quantity of output, and faces the same relative price. The three cases differ in the tariff rate, tariff revenue, national income and consumer demand, which do not change under PXGEM. Therefore, the responses of the remaining supply side variables have to be the same. This provides a good basis against which the predictions of the PEGEM can be compared.

8.3.1.4   A comparison between the predictions of PXGEM and PEGEM
Consider first the shock to the domestic economy, which is initially at almost free trade equilibrium, of a one per cent increase in the relative price of the home importable in the international market - Table 8.4. PXGEM predicts that domestic relative price of good 1 will increase by a one percent. Consequently, the output of good 1 will increase by 0.51 per cent, output of good 2 will fall by 0.52 per cent, the rental rate in sector 1 will increase by 1.52 per cent, the rental rate in sector 2 will fall by 0.52 per cent and the wage rate will rise by 0.78 per cent, all measured in units of commodity 2. These results are consistent with the predictions of standard general equilibrium models.

However, the PEGEM predicts that as the relative price of the home importable good rises in the world market by a one percent the protection awarded to the domestic import competing sector will be reduced through a tariff cut of

0.06 percentage points. So, the new tariff rate will be 1.94 per cent ad valorem on imports of commodity 1. The domestic relative price will increase by 0.94 per cent only. Consequently, the responses of other economic variables are determined accordingly. The output of commodity 1 increases by 0.48 per cent, the output of commodity 2 falls by 0.49 per cent, the rental rate in sector 1 increases by 1.43 per cent, the rental rate in sector 2 falls by 0.49 per cent, the wage rate rises by 0.73 per cent, the payoff of player 1 increases by 0.48 per cent and the payoff of player 2 falls by 0.49 per cent. For each of the variables, the PEGEM has predicted a smaller change (gain or loss) than the PXGEM. This occurs simply because a change in the policy (tariff) prevented a foreign price change to be transmitted fully into the domestic economy.

The simulation results for case (b) are presented in Table 8.5. Note that in this case the economy is in almost autarkic equilibrium, and the tariff rate at the observed equilibrium is 100 per cent ad valorem and so, the value of τ^o is 0.5.

When the models were shocked by a one percent increase in the relative price of good 1 in the international market PXGEM predicted that the output of the import competing sector will increase by 0.51 per cent and the output of the exporting sector will decrease by 0.52 per cent.

The predictions of the PEGEM are quite different. It predicts that the tariff rate will fall by 1.89 percentage points. So, the relative price of commodity 1 in the domestic market will increase by 0.05 per cent only. Consequently, changes in other variables were very small. The output of sector 1 is predicted to rise by 0.02 per cent and that of sector 2 is predicted to fall by 0.02 per cent and so on.

Similarly, as K_1 increased by a one percent, ceteris paribus, PEGEM predicted a decline in the protection awarded to sector 1. The tariff rate is predicted to fall by 0.57 percentage points and the domestic relative price by 0.28 per cent. This change in price partially compensated for the loss in the rental income of player 2 caused by an expansion in sector 1, which otherwise would be biding some of the mobile factor away from sector 2. Consequently, the output and the rental income of sector 2 remained almost unaffected by the shock.

In PEGEM as K_2 increased by a one percent, ceteris paribus, the tariff rate increased by 1.16 percentage points raising the protection to sector 1. The relative price of commodity 1 increased by 0.58 per cent. Consequently, output in sector 1 did not decline by as much as was predicted by the PXGEM. In fact, it remained almost unchanged. Output in sector 2 increased by 0.61 per cent. The most surprising result is that the rental rate in sector 1 has increased by 0.57 per cent! We would expect it to fall as in case (a). The PXGEM predicts that the rental rates in both sectors fall as the capital stock increases in either sector. This unusual result can be explained as follows.

Since, the relative price of commodity 1 increased by 0.58 per cent and the wage rate also increased by 0.58 per cent in the new equilibrium, the real wage rate faced by sector 1 remained unchanged. Output and employment of labour (not shown, but can be inferred from equation (3.37) in Table 8.1) in sector 1 has remained unchanged. Under Cobb-Douglas production functions the distributive shares are constant implying that the share of output of sector 1 that goes to the specific-factor has not changed either. The relative price of commodity 1 has gone up by 0.58 per cent implies, therefore, that the rental rate and the rental income of sector 1 (in units of commodity 2) should go up by 0.58 per cent keeping the payoff to player 1 unchanged. This is precisely what has happened.

Now let us consider the effects of a one percent increase in each of the endowment variables, ceteris paribus, in case (c), which assumes that the economy was initially in an intermediate equilibrium (Table 8.6).

As K_1 increases by a one percent, the bargained tariff rate falls by 0.17 percentage points; the gain in sector 1, obtained through capacity expansion, is partly eroded by a decline in the price of its output. The output in sector 1 grows by 0.38 per cent only, which is less than 0.45 per cent as predicted by the PXGEM. The output of sector 2 falls but by less than that predicted by the PXGEM. Similarly, as K_2 expands by a one percent the tariff rate increases by 0.35 percentage points, which increases the protection awarded to the import competing sector and the decline of the import competing sector is retarded. Consequently PEGEM predicts that an increase in K_2 will cause output in the exporting sector to increase and the output in the import competing sector to fall but by less than those predicted by the PXGEM. A similar interpretation can be given to other figures.

Responses of endogenous variables to a one percent increase in the economy-wide supply of labour displayed the effect of the difference in the factor intensity between the two sectors (Table 7.6 and 7.6). Output of the sector which is more labour intensive expands at a faster rate than the output of the sector which is more capital intensive.

8.3.1.5 Exogenous shocks and the bargaining equilibrium The fundamental question is that why does the tariff rate change in the first place as exogenous variables change? Once this factor is understood properly the responses of all other variables can be explained as in a conventional policy exogenous CGE model. In terms of the arguments developed so far, the perturbation, as the exogenous variables change, in the equality of the players' generalized fear of ruin holds the key.

More precisely, we have seen (in Chapter 6) that the generalized Nash solution to the bargaining problem in the tariff game is characterized by the condition

$$\frac{f_1}{\Theta_1} = \frac{f_2}{\Theta_2}$$

where,

$$\frac{f_1}{f_2} = \frac{\Pi_1^o - \Pi_1^*}{\Pi_2^o - \Pi_2^a}\left(\frac{-1}{d\,\Pi_1\,/\,d\,\Pi_2}\right)$$

is the ratio of the two players' fear of ruin (see Appendix 6A), and Θ_i is the 'exogenous' bargaining power of player i.

Recall that a player's fear of ruin is simply the inverse of his boldness, which is the maximum probability of conflict that the player is prepared to accept for a small gain in the payoff. It has been shown in Chapter 6 that a player's boldness declines as his payoff relative to the minimum expectation payoff increases. In other words, a player's fear of ruin (conflict) will increase if either his payoff has increased with unchanged minimum expectation or his payoff at the minimum expectation has fallen at unchanged current payoff level or a combination of both. Intuitively, this means that the more net gain a player has been able to obtain relative to his minimum expectation the more fearful he will be of a conflict with his bargaining opponent. In a Nash bargaining process the player who fears more relative to his bargaining power will reduce his demand. A Nash equilibrium (in the bargaining process) is attained when both players' fear of ruin are proportional to their bargaining power.

Now, if an exogenous shock does not alter both the minimum expectation payoffs and the bargaining power of the players, then the player, who gains from the shock, will have his fear of ruin increased and the other player, who loses, will have his fear of ruin fallen. A similar reasoning holds when both the current payoffs (after the shock at the unchanged policy) and the payoffs at the point of minimum expectation are affected by the shock. The player who has gained more relative to his new minimum expectation will have his fear of ruin increased by more than that of the other player who has gained less relative to his new minimum expectation payoff.

Let us consider, for simplicity, Cobb-Douglas production functions again. Then, using equation (7.3), which yields the slope of the RTF, we can write

$$\chi \equiv \frac{f_1}{f_2} = \frac{\Pi_1^o - \Pi_1^*}{\Pi_2^o - \Pi_2^a}\left(\frac{S_{K2}P_1^o}{S_{K1}}\right).$$

Therefore, the generalized Nash solution is obtained when we have

$$\chi = \frac{\Theta_1}{\Theta_2}.$$

With an unchanged tariff rate after a shock if $\chi > \Theta_1 / \Theta_2$ in the immediate economic equilibrium, then the political sphere will be out of equilibrium. Player 1's generalized fear of ruin will exceed that of player 2. Therefore, in the new bargaining process player 1 will concede and the tariff rate will fall. The direction of tariff change will be reversed if $\chi < \Theta_1 / \Theta_2$.

After each shock the PXGEM-updated value of χ can be obtained as

$$\chi^u = \frac{\Pi_1^o\left(1 + \dfrac{k_1}{100} + \dfrac{r_1^o}{100} - \dfrac{p_1^o}{100}\right) - \Pi_1^*\left(1 + \dfrac{\pi_1^*}{100}\right)}{\Pi_2^o\left(1 + \dfrac{k_2}{100} + \dfrac{r_2^o}{100}\right) - \Pi_2^a\left(1 + \dfrac{\pi_2^a}{100}\right)}\left(\frac{S_{K2}P_1^o\left(1 + \dfrac{p_1^o}{100}\right)}{S_{K1}}\right),$$

where all endogenous variables are as predicted by PXGEM. Note that the PEGEM predictions of π_1^*, and π_2^a are the same as that of PXGEM.

By comparing the updated value of χ with the relative bargaining power of player 1, in each of the three cases and for each of the shocks, we can predict the direction of change in the bargained tariff rate. For example, in case (a) we have $\Theta_1 / \Theta_2 = 0.0408$, and χ^u equals 0.0421, 0.0412, 0.0404, and 0.0409 respectively as the world relative price of good 1, stock of specific-factor in sector 1, stock of specific-factor in sector 2, and the supply of labour increases by a one percent in turn. That is, at the unchanged tariff rate χ^u exceeds Θ_1 / Θ_2 as the world relative price of good 1, the stock of the specific-factor in sector 1, or the supply of labour in the economy increase by a one percent, and χ^u falls short of Θ_1 / Θ_2 as the stock of specific-factor in sector 2 increases by a one percent. This, in turn, means that player 1's generalized fear of ruin relative to that of player 2 increases and the bargained tariff rate falls, as the world price of commodity 1, the specific-factor in sector 1, or the supply of labour in the economy increases. Similarly, player 2's generalized fear of ruin relative to that of player 1 increases and the bargained tariff rate rises, as the stock of the specific-factor in sector 2 increases.

The exact magnitude of change in the bargained tariff rate is determined by parametric configurations and therefore we need a PEGEM to evaluate them. One can verify that the PXGEM updated value of χ, in each case is equal to Θ_1 / Θ_2 - the relative bargaining power of player 1. This confirms further that at the PEGEM solution players' generalized fears of ruin are equalized.[6] Thus, the simulation results demonstrate the overall consistency and the implementation of the PEGEM developed in the previous chapters.

8.3.2   Recalibration, simulation and discussion of the results: part II

To see the behaviour of the tariff rate under CES production functions we performed two different sets of simulations: one with $\sigma_1 = 1.5$ and $\sigma_2 = 2$, and the other with $\sigma_1 = 2$ and $\sigma_2 = 1.5$. In both simulations the initial characterization of the economy was as in case (c). Therefore, PXGEM was simulated again with new parameter values to obtain the projected state of the economy at autarky and at the free trade, since the elasticities of factor substitution are now different from unity. The data representing the 'observed' equilibrium, simulated autarky and simulated free trade are given in the top portion of Tables 8.8 and 8.9 respectively. The bottom portions of these tables report the predictions of the PEGEM.

The simulation results presented in Tables 8.8 - 8.9 display similar patterns on the behaviour of endogenous variables as was displayed by results presented in Tables 8.4 - 8.6. These results can be explained by the same set of arguments. The differences, as one can expect, are that the responses of the payoffs and the sectorial outputs are no longer identical; the minimum expectation of player 2 now responds to changes in the stock of specific-factor in sector 1. This is simply the consequence of assuming that the production functions are *not* Cobb-Douglas.[7]

The most important observation is that the bargained tariff rate has fallen with an increase in the world relative price of the home importable. It has also fallen with the stock of the specific-factor in the import competing sector, or the supply of labour in the economy (sector 1 is more labour intensive), and has risen with an increase in the stock of the specific-factor in the exporting sector.

The pattern of the response of the tariff rate with respect to world price and sector-specific-factor changes has remained intact even when the factor intensities of the sectors were reversed (see Table 8.7) and CES production functions were considered.

This pattern of response of the bargained tariff rate displayed in simulation results is similar to that observed in the analytical results obtained in the previous chapter with a 'coercive' government. The difference is that the tariff changes in these cases, unlike the case with a 'coercive' government, do not fully insulate the economy from world price changes. This is because the point of minimum expectation responds to changes in exogenous variables, and unlike the case with a coercive government the point of minimum expectation does not coincide with the origin. The responsiveness of the point of minimum expectation to the shocks not only changes the bargaining set, but also alters the curvature of the level curves of the generalized Nash product by shifting their asymptotes.

Intuitively, the mechanism behind the endogenous response of the tariff rate can be explained as follows. An increase in the world relative price of good 1 not only increases the rental income of player 1 at the unchanged tariff rate but also raises the payoff of player 1 at the free trade equilibrium, which is the minimum expectation of player 1. The minimum expectation of player 2 remains unaffected, because the autarkic equilibrium is unaffected by changes in the world prices. Since an increase in the payoff at the minimum expectation has the effect of reducing a player's fear of ruin, therefore, for a given increase in the world price of good 1, the increase in player 1's fear of ruin under a support maximizing

Table 8.8
Simulation results - part II, case (c):
intermediate tariff regime and CES production functions with $\sigma_1=1.5$, $\sigma_2=2$

	Wage	Rent	Value-added	Con. Exp.	Net Imp.	Price Level
The observed data						
Sector 1	70	30	100	125	25	1.00
Sector 2	40	60	100	80	-20	1.00
Simulated autarky						
Sector 1	94	38	132	132	0	1.44
Sector 2	29	55	84	84	0	1.00
Simulated free trade						
Sector 1	40	20	60	111	51	0.80
Sector 2	56	66	122	71	-51	1.00

Simulation results

	Effects of 1% increase in			
Endogenous variables	P_1^*	K_1	K_2	L
PEGEM				
y_1^o	0.45	0.38	-0.07	0.68
y_2^o	-0.45	-0.08	0.67	0.42
r_1^o	0.77	-0.52	0.19	0.34
r_2^o	-0.23	-0.04	-0.17	0.21
w	0.34	0.06	0.25	-0.31
p_1^o	0.47	-0.11	0.23	-0.12
t	**-0.66**	**-0.14**	**0.29**	**-0.15**
π_1^o	0.30	0.59	-0.04	0.45
π_2^o	-0.23	-0.04	0.83	0.21
π_1^*	1.06	0.79	-0.29	0.50
π_2^a	0.00	0.02	0.77	0.21

220

Table 8.9
Simulation results - part II, case (c):
intermediate tariff regime and CES production functions with $\sigma_1=2$, $\sigma_2=1.5$

	Wage	Rent	Value-added	Con. Exp.	Net Imp.	Price Level
The observed data						
Sector 1	70	30	100	125	25	1.00
Sector 2	40	60	100	80	-20	1.00
Simulated autarky						
Sector 1	96	38	134	134	0	1.18
Sector 2	31	54	85	85	0	1.00
Simulated free trade						
Sector 1	41	21	62	111	49	0.80
Sector 2	52	68	120	71	-49	1.00

Simulation results PEGEM

	Effects of 1% increase in			
Endogenous variables	P_1^*	K_1	K_2	L
y_1^o	0.39	0.34	-0.11	0.77
y_2^o	-0.39	-0.04	0.71	0.33
r_1^o	0.67	-0.43	0.20	0.22
r_2^o	-0.26	-0.03	-0.19	0.22
w	0.39	0.04	0.29	-0.33
p_1^o	0.47	-0.10	0.26	-0.16
t	**-0.65**	**-0.12**	**0.33**	**-0.20**
π_1^o	0.19	0.67	-0.06	0.39
π_2^o	-0.26	-0.03	0.81	0.22
π_1^*	0.70	0.79	-0.27	0.48
π_2^a	0.00	0.03	0.71	0.26

government will be lower than that under a coercive government, whereas player 2's fear of ruin declines by the same amount in both cases.

This means that player 1 would be prepared to forgo less, in terms of a tariff cut, to attain a new bargaining equilibrium under a support maximizing government than under a coercive government, in which case the point of minimum expectation remains at the origin irrespective of the shocks. This, in turn, means that endogenous changes in the tariff rate under a support-maximizing government will not be sufficient to offset the effects of world price changes on the domestic price.

We conclude this section with a remark. Since, the simulation results show that the bargained tariff rate and, hence, the domestic relative price respond to changes in the endowment variables even if the bargaining power of the players are unchanged. This means that the domestic relative price could have been anywhere between the autarky and the free trade price had the endowment variables been configured (or change) appropriately.

Therefore, it is important to note the fact that a player holding more bargaining power than his opponent is neither necessary nor sufficient for the location of the full equilibrium either closer to the free trade equilibrium or closer to the autarkic equilibrium. The location of the general equilibrium point depends not only on the bargaining power of the players but also on the configuration of the endowment variables as well.

8.4 Some testable hypotheses

On the basis of these results we list the following hypotheses or refutable propositions regarding the behaviour of the bargained tariff rate. Ceteris paribus -

(H1)   If the international relative price of the home importable good falls (rises) in the world market, then its relative price in the home market also falls (rises), but the bargained tariff rate will rise (fall).

(H2)   If the stock of the specific-factor in the import competing sector increases (decreases) exogenously, then the bargained tariff rate will fall (rise).

(H3)   If the stock of the specific-factor in the exporting sector increases (decreases), then the bargained tariff rate will rise (fall).

(H4)   If the supply of labour (or the mobile factor) in the economy increases (decreases) exogenously, then the bargained tariff rate will fall (rise) provided that the import-competing sector is more labour (capital) intensive compared to the exporting sector. The tariff rate will remain unaffected by changes in the supply of labour if both sectors are equally labour intensive.

Before we go on to apply the model to explain some issues of practical interest it is necessary to examine the validity the model itself. One approach towards the validation of the model is to check whether the hypotheses that follow from the model are consistent with the observed facts. An elaborate statistical test of these hypotheses is beyond our scope. For the present purpose we will simply compare the predictions of PEGEM with the hypotheses, observations, and findings of previous studies.

8.5 Existing literature and credibility of the hypotheses

The first hypothesis is consistent with Hillman's (1982) result that a declining industry will continue to decline even if there are politically motivated tariffs to retard the rate of decline of such industries. Long and Vousden (1991), in a more general setting than that considered by Hillman, found analytical support for Hillman's result. They came to the conclusion that Hillman's hypothesis remains robust provided that the owner of specific-factor in the unprotected sector is not significantly less risk averse than the owner of the specific-factor in the protected sector.

The remaining hypotheses can be related to the findings of Magee, Brock and Young (1989), who have deduced that any increase in the endowment of a factor in an economy always leads to an increase in the policy favoured by the factor (p. 209). This means that an increase in the stock of the specific-factor in sector 1 should lead to an increase in the tariff rate and an increase in the stock of the specific-factor in sector 2 should lead to a fall in the tariff rate. The hypotheses (H2) and (H3), in particular, indicate to the contrary. This apparent disagreement between Magee, Brock and Young's result and the predictions of the PEGEM can be explained by noting that they have not distinguished between the interests of the owners of the specific-factors (capital) in the two sectors because they do not have specific-factors in their model. Theirs is a long-run model. Magee, Brock and Young's result is based on the assumption that capital is capital wherever it is employed, which runs against the implication of their three tests of Stolper-Samuelson Theorem (pp. 101-10; and pp. 293-4). There it is shown that both capital and labour favour protection if they are in the import competing sector and favour free trade if they are in the exporting sector. PEGEM is based on this distinction. Therefore the predictions of the two models differ.

Moreover, observing that tariff rates in the US declined over this century, Brock, Magee, and Young (1989: 189-94) also attempted to correlate this decline with the movements of factor endowments, and the US terms of trade changes. They found that changes in the labour-capital ratio had a statistically insignificant effect on tariff rates, whereas terms of trade changes had the expected sign and significant effect on the tariff rate.[8]

The PEGEM would predict that changes in the capital stock in different sectors will have opposing effects on the tariff rate, and therefore, nothing can be said *a priori* about the effect of a change in the aggregate stock of capital on the tariff rates. For example, if the capital stocks in both sectors increase in such a way that they fully offset the effect of each other on the tariff rate, then one may observe an unchanged tariff rate even with an increase in the aggregate stock of the capital. Several other possibilities can be conceived in which the movement of the tariff rate may appear independent of changes in the aggregate endowments of the factors. Therefore, Brock, Magee, and Young's findings do not provide evidence against the predictions of the PEGEM. We still conjecture that, in a study like BMY have done, if the stock of capital were (dis)aggregated by trade orientation of the industries, then it is likely that we will observe the result as predicted by the PEGEM. In other words, we expect the tariff rate to decline with an increase in the capital stock of the import competing sector and decline with an increase in the capital stock of the exporting sector.

8.6 An application of the model and some additional hypotheses

Of the four hypotheses, (H2) and (H3) relate the level of domestic protection to the structure of capital formation in the domestic industries. These hypotheses imply that if an exogenous increase in the stock of the specific-factor in the import-competing sector is sufficiently large to more than offset the positive effect on the tariff rate of an increase in the stock of capital in the exporting sector, then the country will lower the protection awarded to the import competing sector.

The process of capital formation may take several forms Protection by itself can be a source of surplus generation in the import competing sector which, attracted by the higher rents under protection, can be reinvested within the sector thereby further increasing the stock of the specific-factor in the import competing sector. Moreover, new investors may come in, or the sector may experience specific-factor augmenting technical progress.

Assume that the import competing sector is more capital intensive than the exporting sector. Assume further that the initial equilibrium of the economy is as given in Table 8.7. We may now ask what happens to the bargained tariff rate if sector 1 experiences a sufficiently high growth in its stock of the specific-factor - say, by a 200 per cent? We can use PEGEM to answer this question. It also provides a ground to compare two otherwise similar economies that differ only in the stock of capital in sector 1.

We used the factual and counterfactual data from Table 8.7, and simulated the PEGEM to obtain the result shown in Tables 8.10 and 8.11.

Since the size of the shock was very large a convergence problem was encountered. The numbers of steps were increased to 100, 200 and 400. The three multistep solutions and the extrapolated solution of the model are presented in Table 8.10, and the updates of the base data (based on the extrapolated solution) are given in Table 8.11.

Table 8.10

The response of endogenous variables to an increase of a 200% in K_1

(Details of the multi-step and extrapolated simulation results)

Endogenous variables	100-step results	200-step results	400-step results	Extrapolated results
y_1^o	146.4700	146.3600	146.3140	146.2740
y_2^o	-17.7247	-17.6953	-17.6875	-17.6843
c_1^o	77.6859	77.5900	77.1922	76.5611
c_2^o	27.4964	27.4809	27.2405	26.8450
m_1^o	-198.6090	-198.4000	-197.3930	-195.7830
m_2^o	-198.6090	-198.4000	-197.3930	-195.7830
l_1^o	55.5755	55.4609	55.4240	55.4007
l_2^o	-27.7752	-27.7241	-27.7088	-27.7002
p_1^o	-28.3828	-28.2843	-28.2246	-28.1578
r_1^o	-41.3285	-41.1904	-41.1105	-41.0235
r_2^o	-17.7247	-17.6953	-17.6875	-17.6843
w	13.8654	13.8508	13.8499	13.8531
z (change)	-2.9532	-2.9121	-3.3941	-4.2112
t (change)	-35.4785	-35.3554	-35.2807	-35.1972
π_1^o	146.4700	146.3600	146.3140	146.2740
π_2^o	-17.7247	-17.6953	-17.6875	-17.6843
π_1^*	174.0820	173.9680	173.9110	173.8530
π_2^a	2.19E-07	0.0000	0.0000	7.30E-08

Table 8.11
Effects of a 200% increase in K_1 on the levels of the main variables
(Values are in units of commodity 2)

	Wage	Rent	Value-added	Con. Exp.	Net. Imp.	Price Level
The economy before the shock:						
Sector 1	30	70	100	125	25	1.0
Sector 2	60	40	100	80	-20	1.0
The economy after the shock:						
Sector 1	53.08	123.84	176.92	158.55	-18.37	0.72
Sector 2	49.39	32.93	82.31	101.47	19.16	1.00

The results shown in Table 8.10 display the same features as was seen in the previous results: the output and employment of labour in sector 1 expand while those in sector 2 contract; rental rates in both sectors fall; wage rate increases; tariff rate falls by 35 percentage points, relative price of commodity 1 falls; and so on. The percentage change in sectoral output is identical with the percentage change in the payoff of the respective player, and the minimum expectation of player 2 has remained unaffected - both consequences of the assumption of Cobb-Douglas production functions.[9]

The updated data base (Table 8.11) shows that commodity 1 will be exported at the new equilibrium instead of being imported, and the exports of commodity 1 will be taxed at the rate of 10 per cent ad valorem. Initially, the imports of commodity 1 were being taxed at the rate of 25 per cent ad valorem. On the basis of this exercise we draw the following additional hypotheses:

A sufficient increase in the stock of a specific-factor in the import competing sector may lead to

(H5)   a reversal in the direction of trade: commodity 1 will be exported and commodity 2 will be imported.

During the process of the reversal in the direction of trade, sector 2 contracts and sector 1 expands in terms of output and employment. This result is consistent with the empirical findings of Martin and Warr (1992). They observed that capital accumulation and technical change biased against agriculture have been the most important determinants of the decline in agriculture's share of GDP in Thailand. In case of Indonesia, capital accumulation has been the principal cause of decline in agriculture's share of GDP (Warr, 1991).

Martin and Warr have explained this phenomenon by invoking the Rybczynski effect, which implies that an increase in the stock of capital would lead to an increase in the output of capital intensive sector (non-agriculture) and a decline in the output of labour intensive sector (agriculture). The mechanism of this effect involves a movement of both capital and labour away from agriculture to the non-agriculture sector, which is more capital intensive than agriculture, and therefore this is equivalent to an increase in the stock of capital in non-agriculture sector and a decline in the stock of capital in agricultural sector. Both changes, in PEGEM, imply a decline of agriculture and expansion of non-agriculture sector.

(H6)   A reversal in the direction of tariff protection: exports of commodity 1 or the imports of commodity 2 will be taxed or the production of commodity 2 will be subsidized instead of the imports of commodity 1 being continually taxed.

(H7)   If a country continues to 'over-invest' in the import-competing sector relative to the exporting sector, then over time it will adopt a policy of unilateral trade liberalization. In other words, trade liberalization will eventually turn out to be the dominant strategy for a highly protective economy.

This hypothesis appears to be consistent with Drysdale and Garnaut's (1992) observation that recent trade liberalization in the Western Pacific countries has been mostly non-discriminatory and unilateral. They argue that the 'observation of the highly beneficial effect of one country's liberalization on its own trade expansion, has led each Western Pacific economy to calculate that, whatever the policies of others, it will benefit more from keeping its own borders open to trade than from protection' (p.5).

(H8)   Over a long period, some countries may display tariff cycles.

The base of the rationalized tariff changes as the capital stock in the import competing sector keeps on increasing, and the tariff rate on the imports of previously exported commodity (commodity 2) starts rising. This provides a leverage to sector 2 through protection, and the capital stock in sector 2 may start to accumulate. The tax on exports of good 1 or on imports of good 2 will start to fall as capital accumulation in sector 2 takes momentum, and hence the tariff cycle.

The approach underlying the construction of the PEGEM may help explain the existence of tariff cycles. The current model is too crude to be able to provide a complete description of the tariff cycles. A more detailed explanation can be found in Cassing, McKeown, and Ochs (1986), who, by assuming that players have spatially concentrated asset distribution and markets in such assets are incomplete, have been able to show not only the existence of tariff cycles but also that tariff cycles match the pattern of the business cycles. Some of the empirical evidence cited in their paper are not inconsistent with our hypothesis, however.

(H9)   For given technologies of production, taste of the domestic consumer, and the total supply of the mobile factor (labour), there is a unique configuration of the stocks of sector-specific-factors that will yield the free trade as the generalized Nash solution to the bargaining problem in the tariff game. In other words, any imbalances among factor endowments, tastes and technologies will lead to a positive tax on either domestic exports or on imports, whichever way it is viewed.

Though this hypothesis follows from (H2), it is not easy to check its empirical validity because of its non-refutable character. However, if this hypothesis is correct, then one may expect to find almost every country with a positive tax on trade, since it will be almost impossible to maintain the equilibrium configuration of the factor endowments.

Now, if developing countries had 'comparative advantage' in agriculture and developed countries have 'comparative advantage' in manufactures then it follows from the above that developing countries will tax agriculture and developed countries will tax manufactures (Anderson and Hayami, 1986; Honma and Hayami, 1986; Krueger, Schiff and Valdes, 1988). They both tax their respective export sectors.

8.7 Summary

In this chapter, a computable version of the PEGEM was developed and few illustrative simulations were performed on stylized data sets. The results demonstrate that the bargain-theoretic approach can be used to construct an operational policy-endogenous general equilibrium model, which can be used to predict the behaviour of policies endogenously as parameters of economic and political spheres change.

The numbers that have been used in simulating the model are all hypothetical. Therefore, the magnitudes of the elasticities have no practical significance. However, the simulation results have shown some degree of consistency in the direction of change of the response of the bargained tariff rate with respect to changes in the exogenous variables. They were similar to the directions that were obtained analytically in the previous chapter for the special case of a 'coercive' government. These results prompted a number of hypotheses regarding the behaviour of the tariff rate.

All of the hypotheses, implied by the PEGEM, very closely paralleled the predictions of the approach that maximizes a conservative social welfare function (Corden, 1974), in which increases in income are given relatively low weights and decreases very high weights (Corden, 1974: p.107). At the heart of this function lies the idea that any significant reduction in real incomes of any significant section of the community should be avoided (Corden, 1974: p.107). A number of reasons such as fairness, social insurance, and avoidance of social and political conflict have been forwarded in defence of this approach.

For example, if the relative price of the import competing good falls in the world market, then the tariff rate increases by (H1) implying that the policy change compensates, at least partly, for the loss in the real income of player 1. Similarly, the response of the tariff rate implied by (H2) - (H4) can also be predicted by conservative social welfare theorists on grounds of fairness, and so on.

The predictions of the PEGEM, however, were not derived by maximizing a conservative social welfare function. They are outcomes of bargaining between the two players. The government is viewed as a self-interested agent; it maximizes its political support by implementing the agreement reached by the two players.

Hillman (1982) has suggested a point of difference between the two approaches. He argued that if the government were a CSW maximizer then its policy change ought to be directed at arresting industry decline, whereas a politically motivated behaviour of the government (H1) implies that a declining industry will continue to decline. In other words, the extent to which losers are compensated by policy changes serves as the criteria of distinguishing a self-interested government from a benevolent one. We saw, however, in Chapter 7 that if the government is coercive in nature (or maximizes Stigler-Peltzman type political support function, see Hillman, 1982), then the policy supplied by the government will meet Hillman's criteria of maximizing the conservative social welfare function that policy changes will fully compensate terms of trade changes.

Therefore, it follows that there are problems in differentiating a conservative social welfare-maximizing government and a self-interested, politically motivated (support-maximizing) government simply by observing a government's policy choices. Both self-interested and altruist governments will offer similar policy responses. Some further method needs to be devised.

As far as policy modelling is concerned, therefore, there is a choice between a bargain-theoretic approach and a welfare-theoretic approach. Both offer competing framework for policy modelling. As argued by Posner (1974) and Vousden (1990), however, the social welfare-maximizing approach lacks explanation on how such functions are formed and translated into legislation, whereas the bargain-theoretic approach, while being able to predict as much, does not suffer from this criticism. If, however, the conservative social welfare function is considered an outcome of a (Nash) bargaining process,[10] then this study can be used to reconcile the difference between the conservative social welfare maximizing approach and the political support maximizing approach to policy determination.[11]

Appendix-8A: Generic calculation of share parameters

Table 8A.1
The base year data set

	Wage	Rent	Value Added	Consumption Expenditure	Value of Net Import
Sector 1	WL_1	R_1K_1	P_1Y_1	P_1C_1	P_1M_1
Sector 2	WL_2	R_2K_2	P_2Y_2	P_2C_2	P_2M_2

These data should satisfy the following restriction:

(a) Zero profit condition - that is for each i we must have

$$WL_i + R_iK_i = P_iY_i$$

(b) Market clearing conditions - that is for each i we must have

$$P_iC_i = P_iY_i + P_iM_i.$$

It is clear that conditions (a) and (b) together imply that the aggregate budget constraint of the national consumer holds.

From this data set, we can make the following calculations:

(1) Tariff revenue equals the sum of the values of net imports at domestic price. That is

$$Z = P_1M_1 + P_2M_2$$

by the condition that trade balances at world prices.

(2) The rationalized tariff rate

$$T_1 = -Z/P_2M_2$$

(3) Employment shares:

$$\lambda_i = \frac{WL_i}{WL_1 + WL_2}$$

by the assumption of perfect mobility and homogeneity of labour.

230

(4) Distributive shares:

$$S_{Li} = WL_i \, / \, P_i Y_i \text{ and}$$

$$S_{Ki} = R_i K_i \, / \, P_i Y_i$$

because zero profit condition holds.

(5) Tariff coefficient

$$\tau = 1 \, / \, (1 + T_1) \, .$$

The share parameters H's and J's can be calculated by using the defining equations (8.2) and (8.5) respectively.

Notes

1   The reason why the inclusion of the demand side is essential will become clear shortly.
2   The GEMPACK Software System for solving large economic models was developed by the Impact Project, University of Melbourne, Melbourne Australia. Details of user guidelines, syntax and semantic, etc., can be found in Harrison and Pearson (1994a and 1994b). In the GEMPACK referencing system these documents are identified as GPD-1, and GPD-2 respectively.
3   For details on Richardson extrapolation see Pearson (1991).
4   See Appendix-8A for methods of calculation.
5   The two exceptions are: variables t and z (not listed in the Table). The variable t measures the change in the percentage point of the rationalized tariff rate and the variable z measures change (instead of percentage change) in tariff revenue collected. It is because the tariff rate and the tariff revenue can sometimes take the value zero (for example at the free trade equilibrium) in which case percentage changes of these variables are not defined.
6   Note that the numbers given in these Tables have been rounded several times. Therefore, PEGEM results satisfy this condition only approximately.
7   We have assumed that the long run elasticities of factor substitution are at least unity. The production functions are not Cobb-Douglas implying that the elasticities are greater than unity. Then, it follows from equation (3B.18) and the subsequent discussion in Appendix-3B that the rental income of player 2 will in fact fall as the stock of the specific-factor in sector 1 increases.
8   The following were their hypotheses. A decline in the labour-capital ratio must have been responsible for the decline in the US tariff rate over the

century since labour, which has become less important - *endowment effect*, benefits from protection. Continuous decline in the import prices must have contributed to a rise in the US tariff rate since cheaper imports cause blue collar wage to fall and labour can afford to increase its lobbying activities more intensely - *compensation effect*.

9   However, some of the variables are not showing the sign of convergence. Convergence requires that the difference between 400-step and 200-step solution be less than the difference between 200-step and 100-step solution. Tariff revenue, consumer demand, and quantities of net imports have not satisfied this criterion. Out of these three nonconverging variables, the source of the problem is the tariff revenue change variable. It is fluctuating, thereby affecting the consumer's income which in turn has affected the consumer demand and consequently, the quantities of net imports. Since the size of the error seems very small, we decided not to increase the number of steps any further.

10   For an axiomatic derivation of the Nash social welfare function see Kaneko and Nakamura (1979). For arguments against the use of the Nash social welfare function, see Ng (1981) and Yaari (1981). It is, however, noteworthy that all of these studies are limited up to the original version of Nash's solution that does not allow for unequal bargaining power of the players. Whether the presence of asymmetric bargaining power can dilute Ng's conclusion is a topic for further research.

11   See Martin (1990) for a comparative discussion of both theory and evidence on private and public interest approach in policy formulation.

9 Epilogue

The main purpose of this book was to provide a coherent analytical framework, which can explain the process of formation and the behaviour of a government's redistributive policies. Tariff policy was chosen as the specific subject matter of this study because, among other things, it can be employed to focus sharply on the issue of redistribution, has a methodological basis developed by existing endogenous tariff literature and is an interesting issue on its own account. Consequently, the major questions addressed by this study were phrased in terms of the tariff rate. How the tariff rate in a small open political economy is determined and how does it respond to exogenous shocks were the main questions asked in the beginning of this study.

We have thoroughly and consistently argued that tariffs are instruments of income transfer; their precise rates in a political economy with rationale players are matters of bargaining between the interest groups. Since the bargaining environment is completely explained by parameters of the economic and the political spheres - factor endowment, technology, international market conditions, the type of government and the bargaining power held by each player - the tariff rate responds to changes in these parameters (or exogenous variables). *Because of the fear of losing all the gains, winners tend to give up some of the gains by way of tariff adjustments so that the losers would readily accept adverse changes in exogenous variables.* In arriving at this conclusion this study assumed that the political process admits cooperative behaviour among the conflicting interest groups and derived a general equilibrium model of a small open political economy based on a bargain-theoretic approach to policy modelling. The logical sequence involved in deriving the model that determined the tariff rate endogenously and deducing the above conclusions from the model may be summarized as follows.

9.1 Summary

We reviewed the literature concerned with the endogenous determination of the tariff rate in Chapter 2. It led us to two competing approaches to policy modelling. One approach is based on the assumptions that there exists a social welfare function of some kind (conservative or another), which is maximized by the government while making policies - that the government is a social welfare maximizer. The other approach is based on the assumption that a government is a political support maximizer. This approach puts forward some model of political sphere to describe the process of policy formation. In one type of these models, private interest groups behave strategically in mobilizing political support for the government to enhance their own welfare in the economic sphere and the government also behaves strategically in supplying policies so as to maximize the political support for itself in the political sphere. The most interesting observation is that models based on either approach yields very similar predictions regarding the behaviour of the tariff rate.

The first approach, however, suffers from two major problems: (i) how to ascertain the existence and uniqueness of a social welfare function; and (ii) how can the government be a benevolent agent, while all the other individuals are self-interested. Where do the people in the government come from? The second approach, on the other hand, views all agents, including the government, in the political economy as self-interested; it takes the set of policies as a device of conflict resolution. Because of this consistency, we preferred to follow the political economy approach to the study of policy formation.

Though the political economy approach did provide a consistent analytical framework within which the policy formation process could be modelled, the existing literature subscribing to this view has nevertheless left several fundamental questions unresolved. In particular, the existence of an equilibrium in a productive political economy was an open question. Logically, it is necessary that the existence of an equilibrium in a political economy be established prior to any comparative static exercise is done around this equilibrium point. Hence, by the choice of the modelling approach we accepted the responsibility of showing that the type of economic and political process modelled leads the political economy to an equilibrium.

The modelling work of this study began in Chapter 3, where a Ricardo-Viner type 2-sector model of the economic sphere of a simple, open political economy was described. In the model of the economic sphere was subjected to comparative statics under the assumption that outcomes of the political sphere, the policies of the government (tariff rates), are exogenous.

Results obtained in Chapter 3 were employed in Chapter 4 to derive the rent transformation frontier. The rent transformation frontier summarized the general equilibrium effects of tariff changes on the sectoral rental incomes. The first-order property of the rent transformation frontier showed that the two owners of the specific factors (or simply sectors) have opposing interest in the government's tariff policy. The second-order property of the frontier showed that the real-rent possibility set is convex provided that the elasticities of factor substitution are at least unity.

In Chapter 5, we described the political process of tariff determination as a noncooperative game and studied the existence of a Nash equilibrium in the political economy in the following two steps.

In the first step, as in previous studies, we specified a lobbying game, in which the government offered a lobbying sensitive pricing function, satisfying some reasonable properties, to the conflicting interest groups (players). Each player chose his or her own lobbying effort to maximize his or her real-rental income subject to the general equilibrium of the economic sphere by taking the lobbying effort of the other player as given. It was shown that at least one Nash equilibrium exists in this lobbying game and at each equilibrium, each player spends a non-zero amount of resource in lobbying the government. Furthermore, we also saw that if the government had a budgetary constraint, then a positive tax on trade emerges at all possible equilibria of the game. In this case, although free trade was feasible, a Nash equilibrium necessarily implied a positive tax on trade.

In the second step, it was demonstrated that the assumed properties of the government's pricing function are also sufficient to guarantee the maximum of a Peltzman-type political support function of the government at each Nash equilibrium of the tariff game. These results in together established that there exists an equilibrium in the political economy, where the government behaves as a Stackelberg leader in maximizing its political support, and the private interest groups behave as Nash followers in lobbying the government in order to maximize their real rental income. At this equilibrium everyone lobbies the government and most likely the political economy will deviate from free trade. The key to this result is held by the nature of the pricing function, which makes non-zero lobbying the dominant strategy of the import-competing sector even when the exporting sector is not lobbying. This 'rational-greed' of the import-competing sector and the 'political weakness' of the government drags the exporting sector to active lobbying in order to moderate the tariff change and mitigate its adverse effects.

Interestingly, the results also show that the two strands of the existing political economy approach to endogenous tariff theory, which have either considered support-maximizing behaviour of the government without considering the reactions of the lobbyists, or considered the lobbying equilibrium for a given pricing function without showing how such function was obtained, are mutually compatible. They imply the same policy outcome, if the political economy admits a unique equilibrium.

Though the model thus described as a noncooperative game was capable of integrating the political sphere with the underlying economic sphere of a political economy, it was not yet sufficient to capture a complete description of the political process that would lead to a stable equilibrium of the political economy. In particular, it did not allow for the possibility that the interest groups may communicate and negotiate with each other in order to obtain a cooperative solution that will Pareto dominate the noncooperative outcome in the tariff game. Since a cooperative solution will be the one agreed by the two conflicting parties, the government will maximize its political support by enforcing it. There were no compelling reasons to continue assuming that the political sphere is characterized by noncooperation.

Therefore, in Chapter 6, this study proceeded further and allowed the interest groups to search for a cooperative solution. It is individually rational to do so because as we saw in Chapter 5 that in every (noncooperative) Nash equilibrium each player spends a non-zero amount of resource in lobbying, which can be saved. From this chapter onwards the political activities have been viewed as a bargaining process between the conflicting interest groups, who are pursuing their self-interest through the choice of the tariff rate.

The bargaining problem in the tariff game was formally defined in Chapter 6 assuming that the disagreement payoffs are known a priori. The rent transformation frontier, derived in Chapter 4, was employed to define the bargaining set. Results obtained in Chapters 3 and 4 guaranteed that the bargaining set is compact and convex. The bargaining problem thus defined satisfied the conditions required for the existence and uniqueness of a Nash solution to the bargaining problem set out by earlier studies. The sufficient condition for a unique Nash bargaining solution is that the elasticities of factor substitution be at least unity. On the other hand, if the polity does not admit a cooperative behaviour, then the sufficient conditions for the existence of a noncooperative Nash equilibrium are: (i) the elasticities of factor substitution be at least unity and (ii) the output supply functions in each sector be strictly increasing and concave in own-relative-price. Thus, the question of existence of an equilibrium in a political economy is fully answered. It is shown that an equilibrium exists in a political economy regardless of whether the political sphere admits a cooperative behaviour or not. These results allowed us to conclude that a cooperative equilibrium necessarily dominates noncooperative equilibria. Therefore, we proceeded to obtain the necessary and sufficient condition for a unique Nash bargaining solution in the tariff game in order to address the remaining questions.

The original Nash solution to any arbitrary bargaining game, and issues related to its generalization in the presence of asymmetric bargaining powers were discussed in considerable detail which did yield some useful results. First, it was shown that if the distribution of bargaining power is included in the mathematical description of the bargaining game, then the Nash solution with asymmetric bargaining power is also symmetric. Second, it was shown that an alternative necessary and sufficient conditions for the generalized Nash solution to a bargaining problem are that (i) the players' fear of ruin be strictly positive, and (ii) the players' fear of ruin relative to their bargaining power be equal.

This result implies that a player who expects to gain clearly in the economic sphere under a changed circumstance (after a shock) will concede in the political market. He will offer a concession to the opponent by agreeing on a policy adjustment. It is because he will have greater fear of ruin (disagreement) than the other player who does not expect to gain by as much. This result is important not only from the point of view of the endogenous tariff theory but also from the point of view of the Nash bargaining theory as well. This is because the result provides an intuitive explanation of the Nash bargaining process and justifies why a Nash solution is in fact a solution to a bargaining problem. This result has been employed to explain the results obtained in subsequent chapters. Thus, in summary, Chapter 6 provided the condition characterizing the bargaining equilibrium and a mechanism to summarize the bargaining process, which explains the directions of movement of the bargaining equilibrium in response to exogenous shocks.

In Chapter 7, the condition characterizing the Nash bargaining solution was combined with the conditions of general equilibrium in the economic sphere, described in Chapter 3, and a policy-endogenous general equilibrium model of the political economy was obtained. The bargained tariff rate, which depended on the entire politico-economic environment, was obtained as the solution of the model. This completed the construction of a policy-endogenous general equilibrium model in which the tariff rate is the only policy variable of the government.

However, the condition of a bargaining equilibrium contained terms representing the disagreement payoffs, which were not yet identified. The problem of identification of the disagreement payoffs was resolved by adopting the reference point solution concept. It was further argued that the payoffs at the point of players' minimum expectation in the tariff game could serve as a reference point during the bargaining process. Minimum expectation payoffs were identified for political economies with two different types of the government namely, coercive and popular. The coercive government, introduced for the sake of reference, was defined to be the one that can be captured by the winning player and is prepared to subsidize trade to benefit the winning player. Players' minimum expectation under such a government was shown always to be equal to zero. A popular government, on the other hand, was characterized by support-maximizing behaviour with self-financing policy constraint. Under such a government the free trade and the autarkic equilibria defined the point of minimum expectation. Autarkic equilibrium was the minimum expectation of the exporting sector and the free trade was the minimum of the import-competing sector.

With these two different reference points the model of the political economy was subjected to two different sets of comparative static experiments in order to see how the tariff rate would change as the exogenous variables of the model change. Throughout those experiments it was assumed that the relative bargaining powers of the players remained unaffected by the shocks.

The model did admit conclusive analytical solutions under a coercive government. It was shown that the bargained tariff rate with a coercive government provides a perfect insulation to the domestic relative price from the international terms of trade shocks. Moreover, the bargained tariff rate was also found to be responsive to changes in the domestic endowments of the factors of production. In general, it was observed that tariff changes tend to compensate the loser for the relative loss arising out of the exogenous shocks. The results were explained intuitively.

However, analytical results of the comparative static exercise with a popular government were not entirely conclusive. This was because the point of minimum expectation responded to the shocks; the expressions yielding the response of the bargained tariff rate proved complex enough to make any deductions very difficult. Nevertheless, with Cobb-Douglas production functions it was shown that domestic relative price moves in the same direction as the international relative price.

In Chapter 8, the policy-endogenous general equilibrium model was simulated numerically using hypothetical data sets that covered some extreme cases. The procedures adopted in obtaining the minimum expectation payoffs and the calibration of the model were also discussed in detail. Simulation results showed that, in general, the directions of response of the bargained tariff rate under a popular government were not different from that under a coercive government. The magnitudes of the responses were, of course, different. Some hypotheses that followed from these comparative exercises were stated formally. Those hypotheses were then checked and found to be consistent with the results of previous studies. It was seen that, in general, the bargained tariff rate changes in response to an exogenous shock so as to compensate, at least partly, for the relative loss of the losing player as a result of the shock. Uneven changes in the players' generalized fear of ruin were shown to be the principal mechanism leading to the comparative static results obtained in this study.

Furthermore, the policy-endogenous general equilibrium model was simulated to predict the consequence of a very large growth in the stock of the specific-factor in the import-competing sector. The results showed a reversal in the direction of trade. The commodity that was imported before the shock was exported after the shock and vice versa. The commodity that was being taxed before the shock was subsidized after the shock. Several interesting hypotheses followed from the results of this simulation, which are consistent with the predictions of previous studies and the stylized facts. For example, if the characteristic feature that differentiates between developed and developing countries is the faster rate of capital accumulation and technological growth in the non-agricultural sector relative to the agricultural sector, then on the basis of the simulation results one would predict that a developing country exporting agricultural products will be taxing the farmers and a developed country exporting mainly non-agricultural products will be taxing the producers of non-agricultural products. Thus, we may employ the political economy approach to explain why all countries tax their exporting sectors.

9.2 Central conclusions

The central conclusions of this study can be stated as follows.

Whether a political economy admits a cooperative behaviour or not, there exists at least one equilibrium under fairly general conditions. At this equilibrium, exports will, ultimately, be taxed.

A government's redistributive policy can consistently be viewed as an equilibrium outcome of a bargaining process between the organized interest groups holding conflicting interests on the level of the redistributive policy. If an exogenous shock disturbs the bargaining equilibrium, then at the new equilibrium the level of the redistributive policy of the government will change so as to compensate, at least partly, for the relative loss of the losing player.

The distribution of the relative bargaining power between the interest groups is one of the factors that determine the equilibrium *level* of the redistributive policy. So long as the distribution of the relative bargaining power is unaffected by exogenous shocks in the economic sphere, consequent *changes* in the redistributive policy in response to the shocks will remain independent of the distribution of the bargaining power.

The mechanism underlying the process of policy adjustments is the dynamics of the fear of ruin, which moves in the same direction as the relative gain of the player. In particular, if an exogenous shock causes (a) a decline in the gain perceived by the owner of the specific-factor in the import-competing sector relative to his minimum expectation, and/or (b) an increase in the gain perceived by the owner of the specific-factor in the exporting sector relative to his minimum expectation, then the fear of ruin held by the owner of the specific factor in the import-competing sector falls, while that of the owner of the specific factor in the exporting sector rises. In the new bargaining equilibrium the rationalized tariff rate (the redistributive policy) will rise.

9.3 Implications

The results obtained so far have two implications to policy modelling. First, it demonstrates that the bargain-theoretic approach can provide a theoretically consistent and numerically implementable analytical framework in modelling the policy formation process in a political economy. Second, this approach is potentially capable of reconciling the two diverging approaches to policy modelling that are based on two different views on the motivation of the government, namely, that of self-interest and that of the public-interest. Such a possibility arises because the comparative static behaviour of the bargained tariff rate turns out to be strikingly similar to the predictions that follow from the maximization of a conservative social welfare function (see Chapter 2). So, if bargaining is accepted as the underlying process that generates the (positive) conservative social welfare function (CSWF), then the problem of identification of the social welfare function vanishes. Furthermore, the implementation of a social welfare function will not be inconsistent with the self-interested behaviour of the government. The difference between the political economy approach and the welfare function maximizing approach can be disregarded.

The fact that the predictions of Corden's CSWF and that of the policy-endogenous general equilibrium model (PEGEM) based on the bargain-theoretic approach are indistinguishable prompts us to investigate the internal relationship between the two approaches. CSWF maintains that policy changes should be directed to avoid *any significant* absolute reductions in real incomes of any significant section of the community. No function has been specified to represent this CSWF, however.

What constitutes a significant level of reduction and what defines a significant section of the community, are questions which are yet to be addressed by the CSWF theorists. However, we can now specify one functional form that is consistent with the CSWF by assuming some answers to the above questions.

The first question concerns the segments of population whose welfare is considered important by the state. This is essentially equivalent to the question of number of players in the game. The second question is essentially related to the question of the reference point in the Nash bargaining game, since in a Nash bargaining game the payoff of no player is allowed to fall below the 'disagreement' payoffs, that is, the level of reference payoffs. One may logically disagree on a particular choice of the reference point, but to solve a Nash bargaining problem one has to assign a value to it in one way or the other.

If players in the bargaining game represent all significant sections of the community; and the reference point used in the bargaining problem is the same as the reference point implied by the CSWF; then it follows that the CSWF is indistinguishable from the generalized Nash product which will be maximized by the choice of the tariff rate subject to the rent transformation function. Therefore, the generalized Nash product may be viewed as a specific form of the conservative social welfare function and the bargaining process in the political sphere as the underlying mechanism of generating it.

9.4 Limitations

Despite its analytical rigour, this study, nevertheless, has limitations some of which were simply due to assumptions made to keep the model tractable and simple. Major limitations can be described as follows.

First, this study assumed that the trade tax is the only redistributive policy instrument available to a government. This was, of course, a simplification. The government has numerous instruments of intervention, none of which is in the real world completely equivalent to any other in every respect (see, Warr and Parmenter, 1986; Hertel, 1989). The choice of instruments itself may require separate politico-economic explanations (see Lloyd and Falvey, 1986, and Falvey and Lloyd, 1991). These may eventually extend the generality of the model presented in this study. In order to keep the analysis simple, well focused on a specific issue and to understand the process of policy determination as clearly as possible an assumption of this sort was necessary.

Second, this study did not consider how the tariff revenue was distributed. It assumed that the tariff revenue is simply a transfer to the consumer. But, the response of the tariff rate with respect to the exogenous shocks could be sensitive to the way tariff revenue is distributed among the factor groups (Long and Vousden, 1991). The purpose in not modelling the distribution of tariff revenue explicitly was to make the rationalized tariff rate the only instrument of income redistribution. Otherwise, tariff revenue itself would be another instrument in affecting the income distribution. Consistency in the model of a political economy would require that some sort of revenue-seeking activity also be modelled.

Third, this study has ignored other policies of a government that could be directed to macroeconomic stabilization and growth. Rausser (1982) and Rausser and Foster (1990) have argued that a model that does not consider both 'pie-expanding' and 'pie-sharing' policies together is likely to yield incorrect answers to the questions of endogenous policy responses. In this sense, the model described in this study is not exhaustive, as it described only a sub-game of a much larger policy game actually played in a political economy. A direct reflection of this limitation was observed in Chapter 7 while determining the minimum expectation of the players.

Fourth, this study also assumed that the mobile factor is fully employed at the wage rate that clears the market. This is another simplification. However, this assumption could be relaxed by specifying the mobile factor market in a more realistic way. For example, one may consider that the wage rate is exogenously determined and model the unemployment/ employment level as an endogenous variable. Alternatively, a labour supply function that responds to changes in the wage rate can be built into it. These are possible extensions that can be handled easily within the present framework.

Fifth, this study has not modelled a coalition of the owners of the mobile factor as a separate, independent player. In the political sphere, they are considered as rationally ignorant voters. However, one may model enterprise bargaining, and then consider the existence of unemployment and the strategic behaviour of the owners of the mobile factors at the same time. Wallerstein (1987) could provide some guidelines in modelling these two issues related to the labour market.

Sixth, the interest groups in this study were assumed to maximize the real rental income, not the utility that they can obtain from it. Hence the existence result obtained in this study needs to be understood with appropriate qualifications. Moreover, since in the standard Nash bargaining theory players' payoffs are defined in terms of utilities, the solution to the bargaining problem obtained in this study is therefore a Nash-like solution, because players' payoffs are measured in terms of real rental income. This simply underscores the importance of further research in this area. Binmore (1987c) and Rubinstein, Safra and Thomson (1992) may provide the axiomatic foundation for such studies.

Seventh, in a more realistic model, one may introduce the inter-industry relationship by incorporating the input-output structure into the model of the economic sphere. The technique for doing so is already well developed in the literature (see, for example, Dixon, et al., 1982).

Eighth, the solution to the bargaining problem has been made operational by taking a somewhat ad hoc approach in specifying the disagreement payoffs. The point of minimum expectation, which has been assumed to summarize the worst scenario in disagreement, has been identified by imposing a particular restriction, namely the self-financing, on the government's behaviour. This restriction is justified so long as the tariff rate is the only policy instrument available to the government. One may, however, systematically disagree on the imposition of this restriction and on the use of minimum expectation payoffs as the reference point in the bargaining process. A better theory of disagreement, if available, could improve the theoretical structure of the policy-endogenous general equilibrium model.

Ninth, this study also assumed that the distribution of relative bargaining power among the players is exogenously given. This was justified by Binmore, Rubinstein, and Wolinsky's demonstration that difference among players in their time preference rates, and the fear of disagreement due to exogenous intervention could be captured in the static representation of the game by the asymmetric distribution of the bargaining power. However, there could be other strategic behaviours of the players, not modelled, that affect the opponent's perception of exogenous risk, and hence the distribution of the relative bargaining power. A systematic analysis of factors that determine a player's bargaining power would therefore enrich the model presented in this study.

Finally, we come to the bottom line. This study conclusively shows that a positive tariff rate emerges at the bargaining equilibrium of a political economy in which all agents are rational and hence cooperative. The agents jointly select the best policy option which maximizes the benefit of each and every agent. In every situation considered in Chapter 8, however, the bundle of goods available to the consumer under simulated free trade scenario dominates the bundle of goods available under both the simulated autarky or the observed equilibrium (see Table 8.2). In other words, that means, the country as a whole benefits from free trade while the political economy equilibrates at some other point unless a unique configuration of factor endowment has been achieved. Why don't the players choose free trade and redistribute the extra gain among themselves using some other side payment mechanism? This option could potentially be preferable to an equilibrium with a positive tariff rate.

Here it is important to note that the model we have considered has got only one policy variable - the rationalized tariff rate. Certainly free trade is better than any other equilibrium for the society as a whole, but in the absence of another superior instrument to make side payments it is worse than the observed equilibrium as far as the import competing sector is concerned - therefore a tax on trade. To answer whether or not tariff rates will be employed to make the required compensation as situations change, we need an elaborate model of the political economy with at least one another redistributive instrument and the cost of identifying gainers, losers and of making side payments. Only then the baffling question that why tariffs exist in the real world can be answered conclusively. One may, nevertheless, start with the following conjecture - that the cost of identifying the gainers and losers and the cost of making side-payments exceeds the efficiency cost of the tariff rate and hence it has survived over the centuries and served as an instrument of redistribution between the import-competing and the exporting sectors. The advantage of tariff rate over other instruments in making compensation when foreign prices change is well known in the literature (Corden, 1974).

9.5 Suggestions for further research

The above limitations of this study suggest some areas of future research in policy modelling that may extend this study in three directions.

The first direction of research might be towards the application of the general equilibrium model of a political economy described in this study to country specific data sets which could then be pooled together to obtain a regional model of general equilibrium. Such work has already been done with policy-exogenous models (see, for example, Industry Commission, 1991; Whalley, 1985). Use of policy-endogenous framework in the construction of a regional model would allow for the political constraints faced by the governments of each country. Such models would, therefore, offer a more general analytical framework to study the possibilities of regional cooperation than policy exogenous models. Policy endogenous national models would provide sufficient 'behind-the-scene' information to models of trade wars and negotiation such as studied by Harrison,

Rutstrom and Wigle (1989), Markusen and Wigle (1989) and Harrison and Rutstrom (1991).

The second direction of research could be towards the generalization of the present model. As indicated above, the present model suffers from many limitations due to several simplifying assumptions. In particular, the following areas of research seem to be interesting and feasible.

(a)   The existence result provided in this study is based on a particular structure of the production functions, namely the CES functions, and real rent maximizing behaviour of the owners of the specific factors. An analytically challenging work is to study the existence of an equilibrium in a political economy with general production functions, and utility maximizing behaviour on the part of the owners of the specific factors. As a first step one may impose some restrictions on the nature of the utility functions that would define a one-to-one correspondence with the real rental income and the utility level it yields.

(b)   This study followed Nash's theory in solving the bargaining problem in the tariff game. One may test the robustness of the results obtained in this study by following other solution concepts provided in cooperative game theory. Moreover, to operationalize the concept of disagreement one might also examine whether there exist other uniquely defined reference points which are more appealing in terms of their empirical relevance than the point of minimum expectation and whether a shift in the reference point affects the conclusion of this study qualitatively.

(c)   A more challenging area of research in policy modelling would, of course, be to attempt to model the government expenditure on productive activities as well rather than to assume that the (tariff) revenue of a government is transferred to the 'individuals' in a lump-sum manner. A model of political economy that also describes government expenditures more realistically would bring the 'pie-expanding' policies of the government into the purview of general equilibrium modelling. In such models, government policies will create not only a movement along a given rent transformation frontier but also the possibilities of shifts on the frontier as well. The results obtained from such models would be more realistic than the results obtained from models that allow for the redistributive policies only, such as the predictions of the present study (see, Weingast, et al., 1981; Rausser, 1983; and Rausser and Foster, 1990).

(d)   There exist several possibilities to extend the structure of the present model by improving the specification of the general equilibrium structure of the economic sphere. For example, one may consider the following straightforward cases. (i) One may introduce a non-traded good into the model and study the endogenous behaviour of the tariff rate. The model presented in Cassing and Warr (1985) could be employed to describe the behaviour of the economic sphere of a political economy with three goods of which one is non-traded. A model of the political economy could be obtained by superimposing the political sphere onto it. (ii) One may also consider introducing inter-industry dependency by incorporating the input-output structure in the description of the economic sphere. A simple modification of the description of the economic sphere of the present study is sufficient to do this exercise. Dixon, et al., (1982) provides the required methodology for that. In fact, one may consider a generalization to n-commodity case. However, with arbitrarily chosen n-commodity aggregates and the corresponding input-output structure one may not always obtain a well-behaved bargaining set. This will make the model solution sufficiently complex and one may have to look into mixed strategy space for the solution.

(e)   The third direction of research could be towards empirical validation of the political economy approach in policy modelling. This can be done in two ways. First, one may take the predictions of the analytical models or calibrated numerical models and test whether the predictions are consistent with history. For example, the prediction of this study that if capital accumulation and/or technological progress in the import competing sector dominates that in the exporting sector, then the protection afforded to the import competing sector declines is refutable. Second, one may attempt to estimate the game econometrically and administer the diagnostic tests rigorously. Data limitation to the second type of tests is likely to be a limiting factor.

Finally, we note that if policy changes are actually governed by the politico-economic structure of the society, then the mere realization of this fact may save resources of the society at large from going to the design and implementation of policies that do not confirm to this reality. The society as a whole can be made better off by policy changes that were from the beginning directed to the political reality of the society. Bargaining is a fact of life. Economists may better guide the society by predicting the policy changes than by proposing policy changes that will never be implemented.

Bibliography

Adelman, I. and Robinson, S. (1986), 'U.S. agriculture in a General Equilibrium Framework: Analysis with a Social Accounting Matrix', *American Journal of Agricultural Economics*, 68: 1196-1207.

Anderson, J. E. and Neary, J. P. (1992), 'Trade Reforms with Quotas, Partial Rent Retention, and Tariffs', *Econometrica*, 60: 57-76.

Anderson, K. and Hayami, Y., Ed. (1986), *The Political Economy of Agricultural Protection: East Asia in International Perspective*, Allen and Unwin: Sydney.

Anderson, K. and Warr, P. G. (1987), 'General Equilibrium Effects of Agricultural Price Distortions: A Simple Model for Korea', *Food Research Institute Studies*, 20: 245-263.

Appelbaum, E. and Katz, E. (1986), 'Rent-Seeking and Entry', *Economic Letters*, 20: 207-212.

Appelbaum, E. and Katz, E. (1987), 'Seeking Rents by Setting Rents', *The Economic Journal*, 97: 685-699.

Asheim, G. B. (1992), 'A Unique Solution to n-Person Sequential Bargaining', *Games and Economic Behaviour*, 4: 169-181.

Aumann, R. J. and Kurz, M. (1977a), 'Power and Taxes', *Econometrica*, 45: 1137-1161.

Aumann, R. J. and Kurz, M. (1977b), 'Power and Taxes in a Multi-Commodity Economy', *Israel Journal of Mathematics*, 27: 185-234.

Baldwin, R. (1982), 'The Political Economy of Protectionism', in Bhagwati, J. (ed.), *Import Competition and Response*, Chicago University Press: Chicago.

Baldwin, R. (1986), *The Political Economy of US Import Policy*, MIT Press: Cambridge, MA.

Baldwin, R. (1987), 'Politically Realistic Objective Functions and Trade Policy', *Economics Letters*, 24: 287-290.

Baldwin, R. E. (1984), 'Trade Policies in Developed Countries', in Jones, R. W. and Kenen, P. B. (ed.), *Handbook of International Economics*, North-Holland: Amsterdam.

Becker, G. S. (1983), 'A Theory of Competition among Pressure Groups for Political Influence', *Quarterly Journal of Economics*, 98: 371-400.

Beghin, J. C. (1990), 'A Game-Theoretic Model of Endogenous Public Policies', *American Journal of Agricultural Economics*, 72: 138-148.

Beghin, J. C. and Karp, L. S. (1991), 'Estimation of Price Policies in Senegal - An Empirical Test of Cooperative Game Theory', *Journal of Development Economics*, 35: 49-67.

Bell, C. and Zusman, P. (1976), 'A Bargaining Theoretic Approach to Crop Sharing Contracts', *American Economic Review*, 66: 578-587.

Bhagwati, J. and Srinivasan, T. N. (1980), 'Revenue Seeking: A Generalization of the Theory of Tariffs', *Journal of Political Economy*, 88: 1069-1087.

Bhagwati, J. N. (1971), 'The Generalized Theory of Distortions and Welfare', in Bhagwati, J. N., et al. (ed.), *Trade, Balance of Payments and Growth: Papers in International Economics in Honour of Charles P. Kindleberger*, North-Holland: Amsterdam.

Bhagwati, J. N. (1980), 'Lobbying and Welfare', *Journal of Public Economics*, 47: 355-363.

Bhagwati, J. N. (1982a), 'Directly Unproductive Profit-Seeking (DUP) Activities: A Welfare-Theoretic Synthesis and Generalization', *Journal of Political Economy*, 90: 988-1002.

Bhagwati, J. N., Ed. (1982b), *Import Competition and Response*, Chicago University Press: Chicago.

Binmore, K. (1987a), 'Nash Bargaining Theory I', in Binmore, K. and Dasgupta, P. (ed.), *The Economics of Bargaining*, Basil Blackwell: Oxford.

Binmore, K. (1987b), 'Nash Bargaining Theory II', in Binmore, K. and Dasgupta, P. (ed.), *The Economics of Bargaining*, Basil Blackwell: Oxford.

Binmore, K. (1987c), 'Nash Bargaining Theory III', in Binmore, K. and Dasgupta, P. (ed.), *The Economics of Bargaining*, Basil Blackwell: Oxford.

Binmore, K. (1987d), 'Perfect Equilibria in Bargaining Models', in Binmore, K. and Dasgupta, P. (ed.), *The Economics of Bargaining*, Basil Blackwell: Oxford.

Binmore, K. and Dasgupta, P., Ed. (1987), *The Economics of Bargaining*, Basil Blackwell: Oxford.

Binmore, K., Rubinstein, A. and Wolinsky, Asher (1986), 'The Nash Bargaining Solution in Economic Modelling', *Rand Journal of Economics*, 17: 176-188.

Brennan, G. (1992), 'Taking Political Economy Seriously', *Methodus*, 4: 11-15.

Brock, W. A. and Magee, S. P. (1978), 'The Economics of Special Interest-Politics: The Case of the Tariff', *American Economic Review*, 68: 246-250.

Brook, W. A. and Magee, S. P. (1980), 'Tariff Formation in a Democracy', in Black, J. and Hindley, B. (ed.), *Current Issues in Commercial Policy and Diplomacy*, Macmillan: London.

Buchanan, J. M., Tollison, R. D. and Tullock, Gordon, Ed. (1980), *Towards a Theory of the Rent-Seeking Society*, A & M University Press: Texas.

Bullock, D. S. (1992), 'Redistributing Income Back to European Community Consumers and Taxpayers through the Common Agricultural Policy', *American Journal of Agricultural Economics*, 74: 59-67.

Byerlee, D. and Sain, G. (1986), 'Food Pricing Policies in developing Countries: Bias against Agriculture or for Urban Consumers?', *American Journal of Agriculture Economics*, 68: 961-969.

Carlson, H. (1991), 'A Bargaining Model Where Parties Make Errors', *Econometrica*, 59: 1487-1496.

Cassing, J. (1981), 'On the Relationship between Commodity Price Changes and Factor Owner's Real Positions', *Journal of Political Economy*, 89: 593-595.

Cassing, J., Hillman, A. and Long, N. V. (1986), 'Risk Aversion, Terms of Trade, and Social-consensus Trade Policy', *Oxford Economic Papers*, 38: 234-42.

Cassing, J., McKeown, T. and Ochs, Jack (1986), 'The Political Economy of the Tariff Cycle', *American Political Science Review*, 80: 843-62.

Cassing, J. H. (1980), 'Alternatives to Protectionism', in Leveson, J. and Wheeler, J. W. (ed.), *Western Economies in Transition*, Westview Press: Boulder.

Cassing, J. H. and Hillman, A. L. (1985), 'Political Influence Motives and the Choice between Tariffs and Quota', *Journal of International Economics*, 19: 279-90.

Cassing, J. H. and Hillman, A. L. (1986), 'Shifting Comparative Advantage and Senescent Industry Collapse', *American Economic Review*, 76: 516-23.

Cassing, J. H. and Warr, P. G. (1985), 'The Distributional Impact of a Resource Boom', *Journal of International Economics*, 18: 301-19.

Chamberlain, N. W. and Kuhn, J. W. (1965), *Collective Bargaining*, McGraw-Hill: New York.

Chun, Y. (1988a), 'The Equal-Loss Principle for Bargaining Problems', *Economics Letters*, 26: 103-106.

Chun, Y. (1988b), 'Nash Solutions and Timing of Bargaining', *Economics Letters*, 28: 27-31.

Chun, Y. and Thompson, W. (1990), 'Nash Solution and Uncertain Disagreement Points', *Games and Economic Behaviour*, 2: 213-223.

Clarete, R. L. and Whalley, J. (1988), 'Interactions Between Trade Policies and Domestic Distortions in a Small Open Developing Country', *Journal of International Economics*, 24: 345-58.

Coggins, J. S. (1989), *On the Existence and Optimality of Equilibria in Lobbying Economies*, Unpublished PhD Thesis, University of Minnesota.

Coggins, J. S., Grahm-Tomasi, T. and Roe, Terry (1991), 'Existence of Equilibrium in a Lobbying Economy', *International Economic Review*, 32: 533-549.

Colander, D., Ed. (1986), *Neoclassical Political Economy: The Analysis of Rent-Seeking and DUP Activities*, Cambridge: Mass.

Corden, W. M. (1974), *Trade Policy and Economic Welfare*, Oxford University Press: Oxford.

Cross, J. G. (1966), 'A Theory of the Bargaining Process', *American Economic Review*, 56: 67-94.

Datt, G. (1989), *Wage and Employment Determination in Agricultural Labour Markets in India*, Unpublished PhD Thesis, The Australian National University, Canberra.

de Melo, J. (1988), 'Computable General Equilibrium Models for Trade Policy Analysis in Developing Countries: A Survey', *Journal of Policy Modelling*, 10: 469-503.

Debreu, G. (1982), 'Existence of Competitive Equilibrium', in Arrow, K. and Intrilligator, M. (ed.), *Handbook of Mathematical Economics*, North-Holland: Amsterdam.

Decaluwe, B. and Martens, A. (1988), 'CGE Modelling and Developing Economies: A Concise Empirical Survey of 73 Applications to 26 Countries', *Journal of Policy Modelling*, 10: 529-568.

Derpanopoulos, J. (1986), 'Optimum Control of General Equilibrium Models', *American Journal of Agricultural Economics*, 68: 1208-1211.

Dervis, K., De Melo, J. and Robinson, Sherman (1982), *General Equilibrium Models for Development Policy*, Cambridge University University Press: Cambridge.

Dixit, A. (1985), *Optimal Trade and Industrial Policies for the US Automobile Industry, (mimeo)*, Princeton University: Princeton, NJ.

Dixit, A. (1987a), 'Trade and Insurance with Moral Hazard', *Journal of International Economics*, 23: 201-10.

Dixit, A. (1987b), 'How should the United States Respond to Other Countries', in Stren, R. (ed.), *U. S. Trade Policies in a Changing World*, MIT Press: Boston.

Dixit, A. (1989a), 'Trade and Insurance with Adverse Selection', *Review of Economic Studies*, 56: 235-48.

Dixit, A. (1989b), 'Trade and Insurance with Imperfectly Observed Outcomes', *Quarterly Journal of Economics*, 104: 195-203.

Dixon, P. B., Parmentor, B. R., et al. (1982), *ORANI: A Multisectoral Model of the Australian Economy*, North-Holland Publishing Company:

Douglas, N. (1989a), 'The Political Economy of Trade Policy', *Economics and Politics*, 1: 301-14.

Downs, A. (1957), *An Economic Theory of Democracy*, Harper and Row: New York.

Drysdale, P. and Garnaut, R. (1992), '*The Pacific: An Application of a General Theory of Economic Integartion*', A Paper Presented in the Twentieth Pacific Trade and Development Conference, Institute of International Economics, Washington, 10-12 September,

Eaton, J. and Grossman, G. M. (1985), 'Tariffs as Insurance: Optimal Commercial Policy when Domestic Markets are Incomplete', *Canadian Journal of Economics*, 18: 258-272.

Favley, R. E. and Lloyd, P. J. (1991), 'Uncertainty and the Choice of Protective Instrument', *Oxford Economic Papers*, 43: 463-78.

Feehan, J. P. (1992), 'The Optimal Revenue Tariff for Public Input Provision', *Journal of Development Economics*, 38: 221-231.

Feenstra, R. and Bhagwati, J. (1982), 'Tariff Seeking and the Efficient Tariff', in Bhagwati, J. (ed.), *Import Competition and Response*, Chicago University Press: Chicago.

Feltenstein, A. (1984), 'Money and Bonds in a Disaggregated Open Economy', in Scarf, H. E. and Shoven, J. B. (ed.), *Applied General Equilibrium Analysis*, Cambridge University Press: Cambridge.

Ferguson, T. (1984), 'From Normalcy to New deal: Industrial Structure, Party Competition and American Public Policy in the Great Depression', *International Organization*, 38: 41-94.

Findlay, R. and Wellissz, S. (1982), 'Endogenous Tariffs, The Political Economy of Trade Restrictions and Welfare', in Bhagwati, J. N. (ed.), *Import Competition and Response*, University of Chicago Press: Chicago.

Findlay, R. and Wellissz, S. (1983), 'Some Aspects of the Political Economy of Trade Restrictions', *Kyklos*, 36: 469-81.

Findlay, R. and Wellissz, S. (1984), 'Towards a Model of Endogenous Rent-Seeking', in Colander, D. C. (ed.), *Neoclassical Political Economy: The Analysis of Rent-Seeking and DUP Activities*, Ballinger Publishing Company: Cambridge.

Finger, J. M., Hall, H. K. and Nelson, D. R. (1982), 'The Political Economy of Administered Protection', *American Economic Review*, 72: 452-66.

Frey, B. S. and Schneider, F. (1979), 'An Econometric Model with an Endogenous Government Sector', *Public Choice*, 34: 29-43.

Friedman, J. W. (1986), *Game Theory with Applications to Economics*, Oxford University Press: Oxford.

Fudenberg, D. and Maskin, E. (1986), 'The Folk Theorem in a Repeated Games with Discounting and Incomplete Information', *Econometrica*, 54: 533-555.

Gale, D. (1986a), 'Bargaining and Competition Part I: Characterization', *Econometrica*, 54: 785-806.

Gale, D. (1986b), 'Bargaining and Competition Part II: Existence', *Econometrica*, 54: 807-818.

Gallaroti, G. M. (1985), 'Towards a Business-Cycle Model of Tariffs', *International Organization*, 39: 155-87.

Gardner, B. L. (1983), 'Efficient Redistributions through Commodity Markets', *American Journal of Agricultural Economics*, 65: 225-34.

Gardner, B. L. (1987), *The Economics of Agricultural Policies*, Macmillan: New York.

Glismann, H. H. and Weiss, F. D. (1980), *On the Political Economy of Protection in Germany*, World Bank: Washington D.C.

Hall, H. K. and Nelson, D. (1992), 'Institutional Structure in the Political Economy of Protection: Legislated V. Administered Protection', *Economics and Politics*, 4: 61-77.

Hamilton, B., Mohammad, S. and Whalley, John (1984), 'Rent Seeking and North South Terms of Trade', *Journal of Policy Modelling*, 6: 485-511.

Harrison, Jill and Pearson, Ken (1994a), 'An Introduction to GEMPACK', (GPD -1), KPSOFT and IMPACT Project, Monash University, Australia.

Harrison, Jill and Pearson, Ken (1994b), 'User's guide to TABLO, GEMSIM and TABLO-Generated Programs', (GPD-2), KPSOFT and IMPACT Project, Monash University, Australia.

Harsanyi, J. C. (1956), 'Approaches to the Bargaining Problem before and after the Theory of Games: A Critical Discussion of Zuthen's, Hicks', and Nash's Theories', *Econometrica*, 24: 144-157.

Harsanyi, J. C. (1962), 'Measurement of Social Power, Opportunity Costs, and the Theory of Two- Person Bargaining Games', *Behavioural Science*, 7: 67-80.

Harsanyi, J. C. (1963), 'A Simplified Bargaining Model for the n-Person Cooperative Game', *International Economic Review*, 4: 195-220.

Harsanyi, J. C. and Selton, R. (1972), 'A Generalized Nash Solution for Two-Person Bargaining Games with Incomplete Information', *Management Science*, 18: 80-106.

Hertel, T. W. (1989), 'Negotiating Reductions in Agricultural Support: Implications of Technology and Fcator Mobility', *American Journal of Agricultural Economics*, 71: 559-573.

Hertel, T. W. (1990), 'General Equilibrium Analysis of U.S. Agriculture: What does it Contribute?', *Journal of Agricultural Economics Research*, 42: 3-9.

Hertel, T. W. and Tsigas, M. E. (1988), 'Tax Policy and U.S. Agriculture: A General Equilibrium Analysis', *American Journal of Agricultural Economics*, 70: 288-302.

Hillman, A. L. (1977), 'The Case for Terminal Protection for Declining Industries', *Southern Economic Journal*, 44: 155-60.

Hillman, A. L. (1982), 'Declining Industries and Political-Support Protectionist Motives', *American Economic Review*, 72: 1180-87.

Hillman, A. L. (1989), *The Political Economy of Protection*, Harwood: Chur.

Hillman, A. L. and Katz, E. (1984), 'Risk-averse Rent Seekers and the Social Cost of Monopoly Power', *Economic Journal*, 94: 104-110.

Honma, M. and Hayami, Y. (1986), 'Structure of Agriculture Protection in Industrial Countries', *Journal of International Economics*, 20: 115-29.

Hughes, H. (1986), 'The Political Economy of Protection in Eleven Industrial Countries', in Snape, R. (ed.), *Issues in World Trade Policy: GATT at the Cross-roads*, Macmillan: London.

Industry Commission (1991), *SALTER: A General Equilibrium Model of World Economy*, (Draft Working Document), A Study Undertaken by the Industry Commission on behalf of the Department of Foreign Affairs and Trade, Canberra.

Johansen, L. (1960), *A Multi-sectoral Study of Economic Growth*, North-Holland: Amsterdam.

Johnson, H. G. (1965), 'An Economic Theory of Protectionism, Tariff Bargaining and the Formation of Custom Unions', *Journal of Political Economy*, 73: 256-83.

Jones, R. W. (1971), 'A Three Factor Model in Theory, Trade, and History', in Bhagwati, J. N., et al. (ed.), *Trade, Balance of Payments and Growth: Papers in International Economics in Honour of Charles P. Kindleberger*, North-Holland: Amsterdam.

Jones, R. W. (1975), 'Income Distribution and Effective Protection in a Multi-Commodity Trade Model', *Journal of Economic Theory*, 11: 1-15.

Kaempfer, W. H. and Tower, E. (1982), 'The Balance of Payment Approach to Trade Tax Symmetry Theorems', *Weltwirtschaftliches Archiv*, 118: 148-65.

Kalai, E. (1977a), 'Nonsymmetric Nash Solutions and Replications of 2-Person Bargaining', *International Journal of Game Theory*, 6: 129-133.

Kalai, E. (1977b), 'Proportional Solutions to Bargaining Situations: Interpersonal Utility Comparisons', *Econometrica*, 45: 1623-1630.

Kaneko, M. and Nakamura, K. (1979), 'The Nash Social Welfare Function', *Econometrica*, 47: 423-35.

Kreps, D. M. (1990), *A Course in Microeconomic Theory*, Princeton University Press: Princeton.

Krueger, A. (1974), 'The Political Economy of the Rent-Seeking Society', *The American Economic Review*, 64: 291-303.

Krueger, A. O., Schiff, M. and Valdes, A. (1988), 'Agricultural Incentives in developing Countries: Measuring the Effects of Sectoral and Economywide Policies', *World Bank Economic Review*, 2: 255-272.

Kundsen, O., Nash, J., et al. (1990), *Redefining the Role of Government in Agriculture for the 1990s*, The World Bank: Washington, D.C.

Laffont, J.-J. and Tirole, J. (1991), 'A Theory of Regulatory Capture', *Quarterly Journal of Economics*, 106: 1089-1127.

Lerner, A. P. (1936), 'The Symmetry between Export and Import Taxes', *Economica*, 3: 306-13.

Lloyd, P. (1987), 'Protection Policy and the Assignment Rule', in Kierzkowsky, H. (ed.), *Protection and Competition in International Trade*, Blackwell: Oxford.

Lloyd, P. and Falvey, R. E. (1986), 'The Choice of Instrument for Industry Protection', in Snape, R. H. (ed.), *Issues in World Trade Policy*, MacMillian: London.

Long, N. V. and Vousden, N. (1991), 'Protectionist Response and Declining Industries', *Journal of International Economics*, 30: 87-103.

Magee, S. M. (1984), 'Endogenous Tariff Theory: A Survey', in Colander, D. C. (ed.), *Neoclassical Political Economy*, Ballinger Press: Cambridge.

Magee, S. P. and Brock, W. A. (1983), 'A Model of Politics, Tariffs and Rent-Seeking in General Equilibrium', in Hughs, H. (ed.), *Proceedings of International Economic Association Sixth World Congress*, Macmillan: London.

Magee, S. P., Brock, W. A. and Young, Leslie (1989), *Black Hole Tariffs and Endogenous Policy Theory*, Cambridge University Press: Cambridge.

Mansur, A. and Whalley, J. (1984), 'Numerical Specification of Applied General Equilibrium Models: Estimation, Calibration, and Data', in Scarf, H. E. and Shoven, J. B. (ed.), *Applied General Equilibrium Analysis*, Cambridge University Press: Cambridge.

Martin, W. (1990), *Public Choice Theory and Australian Agricultural Policy Reform*, Working Paper No. 90/2, National Centre for Development Studies, The Australian National University, Canberra.

Martin, W. and Warr, P. G. (1992), *The Declining Economic Importance of Agriculture: A Supply Side Analysis for Thailand*, Working Paper in Trade and Development, No. 92/1, Department of Economics, The Australian National University, Canberra.

Mayer, W. (1974), 'Short-Run and Long-Run Equilibrium for a Small Open Economy', *Journal of Political Economy*, 82: 955-68.

Mayer, W. (1984), 'Endogenous Tariff Formation', *American Economic Review*, 74: 970-985.

Mayer, W. and Riezman, R. (1987), 'Endogenous Choice of Trade Policy Instruments', *Journal of International Economics*, 23: 377-81.

Mayer, W. and Riezman, R. (1989), 'Tariff Formation in a Multi-dimensional Voting Model', *Economics and Politics*, 1: 61-79.

Mayerson, R. B. (1977), 'Two-Person Bargaining Problems and Comparable Utility', *Econometrica*, 45: 1631-1637.

Messrlin, P. A. (1981), 'The Political Economy of Protectionism: The Bureaucratic Case', *Weltwirtschaftliches Archiv*, 117: 469-96.

Muller, D. C. (1979), *Public Choice*, Cambridge University Press: Cambridge.

Mussa, M. (1974), 'Tariffs and the Distribution of Income: The Importance of Factor Specificity, Substitutability, and Intensity in the Short and Long Run', *Journal of Political Economy*, 82: 1191-1203.

Nash, J. (1950), 'The Bargaining Problem', *Econometrica*, 18: 155-162.

Nash, J. (1953), 'Two-Person Cooperative Games', *Econometrica*, 21: 128-140.

Neary, J. P. (1978), 'Short-Run Capital specificity and the Pure Theory of International Trade', *Economic Journal*, 88: 488-510.

Neary, J. P. and Roberts, K. W. S. (1980), 'The Theory of Household Behaviour under Rationing', *European Economic Review*, 13: 25-42.

Nelson, D. (1988), 'Endogenous Tariff Theory: A Critical Survey', *American Journal of Political Science*, 32: 796-837.

Nelson, D. (1989a), 'Political Economy of Trade Policy', *Economics and Politics*, 1: 301-14.

Nelson, D. (1989b), 'Domestic Political Preconditions of US Trade Policy: Liberal Structure and Protectionist Dynamics', *Journal of Public Policy*, 9: 83-108.

Newbery, D. M. G. and Stiglitz, J. E. (1984), 'Pareto Inferior Trade', *Review of Economic Studies*, 51: 1-12.

Ng, Y.-K. (1981), 'Bentham or Nash? On the Acceptable Form of Social Welfare Function', *Economic Record*, 57: 238-50.

Oehmke, J. F. and Xianbin, Y. (1990), 'A Policy Preference Function for Government Intervention in the U. S. Wheat Market', *American Journal of Agricultural economics*, 72: 631-640.

Ohyama, M. (1989), 'Bargaining with Differential Skills', *KEIO Economic Studies*, 26: 1-4.

Pearson, K. P. (1991), *Solving Nonlinear Models Accurately via a Linear Representation*, Impact Working Paper No. IP-55 (July), Impact Project, Melbourne.

Peltzman, S. (1976), 'Toward a More General Theory of Regulation', *Journal of Law and Economics*, 19: 211-40.

Piggott, J. and Whalley, J., Ed. (1985), *New Developments in Applied General Equilibrium Analysis*, Cambridge University Press: Cambridge.

Pincus, J. (1975), 'Pressure Groups and Pattern of Tariffs', *Journal of Political Economy*, 83: 757-78.

Posner, R. A. (1974), 'Theories of Economic Regulation', *Bell Journal of Economics and Management Science*, 5: 335-338.

Pugel, T. A. and Walter, I. (1985), 'U.S. Corporate Interests and the Political Economy of Trade Policy', *Review of Economics and Statistics*, 67: 465-73.

Rausser, G. C. (1982), 'Political Economic Markets: PERTS and PESTs in Food and Agriculture', *American Journal of Agricultural Economics*, 64: 821-33.

Rausser, G. C. and Foster, W. E. (1990), 'Political Preference Functions and Public Policy Reform', *American Journal of Agricultural Economics*, 72: 641-52.

Rausser, G. C. and Freebairn, J. W. (1974), 'Estimation of Policy Preference Functions: An Application to U. S. Beef Quotas', *The Review of Economics and Statistics*, 56: 437-449.

Ray, E. J. (1981), 'The Determinants of Tariff and Nontariff Restrictions in the United States', *Journal of Political Economy*, 89: 105-121.

Robinson, S. (1989), 'Mulitsectoral Models', in Chenrey, H. and Srinivasan, T. N. (ed.), *Handbook of Development Economics, Volume II*, Elsevier Science Publishers:

Rodrik, D. (1986), 'Tariffs, Subsidies, and Welfare with Endogenous Policy', *Journal of International Economics*, 21: 285-99.

Roth, A. E. (1977), 'Independence of Irrelevant Alternatives, and Solutions to Nash's Bargaining Problem', *Journal of Economic Theory*, 16: 247-251.

Roth, A. E. (1978), 'The Nash Solution and the Utility of Bargaining', *Econometrica*, 46: 587-594.

Roth, A. E. (1979), *Axiomatic Models of Bargaining*, Springer-Verlag: Berlin.

Rowley, C. K., Tollison, R. D. and Tullock, Gordon Ed. (1988), *The Political Economy of Rent Seeking*, Kluwer Academic Press: Boston.

Rubinstein, A. (1982), 'Perfect Equilibrium in a Bargaining Model', *Econometrica*, 50: 97-110.

Rubinstein, A. (1985), 'A Bargaining Model with incomplete Information about Time Preference', *Econometrica*, 53: 1151-1172.

Rubinstein, A., Safra, Z. and Thomson, William (1992), 'On the Interpretation of the Nash Bargaining Solution and Its Extension to Non-Expected Utility Preferences', *Econometrica*, 60: 1171-86.

Rubinstein, A. and Wolinsky, A. (1985), 'Equilibrium in a Market with Sequential Bargaining', *Econometrica*, 53: 1133-1150.

Sah, R. K. and Stiglitz, J. (1987), 'The Taxation and Pricing of Agricultural and Industrial Goods in Developing Economies', in Newbery, D. and Stern, N. (ed.), *The Theory of Taxation in Developing Countries*, A World Bank Research Publication:

Sen, A. (1979), 'Personal Utilities and Public Judgements: Or What's Wrong with Welfare Economics', *The Economic Journal*, 89: 537-58.

Shoven, J. B. (1974), 'A Proof of the Existence of a General Equilibrium with ad Valorem Commodity Taxes', *Journal of Economic Theory*, 8: 1-25.

Shoven, J. B. and Whalley, J. (1984), 'Applied General-Equilibrium Models of Taxation and International Trade: An Introduction and Survey', *Journal of Economic Literature*, 22: 1007-51.

Staiger, R. W. and Tabellini, G. (1987), 'Discretionary Trade Policy and Excessive Protection', *The American Economic Review*, 77: 823-37.

Stigler, G. J. (1971), 'The Theory of Economic Regulation', *Bell Journal of Economics and Management Science*, 2: 3-21.

Subik, M. (1982), *Game Theory in Social Sciences, Concepts and Solutions*, The MIT Press: Cambridge.

Sutton, J. (1986), 'Non-Cooperative Bargaining Theory: An Introduction', *Review of Economic Studies*, 53: 709-724.

Svejnar, J. (1986), 'Bargaining Power, Fear of Disagreement, and Wage Settlements: Theory and Evidence from U.S. Industry', *Econometrica*, 54: 1055-1078.

Thomson, W. (1981), 'A Class of Solutions to Bargaining Problems', *Journal of Economic Theory*, 25: 431-441.

Tullock, G. (1967), 'The Welfare Costs of Tariffs, Monopolies and Theft', *Western Economic Journal*, 5: 224-32.

Tyers, R. (1990), 'Implicit Policy Preference and the Assessment of Negotiable Trade Policy Reforms', *European Economic Review*, 34: 1399-1426.

van Damme, E. (1986), 'The Nash Bargaining Solution is Optimal', *Journal of Economic Theory*, 38: 78-100.

Vousden, N. (1990), *The Economics of Trade Protection*, Cambridge University Press: Cambridge.

Vousden, N. and Long, N. V. (1991), 'Protectionist Responses and Declining Industries', *Journal of International Economics*, 30: 87-103.

Wallerstein, M. (1987), 'Unemployment, Collective Bargaining, and the Demand for Protection', *American Journal of Political science*, 31: 729-52.

Wellisz, Stanislaw and Wilson, John (1986), 'Lobbying and Tariff Formation: A Deadweight Loss Consideration', *Journal of International Economics*, 20: 367-75.

Willig, R. D. (1976), 'Integrability Implications for Locally Constant Demand Elasticities', *Journal of Economic Theory*, 12: 391-401.

Yeldan, A. E. and Roe, T. L. (1991), 'Political Economy of Rent-Seeking under Alternative Trade Regimes', *Weltwirtschaftliches Archiv*, 127: 563-583.

Young, L. and Magee, S. P. (1986), 'Endogenous Protection, Factor Returns and Resource Allocation', *Review of Economic Studies*, 53: 407-419.

Yunker, James A. (1989), 'Some Empirical Evidence on the Social Welfare Maximization Hypothesis', *Public Finance*, 44: 110-33.

Zuthen, F. (1930), *Problem of Monopoly and Economic Welfare*, G. Routledge: London.

For Product Safety Concerns and Information please contact our EU representative GPSR@taylorandfrancis.com Taylor & Francis Verlag GmbH, Kaufingerstraße 24, 80331 München, Germany

Printed and bound by CPI Group (UK) Ltd, Croydon, CR0 4YY
08/05/2025
01864396-0003